D1186658

Limerick City Library

3 0002 00117887 0

Ramses

Under the Western Acacia

Also by Christian Jacq

The Son of the Light
The Temple of a Million Years
The Battle of Kadesh
The Lady of Abu Simbel

About the translator

Dorothy Blair is the author of critical works on the history of literature in French from Africa and the Caribbean. She has published translations of some two dozen works written in French from or about Africa and the Middle East.

Ramses

Under the Western Acacia

Christian Jacq

Translated by Dorothy S. Blair

SIMON & SCHUSTER
A VIACOM COMPANY

First published in Great Britain by Simon & Schuster UK Ltd, 1998
A Viacom Company

Copyright © Éditions Robert Laffont, S.A., Paris, 1997

This book is copyright under the Berne Convention.
No reproduction without permission.
All rights reserved.

The right of Christian Jacq to be identified as author of
this work has been asserted in accordance with sections
77 and 78 of the Copyright Designs and Patents Act,
1988

1 3 5 7 9 10 8 6 4 2

Simon & Schuster UK Ltd
Africa House
64-78 Kingsway
London WC2B 6AH

Simon & Schuster Australia
Sydney

A CIP catalogue record for this book is available
from the British Library.

ISBN Hardback 0 684-82140 0
Trade Paperback: 0 684 82123 0

Typeset by SX Composing DTP, Rayleigh, Essex
Printed and bound in Great Britain by
The Bath Press, Bath

45517
CITY OF LIMERICK
PUBLIC LIBRARY

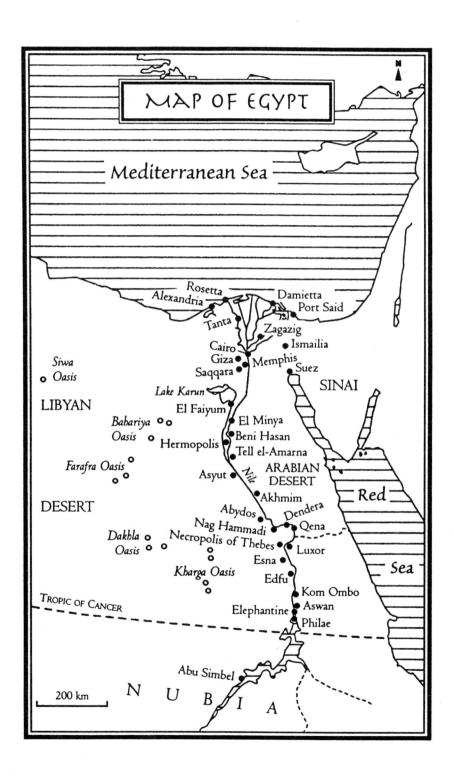

MAP OF EGYPT

Mediterranean Sea

Rosetta
Alexandria
Damietta
Port Said
Tanta
Zagazig
Cairo
Ismailia
Giza
Memphis
Saqqara
Suez
SINAI

Siwa
Oasis

LIBYAN

Lake Karun
El Faiyum

Bahariya
Oasis
Hermopolis

El Minya
Beni Hasan
Tell el-Amarna
ARABIAN
DESERT

Farafra Oasis

Asyut

Nile

Akhmim

DESERT

Abydos
Dendera
Nag Hammadi
Qena
Dakhla
Oasis
Necropolis of Thebes
Luxor
Esna
Kharga Oasis
Edfu
Kom Ombo

TROPIC OF CANCER

Elephantine
Aswan
Philae

Abu Simbel

200 km

N U B I A

Red

Sea

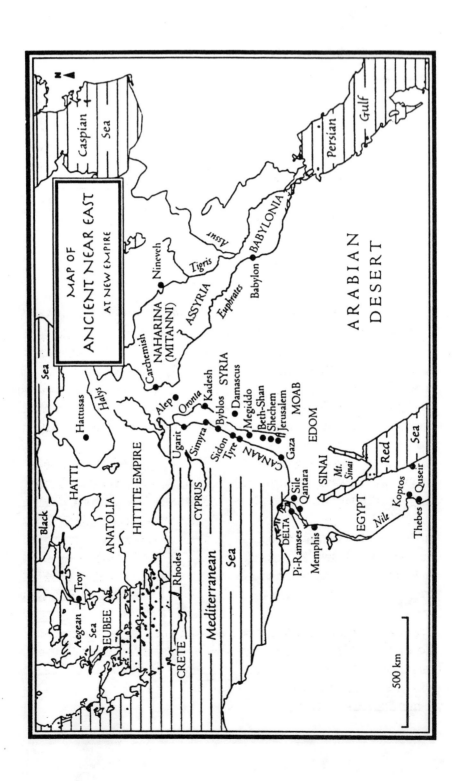

Glossary of Egyptian Deities mentioned in the Text

Amon (also **Amun**). The 'hidden god', originally a local Theban deity, god of fertility and reproduction, then taken up widely as a war-god, procuring victory to the pharaohs. Assimilated with Ra (q.v.), as Amon-Ra, to become the most powerful god in the Egyptian pantheon, sometimes known as the King of the Gods, with temples at Karnak, Luxor, Memphis. Portrayed as a ram or a handsome young man with a plumed crown.

Aton (also **Aten** or **Adon**). Another name for Ra, the sun-god. Aton was the one, or universal, god of Akhenaton, the 'heretic king', probably the pharaoh whose dreams Joseph interpreted, thereby gaining his favour. Akhenaton may have been influenced by Joseph to adopt the idea of one god.

Bastet (or **Bast**). A cat-headed goddess holding a musical instrument, the guardian of the Delta, of music and dance and of pregnant women. The centre of her cult was the city of Bubastis in the Delta.

Hathor (or **Hather**). Wife/mother of Horus. A major goddess, the Lady of Heaven, Earth and the Underworld, a gentle deity, particularly helpful to women. Depicted as a cow or a woman with the head of a cow. Also given the name of Sekhmet (q.v.) in her aggressive form.

Horus. The son of Osiris (q.v.), the hawk-god and special protector of kings.

Isis. The wife of Osiris; had a reputation as a sorceress, but also represented the rich plains fertilized by the annual flooding of the Nile.

Ma'at. The wife of Thoth (q.v.); goddess of truth and justice, who presided over the judgment of the dead. She was regarded as a moral concept of reason, harmony and the right attitude of individuals to others.

Mut. The goddess-mother, wife of Amon-Ra, depicted as vulture-headed; the centre of her cult was a splendid temple in Thebes.

Osiris. The most widely worshipped of all the Egyptian gods. Identified with the fertile black soil of the Nile Valley, the annual cycle of flooding and new growth corresponding to the cycle of his life, death and rebirth.

Ptah. The local god of Memphis, regarded as the creator of all things, the source of moral order, the Lord of Truth and Justice. The patron of artisans and builders.

Ra. A sky-god, identified with the sun, the oldest and one of the greatest in the Egyptian pantheon. The centre of Ra's cult was Heliopolis (Greek: 'sun-city'). Akhenaton's universal god, Aton, was linked to Ra.

Sekhmet. The wife of Ptah, a lioness-headed goddess of war and healing, associated with Memphis; a figure to be placated. Took the form of a lioness to attack men who turned against Ra.

Set (Seth; also **Setekh)**. One of the principal gods, sometimes seen as a Satan figure, representing powers of evil and destruction, requiring respect and placating. Storms, thunder, whirlwinds and hail were his instruments.

Thoth. The scribe of the gods, the god of wisdom and patron of science, literature and inventions and of the scribes in the temple. The inventor of writing, language and magic. Depicted as a man with the head of an ibis or as a baboon or dog-headed ape.

D. S. Blair

1

The rays of the setting sun gilded the façades of the temples of Pi-Ramses, the new capital which Ramses the Great had built in the Delta. The City of Turquoise, so named on account of the blue glazed tiles which adorned the façades of the houses, was the embodiment of wealth, power and beauty.

Life was good there, but this evening Serramanna, the former pirate who had become head of Ramses' personal bodyguard, was in no mood to enjoy either the mild evening air or the delicate rosy tints that suffused the sky. The huge Sardinian was in a very bad temper as, wearing a horned helmet, with his short sword at his side and his moustache curled, he galloped to the villa where the Hittite prince, Uri-Teshup, had been living under house arrest for several years.

Uri-Teshup was the deposed son of the late Muwatallis, Emperor of Hatti, and the sworn enemy of Ramses. The prince had assassinated his own father in order to take his place. But he had been less cunning than Hattusilis, the emperor's brother. Just when Uri-Teshup thought he had the country in his grasp, Hattusilis had seized the throne, forcing his rival to flee (his flight was organized by the diplomat Ahsha, Ramses' childhood friend).

Seramanna smiled. The ruthless Anatolian warrior a fugitive! And – the height of irony – it was Ramses, the man whom Uri-Teshup hated more than anyone else in the world, who had granted him political asylum, in exchange for information about the Hittite troops and their weaponry – which the prince, as former commander-in-chief of those troops, was well able to provide.

In the twenty-first year of Ramses' reign, to the surprise of the two peoples, Egypt and Hatti had concluded a treaty of peace and a mutual-assistance agreement in the event of external aggression. Uri-Teshup had thought his last hour had come, that he would be the ideal expiatory victim, the perfect gift for Ramses to offer Hattusilis, to seal their alliance. But the pharaoh had respected the right to asylum and refused to extradite his guest. Today, Uri-Teshup counted for nothing.

Serramanna did not relish the mission Ramses had entrusted to him, but he admired Ramses and would be loyal to him to his dying day. So, albeit reluctantly, he would carry out the terrible order the king had given him.

Uri-Teshup's villa was situated on the northern edge of the city, in the heart of a palm grove. At least he must have enjoyed a luxurious existence in this land which he had dreamed of destroying.

At the entrance to the villa were two guards armed with daggers and sticks, two men chosen by Serramanna. (Two other guards kept permanent watch over the prince, who spent his time eating, drinking, swimming and sleeping.)

'Anything to report?' he asked.

'Nothing, sir. The Hittite is sleeping off his wine in the garden, near the pool.'

The Sardinian entered the property, and hurried down the gravel path that led to the pool. Swallows circled high in the sky, and a hoopoe flitted past Serramanna's shoulder. With set jaw, clenched fists and a nasty look in his eyes, he prepared to act. For the first time, he regretted being in Ramses' service.

Like a wild animal sensing the approach of danger, Uri-Teshup woke before hearing the giant's heavy tread. The

2

prince was tall and muscular; he wore his hair long and on his chest there was a mat of red hair. He never felt the cold, even during the Anatolian winter, and had lost nothing of his strength.

Lying on the paving-stones surrounding the pool, the Hittite watched through half-closed eyes as Serramanna approached.

So, the time had come.

Since the signing of the monstrous treaty between Egypt and Hatti, Uri-Teshup no longer felt safe. A hundred times he had thought of escaping, but Serramanna's men had never given him the opportunity. He had escaped extradition only to be bled like a pig by a brute as ruthless as himself.

'Get up,' ordered Serramanna.

Uri-Teshup was not accustomed to taking orders. Slowly, as if he were savouring his last movements, he got to his feet and faced the man who was going to slit his throat. There was barely suppressed fury in the Sardinian's eyes.

'Strike, butcher,' said the Hittite contemptuously, 'since that's what your master demands. I shall not even give you the pleasure of defending myself.'

Serramanna's fingers tightened on his sword-hilt. 'Clear off!'

Uri-Teshup thought he must have misheard. 'What do you mean?'

'You're free.'

'Free . . .? What d'you mean, "free"?'

'You're to leave this house and go wherever you like. The pharaoh is applying the law. There's no reason to keep you here.'

'You're joking!'

'It's peace, Uri-Teshup. But if you make the mistake of remaining in Egypt and causing the slightest trouble, I shall arrest you. You won't be considered a foreign dignitary any more, just a common criminal. When the moment comes to sink my sword into your belly, I shan't hesitate.'

'But for the moment, you can't touch me. That's right, isn't it?'

'Clear off!'

A mat, a loincloth, sandals, a loaf of bread, a bunch of onions and two earthenware amulets which he could exchange for food: such were the meagre supplies granted to Uri-Teshup. For a few hours, he wandered about the steets of Pi-Ramses like a sleepwalker. He felt drunk with his new-found freedom and could no longer think clearly.

'There is no more beautiful city than Pi-Ramses', went the words of a popular song. 'The humble person is as respected as the great, acacias and sycamores bestow their shade on those who walk beneath them, the palaces are resplendent in gold and turquoise, the wind is gentle, birds frolic around the ponds.' Uri-Teshup fell under the spell of the capital. It had been built in a fertile region, near one arm of the Nile, framed by wide canals. Its meadows offered lush pastureland, its many orchards the famous apple trees; its extensive olive groves were said to produce more oil than there was sand on the river banks; vineyards provided a sweet, fruity wine; everywhere the houses were bedecked with flowers . . . Pi-Ramses was very different from rugged Hattusa, the capital of the Hittite empire, a fortified city built on a high Anatolian plateau.

Then Uri-Teshup was stung by a painful thought: he would never be Emperor of Hatti. That thought woke him from his torpor. He would avenge himself on Ramses, who had made the mistake of granting him his liberty. The pharaoh was thought the equal of a god since his victory at Kadesh over the coalition which should have crushed him. By killing him, Uri-Teshup would plunge Egypt, and possibly the whole of the known world, into chaos. He did not care. He had nothing left except his burning desire to maim and destroy – that would be some consolation for having been the plaything of a cruel fate.

Around him milled a gaily dressed crowd, in which Egyptians mingled with Nubians, Syrians, Libyans, Greeks and many others come to admire this capital. The Hittites had wanted to raze it to the ground, but after Kadesh they had had to yield to Ramses. Uri-Teshup knew he was nothing but a defeated warrior – he had no chance of striking Ramses down.

'My lord,' mumured a voice behind him. 'My lord, do you recognize me?'

Uri-Teshup looked round. He saw a man of average height, with lively brown eyes, a short, pointed red beard, who had a linen bandeau tied round his thick hair and wore a gown of coloured stripes reaching to his ankles.

'Raia! Is it really you?'

The Syrian merchant bowed obsequiously.

'But you're a Hittite spy. What are you doing in Pi-Ramses?'

'It's peace now, my lord. A new era has begun, and old mistakes have been wiped out. I was a rich, respected merchant. I've resumed my business, and no one can accuse me of anything. I'm well thought of again in good society.'

Raia had been a member of the Hittite spy network in Egypt, whose job had been to destabilize Ramses. The ring had been dismantled by the Egyptian investigators but Raia had got away to Hattusa. Now here he was, back in his adoptive country.

'That's all very well for you,' said Uri-Teshup.

'It's all very well for *us*.'

'What do you mean?'

'Do you think this meeting happened by chance?'

Uri-Teshup looked at Raia more attentively. 'Have you been following me?'

'There were various rumours about you: either you'd meet

a violent death, or you'd be freed. For more than a month my men have been keeping constant watch on the villa where you were held. I let you get a taste of this world again and . . . here I am. May I offer you a cool beer?'

Uri-Teshup hesitated, for the day had inspired many strong emotions. But his instinct told him that, with this Syrian merchant's help, he might succeed in realizing his plans.

In the tavern, their discussions made good progress. Raia watched Uri-Teshup's metamorphosis: gradually the exile became once more the cruel warrior, ready for every conquest. The Syrian knew he had not been mistaken: in spite of the years spent in exile, the prince had lost none of his bitter resentment and his violence.

'I'm not in the habit of wasting time in idle talk, Raia. What do you expect of me?'

The Syrian lowered his voice. 'I've only one question to ask you, my lord. Do you want your revenge on Ramses?'

'He humiliated me. I did not make peace with Egypt! But it seems impossible to bring down this pharaoh.'

Raia shook his head. 'That depends, my lord, that depends—'

'Are you saying you doubt my courage?' demanded Uri-Teshup.

'With respect, my lord, it will take more than courage alone.'

'You're a merchant. Why should you run the risks involved in such a dangerous enterprise?'

Raia smiled grimly. 'Because I burn with a hatred just as bitter as yours.'

2

Wearing a wide gold collar, a white kilt like those favoured by the pharaohs of the time of the pyramids, and white sandals, Ramses the Great celebrated the dawn rites in his Temple of a Million Years, the House of Ramses that he had had built on the west bank of Thebes. He quietly awakened the divine power hidden in the temple's innermost sanctuary; it would cause energy to circulate between heaven and earth, Egypt to exist in the image of the cosmos; and would curb the human race's innate urge to destroy.

The fifty-five-year-old Ramses was of athletic build, nearly three and a half cubits tall. His oval head was crowned with red-gold hair; his forehead was broad, his eyebrows were arched and strongly marked, his eyes piercing, his nose long, thin and slightly hooked, and his ears round, with delicate lobes. His person radiated magnetism, strength and natural authority. In his presence, even the strongest characters lost their composure: this pharaoh, who had covered the country with monuments and laid all his enemies low, was sustained by a god.

Thirty-three years of reigning . . . Only Ramses knew the real weight of the trials he had endured. They had begun with the death of his father, Seti, whose loss had left him distraught just when the Hittites were preparing for war. Without the help of Amon, his divine father, Ramses, who had been betrayed by his own troops, would not have triumphed at Kadesh. He had known happiness and peace, to be sure, but his mother, Tuya, who embodied the legitimacy of power, had joined her illustrious husband in the land of light, where the souls of the righteous lived for ever. And inexorable fate had struck him the cruellest of all blows, inflicting on the king a wound which would never heal. His Great Royal Wife, Nefertari had died in his arms at Abu Simbel, in Nubia, where Ramses had built two temples to glorify the indestructable unity of the royal couple.

Pharaoh had lost the three beings dearest to him, the three beings who had fashioned him and whose love was boundless. Yet he had to continue to reign, to make Egypt the embodiment of the same faith and the same enthusiasm.

Four other companions, who at his side had shared in so many victories, had left him: his two horses, so courageous on the battlefield; his lion, Invincible, who had saved his life more than once; and his golden-yellow dog, Wideawake, who had been favoured with mummification in the first class. The first Wideawake had been succeeded by another, and a third had just been born.

The Greek poet Homer had also died; he had ended his days in his garden in Egypt, contemplating his lemon tree. Ramses thought with nostalgia of his conversations with the author of the *Iliad* and the *Odyssey*, who had become enamoured of the civilization of the pharaohs.

After Nefertari's death, Ramses had been tempted to relinquish power and entrust it to his eldest son, Kha; but his circle of friends had opposed this, reminding him that a pharaoh was appointed for life and that he was no longer his own master. Whatever his suffering as a man, he must carry out his duties until the end of his life. Such were the demands of the Rule to which Ramses, like his predecessors, must conform.

It was from here, his Temple of a Million Years,

transmitter of the magic flow which protected his reign, that Ramses had drawn the necessary strength to continue. Although an important ceremony awaited him, he lingered in the halls of the House of Ramses, which was enclosed by a surrounding wall six hundred cubits long, sheltering two vast courtyards with pillars depicting the king as Osiris, an immense hall of forty-eight pillars, sixty cubits deep and eighty cubits wide, and a sanctuary where the divine presence dwelt. Gateways a hundred and forty cubits high, covered with inscriptions saying that they rose up to the heavens, marked the approach to the temple. The palace was situated on the south side of the first courtyard. A huge library, storehouses, a treasury containing precious metals, offices for the scribes and houses for the priests stood all round the holy place. This temple-city worked day and night, for the service of the gods knew no rest.

Ramses remained for a few all-too-short moments in the part of the sanctuary dedicated to Nefertari and Tuya. He gazed at the bas-reliefs depicting the union of the queen with the perfume of the god Amon-Ra, both secret and luminous, and the suckling of the pharaoh, who was thus assured of perpetual youth.

The king wrenched himself away from his memories: in the palace, the people must be getting impatient. He did not pause either before the thirty-five-cubit tall colossus, carved out of one solid block of pink granite, and given the name of 'Ramses, the Light of Kings', or before the acacia planted in the second year of his reign, but made his way to the sixteen-pillared audience chamber where the foreign diplomats were gathered.

Iset the Fair had sparkling green eyes, a small straight nose, delicate lips, and a scarcely defined chin. Though now in her fifties, she was still alert and cheerful. The years had left no mark on her; she was as graceful and attractive as ever. Her headdress was shaped like a vulture and was topped with two tall feathers, and she wore a long white gown tied at the waist with a red girdle whose ends hung loose, and a gold necklace and bracelets.

'Has the king left the temple yet?' she anxiously asked her lady-in-waiting.

'Not yet, Majesty.'

'The ambassadors will be furious!'

'Don't worry. It's such a privilege to see Ramses that no one dares get impatient.'

To see Ramses . . . Yes, that was the greatest of privileges. Iset remembered her first amorous tryst with Prince Ramses, the passionate young man who seemed isolated from power. How happy they had been in their reed hut at the edge of a cornfield, enjoying the secret of their shared pleasure. But then the prince had met the sublime Nefertari, who, without knowing it, possessed the qualities of a Great Royal Wife. Ramses had not been mistaken; and yet it was Iset the Fair who had given him his two sons, Kha and Meneptah. For a brief period she had felt resentful towards Ramses; but Iset knew she was incapable of assuming the crushing role of a queen and had no other ambition than to share, however little, in the life of the man she loved so passionately.

Neither Nefertari nor Ramses had rejected her: as the 'secondary wife' according to protocol, Iset had had the incomparable happiness of being close to the monarch and living in his shadow. Some people thought she had ruined her life, but Iset did not worry about their criticisms. For her it was better to be Ramses' servant than the wife of a stupid, pretentious dignitary.

Nefertari's death had overwhelmed her with profoundest grief; the queen was not a rival but a friend for whom she felt respect and admiration. Knowing that no words could diminish the king's suffering, she had remained in the background, silent and discreet.

10

And the inconceivable had happened.

At the end of the period of mourning, after himself closing up Nefertari's tomb, Ramses had asked Iset to become the new Great Royal Wife. No sovereign could reign alone, for Pharaoh was the union of the masculine and feminine principles, reconciled and in harmony.

She had never dreamt that she would become Queen of Egypt – the comparison with Nefertari terrified her – but one did not argue with the will of Ramses, so she had consented, in spite of her distress. Iset the Fair became the 'sweet love, the one who saw the gods Horus and Set finally placated in the person of Pharaoh, the Lady of the Two Lands, Upper and Lower Egypt, the one whose voice gave joy'. But these traditional titles had no importance. The real miracle was to share Ramses' life, his hopes and his ordeals. Iset was the wife of the greatest monarch the earth had ever known, and the trust he showed her was sufficient for her happiness.

'His Majesty is asking for you,' said the lady-in-waiting.

The Great Royal Wife made her way to the audience chamber. Her upbringing as a noble, wealthy girl had taught her how to conduct herself at official ceremonies; on this occasion she would be, like Pharaoh, the focus of the dignitaries' eyes, and they would show no indulgence.

Iset the Fair halted a few feet away from Ramses. He was her first and only love, and he still awed her. He was far above her – she would never grasp the breadth of his mind – but the magic of passion bridged this immense gap.

'Are you ready?' he asked.

When the royal couple appeared, conversations were silenced. Ramses and Iset the Fair took their places on their thrones.

Ramses' childhood friend, the minister for foreign affairs and head of the diplomatic service, the elegant Ahsha, came forward. Looking at this refined individual, with his well-groomed little moustache, and his eyes sparkling with

PUBLIC LIBRARY

11

intelligence, no one would ever have imagined that he was in love with adventure and had not hesitated to risk his life in Hittite territory while engaged on a dangerous spying mission. A lover of pretty women, fine clothes (he was always dressed in the height of fashion) and good food, Ahsha surveyed the world with an ironic – sometimes cynical – gaze, but he burned with a desire which nothing or nobody would ever quench: to work for the glory of Ramses, the only person for whom he felt wholehearted admiration, although he would never admit it.

'Majesty,' Ahsha said, 'the South submits to you and brings you its wealth, while entreating from you the breath of life. The North begs for the miracle of your presence. The East gathers together its lands to offer to you. The West kneels humbly before you; its chiefs bow down to you.'

The ambassador of Hatti detached himself from the crowd of diplomats and bowed before the royal couple. 'Pharaoh is the master of radiance,' he declared, 'the breath of fire which gives life and destroys. May his *ka* exist for ever, may his time be happy, may the floodwaters rise in due season, for he causes the divine energy to work, he who belongs both to the heaven and to the earth. In the reign of Ramses there are no more rebels: every land is at peace.'

Gifts followed the speeches. From the depths of Nubia to the protectorates of Canaan and Syria, the empire of Ramses the Great paid homage to its master.

The palace slept; only in the king's office were lights still burning.

'What is happening, Ahsha?' asked the king.

'The Two Lands are prosperous, abundance reigns in every province, the granaries touch the sky, you are the life of your people, you—'

'The speeches are over! Why did the Hittite ambassador launch into such fulsome praise?'

'Diplomacy . . .'

'No, there's something else, don't you think?'

Ahsha stroked his perfumed moustache with a manicured finger. 'I confess that I'm worried.'

'Could Hattusilis be challenging the peace treaty?'

'If he were, he'd be sending us different messages.'

'Tell me what you really think.'

'Believe me, I'm puzzled.'

'Where the Hittites are concerned, it would be a fatal mistake to remain in doubt.'

'Are you saying that you wish me to discover the truth?'

'We've had peace for too long. These last few years you've not been as vigilant as you used to be.'

3

Ahmeni, like Ahsha, had been Ramses' friend since childhood. Small and slightly built, he stayed skinny in spite of the enormous quantities of food he consumed at all hours of the day and night. A born scribe and a tireless worker, he ruled over a score of specialists who prepared abstracts for the pharaoh on every important subject. Ahmeni was remarkably efficient and, in spite of a wealth of unfounded criticism from people who were envious of his position, Ramses retained full trust in him.

Although he suffered from a weak back, the scribe insisted on himself carrying piles of wooden tablets and papyri. He was so pale that he often looked as if he was about to faint, yet he wore his subordinates out, needed only short periods of sleep, and handled his brushes for hours on end – his office was always cluttered with documents – drawing up confidential notes for Ramses' eyes alone.

Since Pharaoh had decided to spend several months in Thebes, Ahmeni had moved there with his team of assistants. Officially the king's sandal-bearer, he had no use for titles or honours; like the Lord of Egypt, he was concerned only with the country's prosperity. So he allowed himself no rest, for fear of making some fatal mistake.

Ahmeni was in his office, breakfasting on barley gruel and soft white cheese, when Ramses came in.

'Have you finished your meal?' asked the king.

'It doesn't matter. But, Majesty, your presence here implies that something's wrong.'

'Your last reports seemed fairly reassuring.'

'"Seemed"? Why that reservation? Surely, Majesty, you don't imagine that I keep the smallest detail from you?' With age, Ahmeni was becoming grumpy. He couldn't tolerate criticism, complained about his working conditions and roundly snubbed anyone who tried to give him advice.

'I don't imagine anything of the sort,' said Ramses calmly. 'I'm trying to understand.'

'Understand what?'

'Isn't there anything that worries you, even a little?'

Ahmeni thought aloud. 'The irrigation system is well under control, as is the upkeep of the dykes . . . The provincial governors obey their orders and show no desire for undue independence . . . Agriculture is well managed, and the people have enough to eat and are well housed . . . There's no fault to find in the organization of the festivals . . . Architects, masterbuilders, quarrymen, stone-cutters, sculptors and painters are hard at work in the whole country . . . No, I don't see any problems.'

Ramses should have been reassured, for Ahmeni was unequalled in spotting any weakness in the country's economic and administrative systems, yet he was still worried.

'Is there something important that Your Majesty is keeping from me?' asked Ahmeni.

'You know very well that I couldn't do that.'

'Well, what is happening?'

'The Hittite ambassador was much too flattering towards Egypt.'

'Bah!' said Ahmeni contemptuously. 'Those people only know how to make war and tell lies.'

'I've felt a storm brewing inside Egypt itself, an imminent storm bringing devastating hailstones.'

Ahmeni took the monarch's intuition seriously; like his father Seti, Ramses maintained special links with the terrifying god Set, who was the master of thunderstorms and celestial turbulence but who also defended the solar ship against the monsters that tried to destroy it.

'Inside Egypt itself,' the scribe repeated worriedly. 'What can this omen mean?'

'If Nefertari were still in this world, her eyes would see into the future.'

Ahmeni rolled up his papyrus and put his brushes away – ridiculous actions to try to dispel the sadness that seized his heart, as it did Ramses'. Nefertari had personified beauty, intelligence and grace, the peaceful smile of Egypt at the height of her perfection. Whenever he had had the chance to see her, Ahmeni had almost forgotten his work. But he did not think much of Iset the Fair. Ramses was probably right to share the throne with her, but the burden of queenship was too heavy for the shoulders of this woman, who was so divorced from the realities of power. Still, at least she loved Ramses – a virtue which cancelled out all her faults.

'Can Your Majesty suggest any leads for me to follow?'

'No, unfortunately.'

'So we must be doubly watchful.'

'I don't much like waiting for blows to fall.'

'I know, I know,' grumbled Ahmeni. 'And here was I hoping to take a day off. I shall have to put that privilege off for later.'

The four-foot-long horned viper was mainly white, with red on its back and green on its sides; its head was flattened and its tail thick. After spending the day buried in the sand, the reptile set out at nightfall in search of its prey. In the hot season, its bite meant instant death. It slithered sideways towards the couple making love in the shade of a palm tree.

Clasped in a passionate embrace, neither the man nor the

woman seemed aware of the danger. Feline, and supple as a liana, the lovely Nubian laughingly obliged her lover – a strong, thickset man in his fifties, with black hair and a mat complexion – to use all the resources of his manhood. Sometimes gentle, sometimes urgent, she gave him no respite as he assailed her with all the ardour of a first encounter. In the cool of the night, they shared a pleasure as burning-hot as the summer sun.

The viper was only a few feet away.

With feigned violence, the man turned the woman over on her back. He kissed her breasts, and she opened herself to him. They gazed into each other's eyes and smothered each other with kisses.

With a swift, sure action, Lotus seized the horned viper by the neck. It hissed and bit at the air.

'A fine catch,' commented Setau, without stopping his lovemaking. 'First-quality venom, obtained without effort.'

Suddenly Lotus's thoughts seemed elsewhere. 'I've a premonition of something bad.'

'Because of this viper?'

'Ramses is in danger.'

Setau and Lotus were an independent and unsociable couple, but because of the lifelong friendship between Setau and Ramses, they had agreed to accompany the pharaoh on to the fields of battle in the South and the North, and tend the wounded soldiers. The two snake-charmers had captured countless reptiles, each more dangerous than the last, and collected their valuable venom, which was used to make powerful remedies for serious illnesses. Their happiness had known no bounds when Pharaoh asked them to leave the state laboratory he had set up for them, and take charge of a province of Nubia, the land they loved. True, the Viceroy of Nubia, a conservative, over-cautious individual, tried to hinder their reforms, but he was afraid of this couple, who used cobras to guard their home.

17

Setau took very seriously the warnings of the lovely sorcerer he had married. 'What sort of danger is it?' he asked anxiously.

'I don't know.'

'Can you see a face?'

'No,' replied Lotus. 'I only felt a sort of faintness, but I knew, just for a moment, that Ramses is threatened.' Still clutching the viper in her fist, she got to her feet. 'You must do something, Setau.'

'What *can* I do from here?'

'We must leave for the capital.'

'The viceroy will take advantage of our absence to cancel our reforms.'

'It can't be helped. If Ramses needs our help, we must be at his side.'

For a long time now, the uncouth Setau, to whom no high official could give orders, had known better than to argue with instructions from the gentle Lotus.

Nebu, the High Priest of Karnak, was very old. As the sage Ptah-hotep had written in his famous *Maxims*, great age found its expression in perpetual tiredness, constant weakness and a tendency to fall asleep all the time, even during the day. One's sight grew dim and one's hearing poor. One had no more energy – even one's heart grew weary. Speaking became an effort, one's joints were painful, one lost the sense of taste, one's nose was blocked, and standing and sitting were equally painful.

In spite of these afflictions Nebu continued to carry out the duties Ramses had entrusted to him; to watch over the god Amon's treasures and his city-temple of Karnak. He had delegated almost all the material tasks to Bakhen, the Second Prophet, who had authority over eighty thousand people employed on the building sites, in the workshops, the fields, orchards and vineyards.

When Ramses appointed him high priest, Nebu had been under no illusions: the young monarch had demanded that Karnak obey him and show no vague wish for independence. But Nebu was no straw man, and he had made it his business to see that Karnak was not despoiled for the benefit of other temples. As Pharaoh had been concerned to maintain harmony in the whole country, Nebu's period of office as High Priest had been a happy one.

Kept fully informed by Bakhen, the old man now scarcely ever left his modest three-roomed home near the sacred lake of Karnak. In the evening he loved to water the beds of irises planted on either side of his entrance door. When he no longer had strength to look after them, he would ask the king to relieve him of his duties.

A gardener was bending down, pulling up weeds.

Nebu did not hide his annoyance. 'Nobody has the right to touch my irises!'

'Not even the Pharaoh of Egypt?' Ramses straightened and turned round.

'Majesty, I beg your—'

'You are right to guard this treasure, Nebu. You have worked well for Egypt and for Karnak. To plant, to see things grow, to maintain this fragile life that is so beautiful – is any task more noble? After the death of Nefertari, I thought of becoming a gardener, far from the throne, far from power.'

'You did not have the right, Majesty.'

'I had hoped you'd be more understanding.'

'It's legitimate for an old man like me to aspire to rest, but you . . .'

Ramses gazed at the rising moon. 'A great storm is coming, Nebu. I need reliable, competent men to confront the elements that will be unleashed. Whatever your age and state of health, put off till later your plans for retirement. Continue to govern Karnak with a firm hand.'

4

The ambassador of Hatti was on his way to the Foreign Affairs secretariat. He was a dried-up little man in his sixties, whose fringed beard made his face look more swarthy. He wore a red and blue striped gown, and his black hair was glossy from the application of an aromatic unguent. When he reached the entrance of the secretariat, in accordance with custom he placed a bunch of chrysanthemums and lilies on a stone altar at the foot of a statue of a baboon, a representation of Thoth, patron of scribes and god of sacred language and knowledge.

Then the Hittite turned to an armed officer standing nearby. 'The minister is expecting me,' he said curtly.

'I'll let him know.'

The ambassador paced up and down for a few minutes until Ahsha, smiling, came to meet him.

'I hope I haven't kept you waiting too long,' Ahsha said. 'Let's go into the garden, my friend. We won't be disturbed there.'

The palms and jujube trees shed a pleasant shade round a pool covered with blue water-lilies. A servant placed on a pedestal table alabaster goblets filled with cool beer and a basket of figs, and then slipped away.

'Speak freely,' said Ahsha. 'No one can overhear us.'

He gestured towards a folding wooden chair, on which

there was a cushion covered in green linen, but the ambassador seemed reluctant to sit down.

'What are you afraid of?'

'You, Ahsha.'

The minister smiled again. 'It's true that I have undertaken spying missions, but that's all in the past. I have become an official personality who values his respectability and hasn't the slightest wish to get involved in anything devious.'

'Why should I believe you?'

'Because, like you, I have only one aim: to strengthen the peace between our two peoples.'

'Has Pharaoh replied to Emperor Hattusilis's last letter?'

'Naturally. Ramses has sent him excellent news of Queen Iset and his horses, and is very pleased with the way the treaty which unites Egypt and Hatti for ever has been scrupulously respected.'

The ambassador's face was expressionless. 'From our point of view, that is completely inadequate.'

'What were you hoping for?'

'Emperor Hattusilis was shocked by the tone of Pharaoh's last letters. He had the feeling that Ramses thought of him as a subject, not as an equal.' The diplomat scarcely hid his belligerency.

'His dissatisfaction must have assumed alarming proportions,' said Ahsha.

'I'm afraid so.'

'Surely such a slight disagreement won't put our alliance in doubt.'

'The Hittites are a proud people,' said the ambassador. 'Anyone who hurts their pride is liable to suffer the consequences.'

'But it's absurd to exaggerate such a minor matter!'

'We see it as a major matter.'

'I hope I'm misunderstanding you . . . Couldn't we negotiate about this?'

21

'No.'

Ahsha had been afraid something like this might happen. At Kadesh, Hattusilis had commanded the coalition defeated by Ramses; he was still resentful and sought a pretext to reaffirm his supremacy.

'Would you go so far as . . . ?'

'As to denounce the treaty. Yes,' said the Hittite.

Ahsha decided to use his secret weapon. 'Perhaps this document may persuade you to be a little more conciliatory.' He handed the Hittite a letter drawn up by Ramses.

His curiosity aroused, the diplomat read the letter aloud:

I pray that you, my brother Hattusilis, are in good health, as also are your wife, your family, your horses and your provinces. I have examined your grievances: you think that I have treated you like one of my subjects, and that distresses me. You can be certain that I grant you all the consideration due to your rank; who but you is Emperor of the Hittites? Be assured that I think of you as my brother.

The ambassador seemed astonished. 'Did Ramses really write this letter?'

'There is no doubt of it,' said Ahsha with a smile.

'Would the Pharaoh of Egypt own to his mistake?'

'Ramses wishes for peace. And I have an important decision to announce to you: a palace for foreign countries is to be opened in Pi-Ramses, where you and other diplomats will have a staff of qualified scribes permanently at your disposal. In this way Egypt's capital will be the centre for a permanent dialogue with her allies and vassals.'

'That's remarkable,' conceded the Hittite.

'May I hope that Hatti's warlike attitude will soon be moderated?'

'I'm afraid not.'

This time Ahsha was really anxious. 'Do you mean that

nothing will reduce the emperor's tendency to take offence?'

'To come to the main point, Hattusilis also wishes to consolidate the peace, but he stipulates one condition.'

The Hittite ambassador revealed his emperor's intentions. Ahsha no longer felt like smiling.

As on every morning, the ritualists celebrated the worship of Seti's *ka* in his magnificent temple at Gurnah, on the west bank of Thebes. The priest in charge of the temple – a foundation for honouring the dead – was preparing to place on the altar an offering of grapes, figs and juniper wood, when one of his subordinates whispered a few words in his ear.

'Pharaoh here? But nobody warned me!'

When he turned round, the priest caught sight of the monarch's tall figure dressed in a white linen robe. Ramses' power and magnetism made him stand out from the other celebrants.

Pharaoh took the dish of offerings and entered the shrine where his father's soul dwelt. It was in this very temple that Seti had announced the coronation of his younger son, so ending the initiation to which he had been subjected with love and discipline since his adolescence. The two crowns, 'the Great Crowns of Magic', had been firmly set on the head of the Son of the Light, whose destiny had become synonymous with that of Egypt.

It had seemed impossible to follow in Seti's footsteps. But Ramses' true freedom had consisted not in being able to choose, but in living according to the Rule and satisfying the gods, thus ensuring men's happiness.

Today Seti, Tuya and Nefertari were travelling along the enchanting paths of eternity and sailing in celestial ships. On earth, their temples and tombs immortalized their names. It was to their *ka* that humans would turn when they felt the desire to penetrate the mysteries of the Otherworld.

When the rite was concluded, Ramses made his way towards the temple garden, whose dominant feature was a great sycamore where ash-grey herons nested.

An oboe's soft, low tones held him spellbound: a leisurely air, with sad inflections brightened by a smile, as if hope would always succeed in dispelling grief. The musician was seated on a low wall in the shade of the trees, playing with closed eyes. With her glossy black hair and the flawless, regular features of a goddess, Meritamon, now thirty-three years old, had never been more beautiful.

Ramses' heart was wrung with emotion. She was so like her mother, Nefertari, that she could have been her double. With her talent for music, Meritamon had been chosen very young to enter the temple and to live the life of a recluse in the service of the deity. Such had been Nefertari's own dream, a dream which Ramses had shattered by asking her to be his Great Royal Wife. Meritamon could have been foremost among the sacred musicians of the temple of Karnak, but she preferred to dwell here, near the soul of Seti.

The last notes soared up to the sun and died away. The musician set down her oboe on the wall and opened her blue-green eyes.

'Father! Have you been here long?'

Ramses clasped his daughter in a long embrace. 'I miss you, Meritamon.'

'Pharaoh is wedded to Egypt: his child is the entire nation. You have more than a hundred sons and daughters, and yet you still remember me?'

He stood back and gazed at her in admiration. 'The Royal Children – those are simply honorary titles. You are the daughter of Nefertari, my only love.'

'Iset the Fair is your wife now.'

'Do you reproach me for that?'

'No, you did the right thing. She will never betray you.'

'Will you come to Pi-Ramses?'

'No, father. The world outside wearies me. Nothing is more important than celebrating the rites. Every day I think of my mother; I realize her dream and I am convinced that my happiness sustains her eternity.'

'You have inherited her beauty and her character. Have I no hope of persuading you?'

'None – as you know very well.'

He gently took her hands. 'Really none?'

She smiled with Nefertari's sweetness. 'Will you dare order me to go?'

'You are the only person on whom Pharaoh will never impose his will.'

'That is not a defeat, father. I am more use in the temple than at the court. To bring the spirit of my grandparents and my mother to life seems to me a major task. Without the link with our ancestors, what sort of world would we build?'

'Continue to play your celestial music, Meritamon. Egypt will have need of it.'

The young woman's heart filled with dread. 'What danger are you afraid of?'

'A storm is brewing.'

'But you are the master of storms, aren't you?'

'Play on, Meritamon; play for Pharaoh too. Create harmony, delight the deities, attract them to the Two Lands. The storm is imminent, and it will be terrifying.'

5

Serramanna punched the wall of the guardroom; a piece of plaster fell off. 'What d'you mean, "disappeared"?'

'He's disappeared, sir,' confirmed the soldier responsible for keeping watch on Uri-Teshup.

The huge Sardinian grabbed his subordinate by the shoulders, and the wretched man, although powerfully built, felt as if the life was being squeezed out of him.

'Are you trying to make a fool of me?'

'No, sir, I swear I'm not!'

'So he just made off from under your nose?'

'He vanished into the crowd.'

'Why didn't you have the houses in the district searched?'

'This Uri-Teshup is a free man, sir! We have no reason to set the police after him. The vizier would charge us with unlawful intervention.'

Serramanna roared like an angry bull and let go of his subordinate. The clumsy oaf was right.

'What are the orders, sir?'

'Protection round Pharaoh to be doubled. The first person who relaxes his discipline will get his helmet shoved into his skull!'

The members of Ramses' personal bodyguard didn't take the threat lightly. In a rage, the former pirate was quite capable of carrying out his threat.

To work off his anger, Serramanna hurled a series of daggers at a wooden target. Uri-Teshup disappearing like this augured no good. Eaten up with hatred as he was, the Hittite would make use of his new-found freedom to harm the Lord of Egypt. But when and how?

With Ahsha in attendance, Ramses in person inaugurated the palace for foreigners in the presence of a host of diplomats. With his accustomed flair, Ahsha delivered a cordial speech in which the words 'peace', 'friendly agreement' and 'economic cooperation' recurred at regular intervals. As was the custom, a sumptuous banquet closed the ceremony which marked the recognition of Pi-Ramses as the capital of the known world, offering hospitality to all peoples.

Ramses had inherited from his father the ability to penetrate everyone's secret thoughts. He knew, in spite of Ahsha's histrionic gifts, that his friend was deeply worried and that his worries were related to the storm the king had predicted.

As soon as the social formalities were over, the two men drew aside from the company.

'That was a brilliant speech, Ahsha.'

'One of the obligations of my profession, Majesty. This initiative will make you still more popular.'

'What was the Hittite ambassador's reaction to my letter?'

'Excellent.'

'But Hattusilis is demanding still more, isn't he?'

'Well . . . he may be.'

'We're not among diplomats now, Ahsha. I insist on the truth.'

'I might as well warn you: if you don't accept Hattusilis's conditions, it will be war.'

'That's blackmail – in which case, I don't even want to know what the conditions are!'

'Listen to me, please! You and I have worked too hard for

this peace to see it destroyed in a moment.'

'Speak, then, and don't hide anything from me.'

'You know that Hattusilis and his wife, Putuhepa, have a daughter. She is said to be a young woman of great beauty and penetrating intelligence.'

'All the better for her.'

'Hattusilis wishes to reinforce the peace, and according to him the best way to do so is to celebrate a marriage.'

'Am I to understand . . . ?'

'You understood from my very first words. To set the final seal on our agreement, Hattusilis insists not only that you marry his daughter but, most important of all, that you make her your Great Royal Wife.'

'Aren't you forgetting that Iset the Fair plays that role?'

'For a Hittite, that sort of detail is of minor importance. The wife owes obedience to her husband. If he puts her aside, she just has to agree and say nothing.'

'We are in Egypt, Ahsha, not in some barbaric land. Are you really recommending that I forsake Iset in order to marry a Hittite, the daughter of my worst enemy?'

'At present, he's your best ally,' corrected the minister for foreign affairs.

'This demand is absurd and revolting!'

'It may seem so, yes, but in fact it is not without interest.'

'I shall never inflict such humiliation on Iset,' declared Ramses.

'You are not a husband like others. The greatness of Egypt must come before your feelings.'

'You've mixed with too many women, Ahsha, to the point of becoming cynical.'

'I agree I'm not known for being faithful, but my opinion now is that of your minister and your friend.'

'It's no good asking the opinion of my sons, Kha and Meneptah. I already know what their answer will be.'

'One could hardly expect them not to show respect for

their mother, Iset the Fair, Ramses' Great Royal Wife. Peace or war . . . that is the choice you have to face.'

'Let us dine with Ahmeni,' said Ramses. 'I want to consult him.'

'You will also have the opinion of Setau, who has just arrived from Nubia.'

'Some good news at last!'

Setau the snake-charmer, who loved the land of Nubia, dressed as usual in his hard-wearing antelope-skin tunic, whose many pockets were saturated with antidotes to snake-bite; Ahsha the far-sighted diplomat; Ahmeni the rigorous, faithful scribe . . . Moses was the only one missing. His presence would have completed the little band of students from the Memphis Academy who, so many years before, had shared the joys of friendship and speculated on the nature of true power.

Ramses' cook had surpassed himself: a square of leeks and courgettes in the juices from the meats, roast lamb with thyme, accompanied by fig purée, marinated kidneys, goat's cheese, honey-cakes coated with carob juice. In honour of this reunion, Ramses had produced a red wine from the third year of Seti's reign, whose bouquet sent Setau into ecstasies.

'All praise to Seti!' exclaimed the cobras' friend. 'When a reign produces such marvels, it is truly blessed by the gods.'

'As far as elegance is concerned, you've not made much progress,' deplored Ahsha.

'True!' approved Ahmeni.

'You, scribe, you just go on eating twice your weight!' retorted Setau. 'What's your secret for not getting fat?'

'Work in the service of the kingdom,' said Ahmeni.

'Have you any fault to find with the way I'm making the most of Nubia's resources?'

'If I had, I'd have drawn up an unfavourable report a long time ago.'

'When you two have finished your usual pleasantries,' Ahsha interrupted, 'perhaps we can get down to serious matters.'

'Moses is the only one who's not here,' Ramses said. thoughtfully. 'Where is he, Ahsha?'

'He's still wandering in the desert and waging war. He'll never reach his Promised Land.'

'Moses has taken the wrong road, but that road leads to a destination that he will reach.'

'Like you, I feel nostalgic,' admitted Ahmeni, 'but how can we forget that our Hebrew friend betrayed Egypt?'

'This isn't a time for memories,' declared Setau. 'To me, a friend who goes off like that is no longer a friend.'

'Would you reject him if he made amends?' asked Ramses.

'When a man has crossed certain boundaries he can't turn back. Forgiveness is the alibi of the weak.'

'It's fortunate,' commented Ahsha drily, 'that Ramses didn't entrust our diplomacy to you.'

'With snakes there are no half-measures; the venom either cures or kills.'

'The matter of Moses is no longer up for discussion,' decided Ahmeni.

'I'm here,' explained Setau, 'because of Lotus. With her gifts for clairvoyance, she warned me. Ramses is in danger, isn't he?'

The pharaoh did not deny it.

Setau turned to Ahmeni. 'Instead of gobbling up that cake, tell us what you've discovered.'

'Me? Nothing. As far as I'm concerned, everything is in order.'

'What about you, Ahsha?'

The diplomat rinsed his fingers in a bowl of lemon-scented water. 'Hattusilis has put forward an unexpected demand: to marry his daughter to Ramses.'

'What's the problem?' asked Setau with amusement. 'That

30

type of diplomatic marriage has been practised quite happily in the past, and what's more this Hittite would only be a secondary wife.'

'In this case, the situation is rather more complicated.'

'Why? Is the girl very ugly?'

'The Hittite emperor wants to make his daughter a Great Royal Wife.'

Setau flew into a rage. 'That . . . that means our old enemy will force Pharaoh to kick Iset out!'

'Your wording is a little blunt,' said Ahsha, 'but you have hit the nail on the head.'

'I hate the Hittites,' growled Setau, emptying another cup of wine. 'True, Iset isn't Nefertari, but she doesn't deserve that fate.'

'For once,' said Ahmeni gruffly, 'I agree with you.'

'You are too impulsive,' said Ahsha. 'Peace itself is at stake.'

'We can't let the Hittites impose their law on us!' protested Setau.

'They're no longer our enemies,' the minister for foreign affairs reminded him.

'You're wrong! Hattusilis and his fellows will never give up their ambition to seize Egypt.'

'You're the one who's wrong,' declared Ahsha. 'Hattusilis wants peace, but he stipulates certain conditions. Why reject them without thinking the matter over?'

'I only believe in my instinct.'

'For my part, I have thought about it,' said Ahmeni. 'I haven't a high opinion of Iset the Fair, but she is Queen of Egypt, the Great Royal Wife whom Ramses chose after the death of Nefertari. No one, not even the Emperor of Hatti, has the right to insult her.'

'That's a ridiculous attitude!' snorted Ahsha. 'Do you wish to send thousands of Egyptians to their deaths, to see our northern protectorates bathed in blood, and put our country itself in danger?'

Ahmeni and Setau looked inquiringly at Ramses.

'I shall make my decision alone,' said Pharaoh.

6

The leader of the convoy hesitated. Should he head south along the coast road, pass through Beirut and cross Canaan to reach Sileh, or should he take the inland track that ran down through the hills past Mount Hermon, leaving Damascus to the east?

Phoenicia was not without its attractions: there were forests of oaks and cedars, walnut trees casting cool shade, fig trees with delicious fruit, hospitable villages offering pleasant places to stay.

But it was important to deliver as quickly as possible to Pi-Ramses the oliban, the precious white frankincense which had been collected in the Arabian peninsula, at the cost of immense efforts. Together with this white incense, which the Egyptians called *sonter*, 'that which deifies', there was also the reddish myrrh, no less valuable. These rare substances were needed to celebrate the rites in the temples; their aromatic smoke wafted upward in the sanctuaries, delighting the gods. Embalmers and physicians also used them.

The Arabian incense tree, with its little dark-green leaves, grew to between ten and fifteen cubits in height. It produced its purple-centred golden-yellow flowers in August and September, while beads of white resin formed under the bark. An expert bark-scraper could obtain three crops a year by reciting the old magical words: 'Be happy with me, incense

CITY OF LIMERICK
33
45517
PUBLIC LIBRARY

tree. Pharaoh will make you grow.'

The donkey-drivers were also transporting copper from Asia and tin and glass, but these materials, though much sought after and easy to trade, did not have the same value as frankincense. When this delivery had been made, the merchant would rest at his fine villa in the Delta.

With his receding hairline and spreading paunch, the frankincense merchant was clearly a good trencherman, but he took his work seriously. He personally checked the state of the carts and the health of the donkeys; his employees were well fed and enjoyed long rests, but did not dare complain for fear of losing their jobs.

The leader of the convoy opted for the mountain track. It was more difficult than the coast road but shorter and, besides, there would be plenty of shade and the animals would benefit from the relative coolness.

The score of donkeys advanced at a brisk pace, their drivers singing to themselves; the wind was in their favour.

'Boss . . .'

'What's the matter?'

'I've got a feeling we're being followed.'

The convoy leader shrugged his shoulders. 'Can't you forget you used to be a mercenary? It's peace now and it's safe to travel.'

'That may be so, but all the same we're being followed. There's something odd about it.'

'We're not the only merchants on the road.'

'If they are vagabonds, don't count on me giving them my share.'

'Stop worrying and see to your donkeys.'

The convoy came to a sudden stop. The leader, furious, walked to the head of the column. He saw that a heap of branches was blocking the track.

'Clear all that away!' he ordered.

Just as the men at the head of the column were beginning

the job, they were pinned to the ground by a volley of arrows. Their panic-stricken companions tried to run, but there was no escape from the attackers. The former mercenary brandished a dagger, climbed up the rocky slope and hurled himself on one of the archers. But a long-haired, athletic fellow split his skull with the blade of a short-handled battle-axe.

The action had only lasted a few minutes. Only the leader of the convoy had been spared. Unable to flee, he trembled at the approach of the killer, whose broad chest was covered with a mat of red hair.

'Spare my life,' the merchant pleaded. 'I'll make you a rich man!'

Uri-Teshup burst out laughing and plunged his sword into the wretch's belly. He hated merchants.

His Phoenician assistants recovered their arrows from the corpses. The donkeys obeyed the orders of their new masters.

Uri-Teshup's violence frightened Raia, but the Syrian had not been able to find a better ally in support of the factions which rejected the peace and wanted to overthrow Ramses. During the truce Raia was growing rich, but he was convinced that the war would be resumed and that the Hittites would attack Egypt. Uri-Teshup, the former commander-in-chief, would be elected leader in a poll organized by his troops and would inspire them with the taste for victory. Having helped him to emerge from the abyss, Raia would enjoy a privileged position in a more or less distant future.

When the Hittite appeared in his warehouse, Raia could not help imperceptibly shrinking away. He had the feeling that this cruel creature, at once hotheaded and cold-blooded, might slit his throat simply for the pleasure of killing.

'Back already!'

'Aren't you pleased to see me, Raia?'

'On the contrary, Prince! Your mission was not simple and—'

'I simplified it.'

The Syrian merchant's little pointed beard quivered. He had asked Uri-Teshup to make contact with the Phoenicians and to purchase the frankincense they were delivering from the Arabian peninsula. There had been a risk that the negotiations would take a long time, but Raia had given Uri-Teshup enough pieces of tin to persuade the leader of the convoy to hand over his load. The Syrian had also tipped the scales with contraband silver, some rare vases and fine lengths of fabric.

'Simplified it?' asked Raia. 'How?'

'Merchants talk; I act.'

'You easily persuaded the leader of the convoy to sell you the frankincense?'

Uri-Teshup smiled his predator's smile. 'Very easily.'

'But he's a hard bargainer.'

'No one argues with my sword.'

'All the same, you didn't . . . ?'

'I hired some mercenaries and we killed the donkey-drivers, including their leader.'

'But why?'

'I don't like endless arguments and I've got the incense. That's all that matters.'

'There will be an investigation,' said Raia worriedly.

'We threw the bodies into a ravine.'

Raia wondered if he wouldn't have done better to lead the peaceful life of a real merchant. But it was too late to turn back: at the slightest sign of reluctance on his part, Uri-Teshup would not hesitate to kill him.

'What now?' asked the prince.

'We must destroy the frankincense,' decided Raia.

'But this load's worth a fortune!'

'Yes, but the purchaser, whoever he might be, would betray us; the incense was intended for the temples.'

'I need weapons, horses and mercenaries.'

'We can't take the risk of selling it!'

'I always despise merchants' advice. You will sell it for me, in small lots, to merchants leaving for Greece and Cyprus. And we shall begin to form a network of loyal followers determined to put an end to this damned peace.'

Uri-Teshup's plan was not unreasonable. Through Phoenician intermediaries, Raia could dispose of the frankincense without too much risk. Phoenicia was deeply hostile to Egypt and sheltered a number of people disenchanted with Hattusilis's policies.

'I must look irreproachable,' the Hittite went on. 'Serramanna will go on hounding me unless I seem idle and set on enjoying the pleasures of life.'

Raia thought for a moment. 'Then you need to marry a rich, respectable woman. That's the only solution: a wealthy widow looking for love.'

'Can you lay hands on one?'

Raia scratched his beard. 'I have a large clientele . . . there are two or three possibilities. Next week I'll organize a banquet and introduce you.'

'When will the next delivery of frankincense leave the Arabian peninsula?'

'I don't know yet, but we've plenty of time. My network of informers won't fail to let us know. But won't more violence trigger a reaction by the Egyptian army?'

'There'll be no trace of violence and the Egyptian authorities will be baffled. We'll have got hold of the year's entire crop. Tell me, though, why are you so sure that the lack of frankincense will topple Ramses?'

'For Egypt, it is essential to carry out the rites correctly. If they aren't celebrated according to the rules laid down since the time of the ancestors, the balance of the country is put in danger. When the priests notice the shortage of frankincense and myrrh, they'll turn against Ramses. What can he do, except admit his lack of foresight? He'll be accused of contempt for the gods, and he'll anger the priests and the people. If we spread some false news, to add to the confusion and deprive Ramses of one or two major supporters, serious disturbances will break out in the principal cities.'

Uri-Teshup imagined Egypt put to the fire and the sword, in the hands of looters, Pharaoh's crowns trampled underfoot by the Hittite army, Pharaoh's eyes filled with terror. His face was so distorted by hatred that Raia was frightened: for a few moments Uri-Teshup had entered the realm of darkness, losing touch with the world of men.

'I want to strike hard and swiftly, Raia.'

'Patience is essential, my lord; Ramses is a formidable enemy. Too much haste will lead to failure.'

'I've heard that he enjoys magic protections. But they grow weaker with age, and Nefertari is no longer there to help this cursed monarch.'

'Our spy network succeeded in manipulating Ramses' brother and the minister Meba,' Raia reminded him. 'They are dead, but I still have some useful contacts in the upper ranks of the administration. Government officials are sometimes talkative – one of them told me there's a risk that diplomatic relations between Hatti and Egypt may deteriorate.'

'That's wonderful news! What's caused the friction?'

'That's a closely guarded secret, but I shall find out more.'

'Our luck is turning, Raia! And don't for one minute think I am any less formidable than Ramses.'

7

Iset the Fair's maidservant took her time over soaping the queen's back, and then poured cool, scented water over her slender body. She used a substance rich in saponin, which was extracted from the bark and abundant fruit of the precious balanite tree. In pensive mood, the Queen of Egypt now put herself in the hands of her manicurist and hairdresser. A manservant brought her a goblet of fresh milk.

Iset felt more at ease here in Pi-Ramses than in Thebes, where Nefertari's tomb was situated, on the west bank, in the Valley of the Queens; there too was her House of Ramses shrine, where Ramses himself often worshipped. Here, in the cosmopolitan capital Pharaoh had created, life was bustling and there was less thought of the past and the next world.

Iset gazed at herself in a round mirror of burnished bronze with a handle in the shape of a long-legged naked woman, her head crowned with a papyrus flower. Yes, she was still beautiful; her skin was as soft as any precious fabric, her face had retained an extraordinary freshness, love shone in her eyes. But her beauty could never equal Nefertari's and she was grateful to Ramses for never having lied to her by claiming that he would one day forget his first Great Royal Wife. Iset was not jealous of Nefertari; on the contrary, she missed her. She had never coveted her place; to have borne Ramses two sons was happiness enough.

How different they were! The elder, Kha, was now thirty-seven. He held high religious offices, and spent most of his time in the temple libraries. Meneptah, the younger by ten years, was as athletic as his father and showed a pronounced taste for command. Perhaps one of the two would be called on to reign; but the pharaoh might choose as his successor one of the many Royal Sons, most of whom were brilliant administrators.

Iset did not care about power and gave no thought to the future. She enjoyed every moment of the miracle that fate had granted her. To live close to Ramses, to take part in the official ceremonies at his side and watch him reign over the Two Lands . . . What could be more wonderful?

The maidservant braided the queen's hair, scented it with myrrh and set on it a short wig, to which she added a diadem of pearls and cornelian.

'Forgive my familiarity, but Your Majesty is so beautiful!'

Iset smiled. She had to remain beautiful for Ramses, to make him forget for as long as possible that he was no longer young.

Just as she was rising to her feet, he appeared. He was incomparable. No other man had his intelligence, his strength and his presence. The gods had given him everything, and he gave back this offering to his country.

'Ramses! I'm not dressed yet.'

'I must speak to you about a serious matter.'

Iset had feared this ordeal. Nefertari had had a talent for governing, but she did not. To be associated with the conduct of the ship of state terrified her.

'Whatever you decide will be right,' she said nervously.

'This concerns you directly, Iset.'

'Me? I swear that I haven't intervened in any way, that—'

'You are personally involved, and what is at stake is peace.'

'I don't understand.'

'Hattusilis insists that I marry his daughter.'

'A marriage of convenience?' said Iset, relieved. 'Well, why not?'

'He's demanding much more than that. He wants her to be my Great Royal Wife.'

Iset stood for a few moments as if turned to stone, then her eyes filled with tears. The miracle had just ended. She had to step aside and make way for a pretty young Hittite, the symbol of the peace between Egypt and Hatti. Iset the Fair weighed less than a feather in the balance.

'It's up to you to decide,' declared Ramses. 'Do you agree to give up your position and go into retirement?'

The queen smiled faintly. 'This Hittite princess must be very young.'

'Her age is unimportant.'

'You have made me very happy, Ramses. Your will is that of Egypt.'

'So you agree?'

'It would be criminal to be an obstacle to peace.'

'Well, I do *not* agree! The Emperor of Hatti shall not dictate the Pharaoh of Egypt's decisions. We are not a barbarian people who treat women as inferior creatures. What Lord of the Two Lands has ever repudiated his Great Royal Wife, the one who is part of Pharaoh's existence? How dare a Hittite warlord ask me, Ramses, to violate the law of our ancestors!'

He took Iset's hands affectionately. 'You spoke on behalf of Egypt's interests, as a true queen should do. Now it is up to me to act.'

The light of the setting sun shone through one of the three large stone-framed windows that lit up Ramses' vast office, and gilded the statue of Seti. Made lifelike by the sculptor's magic and the ritual opening of the mouth and eyes, the statue continued to transmit a message of righteousness – which only his son could comprehend – when the calm of evening was adorned with divine splendour.

White walls, a large table on which a map of the known world was spread out, a straight-backed armchair for the pharaoh, cane chairs for visitors, shelves containing books devoted to the protection of the royal soul, and a cupboard for papyri: such was the austere setting in which Ramses the Great alone made the decisions involving the future of his country.

The king had consulted the sages in the Heliopolis House of Life, the high priests of the main temples, Ahmeni, the viziers and ministers, and had then shut himself up in his office and communed with his father's soul. In the past, he would have talked to Nefertari and Tuya; Iset knew her limitations and had been of no help to him. Solitude weighed more and more heavily on him. Soon he would have to put his two sons to the test, to decide if one of them would be capable of continuing the work begun by the first pharaoh.

Egypt was both strong and fragile. Strong because the Rule of the goddess Ma'at endured, beyond human weaknesses; fragile because the world was changing, according an ever-greater place to tyranny, greed and selfishness. The pharaohs would probably be the last to fight for the Rule of Ma'at, the embodiment of the universal Rule of justice and love, which bound together the elements and components of life. For they knew that without Ma'at this world would be nothing but an enclosed field where barbarians fought with increasingly destructive weapons to build up their power and destroy all links with the gods. To replace disorder, violence, injustice, lies and hatred with the Rule of Ma'at: such was Pharaoh's task, carried out under the favourable eyes of the Invisible. And what the Emperor of Hatti demanded was contrary to that Rule.

A guard showed in Ahsha, who was wearing a linen gown and a long-sleeved tunic of exceptionally fine workmanship.

'I wouldn't like to work in a place like this,' he told Ramses. 'It's too bleak.'

'My father didn't like too much decoration, and neither do I.'

'Being the pharaoh doesn't leave much room for flights of fancy – anyone who envies you is either stupid or ignorant. Has Your Majesty come to a decision?'

'I have finished all my consultations.'

'Have I managed to convince you?'

'No, Ahsha.'

The minister for foreign affairs looked down at the map on the table. 'I was afraid of that.'

'Hattusilis's demands are an insult. To give in to them would be to deny all that the pharaohs stand for.'

Ahsha put a finger on the Hittite Empire. 'Refusal will be tantamount to a declaration of war, Majesty.'

'Do you think I've made the wrong decision?'

'It's the decision of Pharaoh, of Ramses the Great. Your father would have done the same.'

'Were you setting a trap for me?'

'I was doing my job as a diplomat, working for peace. I wouldn't be a real friend if I didn't put it to the proof.'

There was a suggestion of a smile on the king's lips.

'When will Your Majesty give the orders for mobilization?'

'For the head of my diplomatic service, you're very pessimistic.'

'Your official reply will make Hattusilis furious,' said Ahsha, 'and he won't think twice about starting hostilities.'

'You should have more confidence in yourself.'

'I am a realist.'

'If anyone can still save the peace, you can,' said Ramses.

'In other words, Pharaoh is ordering me to leave for Hattusa, to explain our position to the emperor and persuade him to change his mind.'

'You've read my mind.'

'I'd have no chance of success.'

'Ahsha, you've brought off other feats that were just as difficult.'

'Yes, but I'm older now, Majesty.'

'So you're more experienced! Mere argument about this impossible marriage won't be enough. We'll have to be more aggressive.'

Ahsha frowned. He thought he knew Ramses well, but once again the pharaoh had surprised him.

'We have concluded a treaty of mutual assistance with our great friend Hattusilis,' the king went on. 'You will explain to him that we fear a Libyan attack on our western border. Now, since the beginning of the peace, our weaponry has aged and we are short of iron. You will ask the emperor to supply us with a significant quantity. Thanks to him, and in accordance with our agreements, we shall be able to defend ourselves against the attackers.'

Ahsha was taken aback. He folded his arms. 'Is that really my mission?'

'I forgot one detail,' said Ramses. 'The iron must be delivered as quickly as possible.'

8

Kha, the elder son of Ramses and Iset the Fair, had refused to make his career in the army or the government. Such secular work did not attract him, whereas he felt a real passion for the writings of the sages and the monuments of the Old Empire. Kha's face was angular and stern, with deep blue eyes, and his head was shaven; he was almost skinny, and walked rather stiffly because of occasional pains in his joints. He was a born researcher. He had won renown in the struggle against Moses and his magic tricks, and he ruled firmly over the priests of the god Ptah in Memphis. For some time now, Kha had been delegating the temporal side of his responsibilities in order to concentrate on examining the hidden forces which manifested themselves in air and stone, in water and wood.

In the Heliopolis House of Life were stored the 'Souls of Light', the sacred archives dating from the golden age when the pharaohs had built the pyramids and the sages had drawn up the rituals. In that blessed age, they had uncovered the secrets of life and death. Not content with exploring the mysteries of the universe, the sages had transcribed them in hieroglyphs, in order to transmit their vision to future generations.

Recognized by everyone as the finest expert on the tradition, Kha had been chosen to organize Ramses' first *sed-*

feast, marking the thirtieth year of his reign. After exercising power for so long, the pharaoh's magic force was considered to be exhausted. It was therefore necessary to gather all the gods and goddesses round him so that they might restore him and renew his life-force. Many demons had tried in vain to prevent Ramses' regeneration.

Kha wanted to do more than simply decipher books of magic spells. He was haunted by vast projects, so vast that he would need the pharaoh's support. Before submitting his dreams to his father, he must first find the means to realize them. That was why, as soon as dawn broke, he was pacing up and down the Red Mountain quarry, near Heliopolis, looking for blocks of quartzite. Here, according to the legend, the gods had massacred the men who had rebelled against the light, and their blood had permeated the stone for all time.

Although he had no training as a quarryman or sculptor, Kha communicated instinctively with the raw material; he sensed the latent energy which ran through the veins of the rock.

Appearing suddenly out of the new, young light of the morning sun, which conquered the darkness and spread its authority over the desert, Ramses gazed at his son.

Kha caught his breath. He knew that Nefertari had given her life to save him from the spells of an evil sorcerer, and he sometimes wondered if Ramses resented him because of it.

'You're wrong, Kha. I know you aren't to blame.'

'You can read my most secret thoughts!'

'You wanted to see me,' said Ramses.

'I thought you were in Thebes, and yet you're here, on the Red Mountain.'

'Egypt is threatened by great danger, which I must confront. It was essential for me to meditate here.'

'But we're at peace with the Hittites, aren't we?' asked Kha.

'It may be only a truce.'

'Either you will avoid war, or you will win. Whatever happens, you will protect Egypt from disaster.'

'Do you want to help me?'

'Politics!' said Kha. 'No, that's beyond me. And your reign will last a long time, if you respect the ancestral rites. That's what I wanted to speak to you about.'

'What do you suggest?'

'We must immediately prepare the next feast of regeneration.'

'Only three years after the first one?' asked Ramses, surprised.

'From now on, we must celebrate this rite at regular, short intervals. That's the conclusion I've reached through my research.'

'Do whatever is necessary.'

'You make me very happy, father. Not one deity will be absent from your next *sed*-feast. Joy will spread in the Two Lands, and the goddess Nut will scatter malachite and turquoise in the heavens.'

'You have another plan, Kha. For which temple do you intend the blocks of quartzite you are looking for?'

'I've been studying our origins for several years. Among the first of our rites there was the hunting of a bull called Apis, who embodied the king's ability to travel through the heavens. It would be advisable to do more to honour this extraordinary animal and to grant him a burial place worthy of his power. Then we must not forget to restore some of the ancient monuments – some of the pyramids have suffered the ravages of time and were damaged by the Hyksos invaders. Will you grant me teams of builders to do this work?'

'You yourself can choose the architect and stone-cutters.'

Kha's stern face lit up.

'This is a strange place,' observed Ramses. 'The blood of the rebels has soaked into these stones. Here the eternal combat of light against darkness has left deep traces. The Red

Mountain is a place of power, where it is advisable to venture only with great caution. You are not here by chance, Kha. What treasure are you looking for?'

Kha sat down on a brownish-coloured rock. 'The *Book of Thoth*, the book which contains the secret of the hieroglyphs. It is somewhere in the Saqqara necropolis. I shall find it, even if I have to search for many years.'

The Lady Tanit was a beautiful Phoenician. Though she was fifty-four, her generous proportions still attracted men – often much younger men. The widow of a rich merchant, a friend of the Syrian Raia, she had inherited a considerable fortune, which she enjoyed to the full, organizing banquet after banquet in her luxurious Pi-Ramses home.

She had quickly got over the death of a husband whom she considered vulgar and boring. After feigning sadness for a few weeks, Tanit had found consolation in the arms of a magnificent Nubian of outstanding attributes. But she had soon tired of him, as she had of her previous lovers; in spite of their virility, they tired more quickly than she did. And a mistress as greedy for pleasure as Tanit could not forgive them this deplorable lack of stamina.

Tanit could have returned to Phoenicia, but she liked Egypt more and more. Thanks to Ramses' authority and radiance, the land of the pharaohs seemed a near-paradise. Nowhere else was a woman so free to live as she thought fit.

At dusk, tonight's guests arrived: rich Egyptians doing business with the Lady Tanit, senior officials fascinated by the exotic Phoenician, fellow-citizens with an eye on her fortune, not to mention some new faces which it amused the lady of the house to discover – there was nothing more exciting than to feel a man's desire-filled eyes on her. Tanit had the knack of appearing now playful, now distant, never letting the man she was talking to guess the outcome of their meeting. In every situation she kept the initiative and made the decisions. A man who tried to dominate her had no chance of winning her.

Tonight, as usual, the food would be delicious, especially the saddle of hare cooked in a beer sauce and served with aubergine sauce, and the wines would be outstanding. Thanks to her contacts at the palace, Tanit had even obtained several jars of Pi-Ramses red wine dating from the twenty-first year of Ramses' reign, the year of the treaty with the Hittites. Also as usual, the Phoenician would cast lascivious eyes on the most handsome men, in search of future prey,

One of the guests came over and greeted her. 'How are you, my very dear friend?'

'Raia, it's good to see you again. I'm very well.'

'If I wasn't afraid of flattering you, I'd say you grow more beautiful every day.'

Tanit smiled. 'The climate suits me. And then my grief at losing my late husband is beginning to fade.'

'Fortunately, such is the law of nature. A woman like you isn't meant for solitude.'

'Men are liars and brutes,' she said archly. 'I have to be on my guard.'

'You are right to be cautious, but I'm sure fate has new happiness in store for you.'

'And how is your business?'

'Work, a great deal of work. Making luxury preserves demands a highly skilled workforce, who claim high wages. As for the exotic vases which society prizes so much, importing them requires interminable negotiations and journeys. Reliable craftsmen are not cheap. My reputation rests on quality, so I constantly need to invest. That's why I never get rich.'

'Luck has smiled on you,' said Tanit. 'I think your worries are at an end.'

'I've been accused of sympathizing with the Hittite cause. The fact is, I have done business with them, but I've kept well clear of politics. At present, collaboration with our foreign partners is even encouraged. That must be Ramses' greatest victory!'

'Pharaoh is *so* attractive,' sighed Tanit. 'It's such a pity he's inaccessible.'

The peace, the treaty concluded by Ramses and Hattusilis, the loss of the Hittite Empire's spirit of conquest, Egypt triumphant . . . Raia could no longer bear the cowardice and defections that had caused this disaster. He had struggled to make the Hittite army supreme in the whole of the known world, and he would never give up the fight.

'May I introduce a friend?' he asked.

Tanit's curiosity was immediately aroused. 'Who is it?'

'A Hittite prince who is staying in Egypt. He has heard a great deal about you, but he's rather shy. It took a lot of persuasion to get him to attend this banquet – he's frightened of society life.'

'Point him out to me.'

'He's over there, near that clump of oleanders.'

A lamp hung from a pillar lit up Uri-Teshup, who stood apart from the groups of guests engaged in idle conversation. The flickering light revealed his brutal face, his long, thick hair, his broad chest covered with red hair, his tough, warriorlike muscles.

Tanit was struck dumb with emotion. Never before had she seen a wild creature that gave off such intense sensuality. The banquet ceased to exist. She now had only one idea in her head: her urgent need to make love to this stallion.

9

Standing in his chariot, Ramses watched the fight between Meneptah and Serramanna – it reminded him of the fight on the seashore in the course of which he had defeated the pirate Serramanna and then made him the head of his personal bodyguard.

Pharaoh had asked Serramanna not to spare his opponent. Meneptah, 'the Beloved of the God Ptah', was a fine athlete, brave, thoughtful and endowed with lightning reflexes. If he wanted to prove his worth in battle, he could not have wished for a better opponent, for the Sardinian, although over fifty, had lost none of his strength and dynamism: to stand up to him was in itself an achievement.

Equipped with an articulated breastplate, a horned helmet topped with a bronze disc, and a round shield, Serramanna struck repeated blows with his sword on Meneptah's rectangular shield, forcing him to fall back. Meneptah gave ground, returned to the attack, parried the blows, moved sideways; he was gradually wearing the older man down.

Suddenly Serramanna stood still and threw down on the ground his shield and his long sword with its triangular blade. 'That's enough skirmishing. We'll fight with bare hands.'

Meneptah hesitated for a moment, then copied the Sardinian.

Serramanna made a sudden rush at the prince, head-butting

him and taking him completely by surprise; at the military college Meneptah had not learnt to fight like a wild animal. He was thrown flat on his back in the dust of the barracks and felt he was suffocating under the weight of his gigantic opponent.

'The lesson is over,' declared Ramses.

The two men got to their feet.

Meneptah was furious. 'He took me off my guard!'

'That's what the enemy always does, my son.'

'I want to finish the fight.'

'There's no need: I've seen what I wanted to see. Since you've been given a useful lesson, I now appoint you commander-in-chief of the Egyptian army.'

Serramanna nodded his approval.

'In less than a month,' Ramses went on, 'you will submit to me a complete and detailed report on the state of our troops and the quality of their weapons.'

While Meneptah was getting his breath back, Ramses took the reins of his chariot and drove away. To whom should he entrust the fate of Egypt: to Kha, the scholar, or Meneptah, the warrior? If their respective qualities had been combined in one and the same person, the choice would have been easy. As for the Royal Sons, many of whom had fine qualities, none of them were such strong characters as either of Iset the Fair's two sons. And Meritamon, Nefertari's daughter, had chosen to live as a recluse in a temple.

If only Nefertari were still there to advise him . . . Ramses had to take heed of the advice given him by Ahmeni that morning: 'Your Majesty must let himself be regenerated by the rites, in order to continue to reign until his energy is totally exhausted. For Pharaoh, there has never been any other way; and there never will be.'

Raia came out of his warehouse, crossed through the workshop district, passed the royal palace and took the grand avenue that led to the temples of Pi-Ramses. Lined with acacias and sycamores which shed a refreshing shade, this avenue gave a true picture of Ramses' capital – majestic and reassuring.

The merchant left the Temple of Amon on his left, and the Temple of Ra on his right. He tried to walk calmly as he made his way towards the Temple of Ptah. Near the building he was tempted to retreat. Embedded in the external walls were stelae on which the sculptors had carved ears and eyes: the god could hear one's most secret words and see one's most deeply hidden intentions.

'Superstition,' thought Raia, but nevertheless he was uneasy and he avoided the extension of the corner of the wall. There, in a niche, a statue of Ma'at had been enshrined, so that the people could contemplate the principal secret of the pharaonic civilization, this unchanging Rule, born beyond time and space.

Raia arrived at the craftsmen's gate. The guard knew him, and they exchanged a few trivialities about the beauty of the city – the merchant complained about the greed of some of his customers. Then he was permitted to enter the part of the temple reserved for the goldsmiths. As a specialist in precious vases, Raia knew many of them and never failed to ask after the family of one or the health of another.

'You'd love to lay your hands on our secrets,' muttered an old master craftsman who was loading some ingots on to a cart.

'I've given up even thinking about that,' said Raia. 'Just seeing you work is enough to make me happy.'

'All the same, you haven't come here for a rest, have you?'

'I'd like to acquire one or two fine pieces.'

'To sell them at three times the price!'

'That's business, my friend.'

The old craftsman turned his back on Raia, who was used to these rebuffs. Discreet, almost invisible, he watched the apprentices bringing ingots to their fellow workers, who weighed them under the supervision of specialist scribes. The precious metal was then placed in a closed vessel and heated over a blown flame; the blowers often had swollen cheeks as a result of keeping up the rhythm. Other craftsmen poured the molten metal into different-shaped receptacles and entrusted the cooled metal to the goldsmiths, who worked with stone hammers on anvils, fashioning necklaces, bracelets, vases, decorations for temple doors and statues. The secrets of the trade were handed on from master to pupil in the course of an apprenticeship which lasted many years.

'Magnificent!' declared Raia to a goldsmith who had just finished a breastplate.

'It will adorn the statue of a god,' explained the craftsman.

The merchant asked in an undertone, 'Can we talk?'

'There's enough noise in the workshop. No one will hear us.'

'I'm told your two boys want to get married.'

'Possibly,' said the goldsmith.

'If I gave them some furniture, would you be satisfied?'

'What would it cost me?'

'A small piece of information.'

'Don't ask me to reveal any of our craft secrets.'

'It's nothing like that!' said Raia hastily.

'What do you want to know?'

'There are some Syrians living in Egypt whom I'd like to help get on in life. Haven't you engaged one or two in your workshop?'

'Yes, one.'

'Does he seem to have settled in all right?'

'More or less.'

'If you'll give me his name, I'll speak to him.'

'Is that all you want, Raia?'

'I'm beginning to get old, and I've no children. I have a certain amount of property and I'd like to help a compatriot.'

'Egypt has taught you not to be so selfish,' said the goldsmith approvingly. 'So much the better. When the judgment of souls takes place, the great god will appreciate your generosity. Your Syrian is one of the flame-blowers – the biggest one, with the sticking-out ears.'

'I hope my gifts will contribute to your sons' happiness,' said Raia. He said goodbye to the goldsmith and walked away.

He waited till the end of the work period to talk to his fellow Syrian. After two recent failures, with a carpenter and a mason who were both satisfied with their lot, this time he had complete success.

The flame-blower, a former prisoner captured near Kadesh, refused to accept the Hittites' defeat and longed for the end of the peace. Embittered, resentful and bent on revenge, he was just the sort of man Uri-Teshup and Raia needed. What was more, he had friends who shared his views.

Raia had no difficulty persuading him to work for him, and to become part of a group of resistance fighters whose mission would be to attack Egypt's vital interests.

Uri-Teshup bit his mistress on the neck and penetrated her violently. Tanit sighed with pleasure. At last she was experiencing true passion, a combination of brutality and perpetually unsatisfied desire.

'More,' she begged.

The Hittite let himself go in uninhibited enjoyment of the lovely Phoenician's mature charms. In the fortresses of Hatti, he had learnt to use women as they deserved.

For a moment Tanit felt unnerved: for the first time, she was not in control of the situation. This barbarian, with his inexhaustible potency, was almost terrifying. She would never find another lover like him, capable of sharing her wildest debauchery.

In the middle of the night she admitted defeat. 'Enough! I can't go on.'

'Already?'

'You're a monster!'

'You've only known youngsters, my dear. I am a man.'

She nestled against him. 'You're wonderful – I'd like the sun never to rise.'

'What does that matter?'

'But . . . you'll have to leave! We'll see each other again tomorrow night.'

'I'm staying.'

'Do you know what that means, in Egypt?'

'When a man and a woman live under the same roof, openly and publicly, they are married. So we are married.'

Shocked, she drew away from him. 'We'll see each other again, but—'

Uri-Teshup pushed her on to her back and lay down on top of her. 'You will do as I say, woman. I am the son of the late Emperor of Hatti and the legitimate heir to the empire. You are nothing but a Phoenician harlot, who will pleasure me and satisfy all my needs. Are you aware of the honour I do you in making you my wife?'

Tanit tried to protest, but Uri-Teshup took her again with tigerish ferocity, and she was carried away in a whirl of delight.

'If you betray me,' he murmured hoarsely, 'I shall kill you.'

10

Setau extracted from a rush basket a triangular loaf of bread, a bowl of barley gruel, a dried fish, a braised pigeon, a roast quail, two kidneys cooked in wine, a rib of beef on a bed of fried onions, some figs and a herb cheese. He slowly placed the dishes, one by one, on Ahmeni's desk.

The scribe had to push aside the papyri he was consulting. 'What's all this?' he asked.

'Are you blind? A decent meal which will satisfy your appetite for two or three hours.'

'I don't need—'

'Yes, you do. Your brain doesn't work properly if you haven't got a full belly.'

'Are you insulting me?' demanded Ahmeni indignantly.

'It was the only way to get your attention.'

'You're not going to talk to me again about—'

'Yes, I am! I want more credits for Nubia, and I'm not going to amuse myself filling out fifty forms like some old papyrus-shuffler.'

'You've got a superior: the Viceroy of Nubia.'

'He's a lazy fool who thinks of nothing except his career, and couldn't care less about my province. Ramses has asked me to turn it to good account, but if I'm to cover it with temples and shrines, and make more land suitable for cultivation, I need men and materials.'

'There are certain regulations I have to obey,' protested Ahmeni.

'Oh, damn the regulations! They stifle life. Forget them!'

'I'm not-all powerful, Setau. I'm accountable to the vizier, Pazair, and to the king himself.'

'Give me what I'm asking for and you can account for it afterwards.'

'In other words, you're making me responsible for your future mistakes.'

Setau looked surprised. 'Of course I am! You, with your scribe's mumbo-jumbo language, you'll be able to justify us.'

Ahmeni took a mouthful of the braised pigeon. It was a miracle, and he didn't hide his appreciation. 'Lotus cooked it, didn't she?'

'My wife is a real witch.'

'We are about collude in the bribery of a public official.'

'Will you give me what I'm asking for, Ahmeni?'

'If Ramses weren't so fond of Nubia . . .'

'Thanks to me, in a few years, it will be richer than an Egyptian province!'

Ahmeni started on the roast quail.

'Now that that little problem is solved,' said Setau, 'I can tell you I'm very worried.'

'What about?'

'Yesterday I was making love to Lotus, and suddenly she sat up and shouted, "There's a monster prowling around!" She wasn't speaking about our two cobras which keep watch at the foot of our bed, or about the Hittite army – which Ramses will defeat a second time if necessary.'

'Do you know who this monster is?'

'For me, there's no doubt about it: it's that Hittite brute Uri-Teshup.'

'We've nothing against him.'

'Have you warned Serramanna?'

'Of course.'

'What was his reaction?'

'Like you, he hates Uri-Teshup and thinks that freeing him was a mistake. But Uri-Teshup hasn't committed any offence. As far as I'm concerned, he's a defeated warrior and a castrated prince. What have we got to fear from him?'

When the first sunbeams shone into his bedchamber, Serramanna opened his eyes. On his left a Nubian girl lay fast asleep. On his right was a Libyan girl, a little younger. He couldn't remember their names.

'Up, girls!'

He was a bad judge of his own strength, and the pat he gave his two companions' delicate posteriors, as thanks for the one-night stand, was less of a caress than he had meant. They screamed like frightened chickens, giving him a headache.

'Get dressed and clear off.'

Serramanna dived into the pool which took up most of his garden, and swam for twenty minutes. He knew no better cure for the after-effects of over-indulgence in wine and amorous frolics.

Back in shape again, he was starting to wolf down a loaf of freshly baked bread, some onions, bacon and dried beef, when his servant announced one of his subordinates.

'Some news, sir. We've traced Uri-Teshup.'

'Dead, I hope.'

'Well and truly alive and . . . married.'

'Who to?'

'A rich Phoenician widow, Tanit.'

'She has one of the largest fortunes in Pi-Ramses! You must be mistaken.'

'Go and see for yourself, sir.'

'Let's go.'

With an enormous piece of dried beef still in his mouth, Serramanna ran to the stables and leapt on to his horse.

*

The guard at Lady Tanit's villa should have asked to see the official document authorizing the head of Pharaoh's bodyguard to question the villa's owner; Serramanna's angry expression dissuaded him. He called the gardener, and asked him to take Serramanna to the lady of the house.

Dressed in a gown of transparent linen which hid scarcely anything of her abundant charms, Tanit was eating her breakfast on a shady terrace in the company of Uri-Teshup, who was dressed in nothing but his mat of red body-hair.

'The illustrious Serramanna!' exclaimed the Hittite, visibly delighted by this visit. 'Shall we invite him to share our meal, my dear?'

'Do you know who this man is, Lady Tanit?' asked the Sardinian.

'Yes, I do.'

'Please be more precise.'

'Uri-Teshup is a Hittite prince, the son of the late emperor.'

'He was also the commander-in-chief of the Hittite army and a barbarian who was utterly relentness in his determination to destroy Egypt.'

'That's in the distant past,' interrupted Uri-Teshup derisively. 'Ramses and Hattusilis concluded a fine peace, the pharaoh granted me my freedom, and we are all living happily ever after. Don't you agree, Serramanna?'

The Sardinian noticed bite-marks on Tanit's neck. 'This Hittite spent the night under your roof and seems resolved to live here. Do you know what that means, my lady?'

'Of course I do.'

'He's threatening to torture you, isn't he, unless you agree to marry him?'

'Answer, my dear,' ordered Uri-Teshup. 'Tell him you're a free woman, like any other Egyptian, and that you alone make your decisions.'

'I love Uri-Teshup,' she said harshly, 'and I've chosen him

as my husband. There's no law against that.'

'Think carefully, Lady Tanit,' said Serramanna. 'If you tell me that this individual has knocked you about, I'll arrest him on the spot and you won't be in any danger. I'll bring him to trial immediately and the punishment won't be light. To ill-treat a woman is a serious crime.'

'Get out of my house!' snapped Tanit.

'I'm surprised,' added Uri-Teshup ironically. 'I thought we were entertaining a friend and I see we're being questioned by an aggressive policeman. Have you an official document authorizing you to enter private property?'

'Take care, my lady,' warned Serramanna. 'You may be getting yourself into serious trouble.'

'My wife and I could lodge a complaint,' said the Hittite, 'but we'll let it go for once. Make yourself scarce, Serramanna, and leave in peace a decent couple who only want to enjoy their happiness.'

Uri-Teshup embraced Tanit passionately. Forgetting the presence of the Sardinian, she began to caress her husband without the slightest inhibition.

The shelves and cupboards in Ahmeni's office threatened to collapse under the weight of administrative documents. Never had he had to deal with so many important dossiers at once; as he checked every detail himself, he no longer slept for more than two hours a night and, in spite of his colleagues' protests, he had cancelled all leave for the coming three months. Substantial bonuses had appeased them.

Ahmeni was busy dealing with Setau's demands concerning Nubia and rejecting the arguments of the viceroy, who was in favour of leaving well alone. He passed on his advice to the vizier, Pazair, who distrusted specialists in economics. In his capacity as Ramses' private secretary, he saw the king every day to request a thousand and one decisions, after carefully preparing summaries of the concrete facts which the sovereign demanded. And then there was all the rest, because Egypt had to remain a great country, a unique land which he had to serve without thought for his own welfare.

When Serramanna burst into his office, the scribe, whose pale face was furrowed with wrinkles, wondered if his shoulders could bear a fresh burden. 'What now?'

'Uri-Teshup is well and truly married to that Phoenician, Tanit.'

'He's fallen on his feet, then. The fortune is as nicely rounded as the lady.'

'It's a disaster, Ahmeni!'

'Why? Our former commander-in-chief will grow weak in a life of pleasure and idleness.'

'I can't keep an eye on him properly any longer. If he spots my men, he'll lodge a complaint and he'll win his case. He's a free man now. Officially I've nothing against him, but he's up to something, I know he is.'

'Have you spoken to Tanit?'

'He's beaten and threatened her, I'm sure. But she's fallen in love with him.'

'And to think there are people who've got so little to do that they've got time to think about love! Don't worry, Serramanna. Uri-Teshup has finally made a conquest, but this one will keep him off the warpath for ever.'

11

Hattusa,* the capital of the Hittite empire, had not changed. Built on the central Anatolian plateau, exposed to scorching summers and icy winters, the fortified city consisted of a lower town, whose most remarkable feature was the Temple of the God of Storms and the Sun Goddess, and an upper town dominated by the emperor's bleak palace, which had been built to keep permanent watch over the vast ramparts bristling with towers and battlements.

It was not without trepidation that Ahsha saw Hattusa again, the embodiment in stone of Hittite military power. He had nearly lost his life there, during a particularly dangerous spying mission shortly before the battle of Kadesh.

His convoy had had to cross barren steppes and pass through inhospitable gorges before reaching the capital, which was surrounded by high mountains that presented considerable difficulties to a would-be attacker. Hattusa seemed an impregnable fortress perched on rocky outcrops, which had made incredible demands on the builders' skills. How different all this was from Egypt and its warm, welcoming and open cities!

Access to the interior of Hattusa was given by five fortified gates, two in the walls of the lower city, and three in those of

*Bogazköy, about 95 miles east of Ankara in present-day Turkey.

the upper city. Ahsha and his party were led by their Hittite escort, which had accompanied them for some sixty miles, to the highest point of access, the Gate of the Sphinx.

Before entering, Ahsha celebrated the Hittite rite. He broke three loaves of bread, poured wine on the stone and uttered the ritual incantation: 'May this rock be eternal.' He noted the presence of vessels filled with oil and honey, intended to prevent demons spreading their noxious effluvia over the city. Emperor Hattusilis had maintained the traditions.

This time, Ahsha had found the journey very tiring. When he was young, he had hated staying in one place; he had loved danger and had never hesitated to take risks. Now that he had reached maturity, it was becoming a burden to leave Egypt. This stay abroad deprived him of the unique pleasure of watching Ramses govern. Pharaoh respected the Rule of Ma'at, knowing that 'the best thing is to listen', according to the maxim of the sage Ptah-hotep, Nefertari's favorite author. The king let his ministers talk at length, and paid heed to their every intonation, every attitude. Suddenly, with the speed of the crocodile-god Sobek rising from the depths of the waters to cause the rebirth of the sun, Ramses would make his decision. One simple sentence, luminous, obvious, definitive. He was at the helm and handled the rudder with incomparable skill, as he was in himself, alone, both the ship of state and its pilot. The gods who had chosen him had not been mistaken; and men had been right to obey them.

Two helmeted and booted junior officers led Ahsha to the imperial palace, which stood imposingly on piles formed by three peaks; elite soldiers kept permanent watch on the battlements of the high towers. The lord of the land was protected from all external attack. That was why claimants to the supreme power had often preferred poison to an attack on the palace, which had no chance of succeeding. Indeed, Hattusilis might well have had recourse to poison to get rid of

Uri-Teshup, if Ahsha, carrying out his mission with rare skill, had not enabled the prince to escape to Egypt, where he had provided Ramses with useful information on the Hittite army.

Only one entrance gave access to the 'Great Fortress', as it was called by the people, who looked on it with dread. When the heavy bronze gate closed behind him, Ahsha had the impression he was a prisoner. The message he had to deliver to Hattusilis did not inspire him with optimism. The emperor did not keep him waiting – a comforting sign. He was shown into the chilly audience chamber, which had heavy columns and walls adorned with military trophies. The emperor and empress were seated on massive thrones that lacked all elegance.

Hattusilis was small and puny. He was dressed in his usual long red and black gown, and wore a silver necklace and, on his left forearm, an iron bracelet; his hair was bound with a head-band. A superficial observer might have concluded that he was rather insignificant, even inoffensive; that would have been to misunderstand his stubborn character and strategist's skill as priest of the Sun Goddess. He had finally got the better of the formidable Uri-Teshup, after a long, ruthless struggle, in which he had been helped by his wife, the beautiful Putuhepa, whose intelligence was feared by the military as well as by the merchant clans.

Ahsha bowed to the sovereigns. 'May all the deities of Egypt and Hatti favour Your Majesties, and may your reign be as enduring as the heavens.'

'We have known you long enough, Ahsha, for you to dispense with formalities,' said Hattusilis. 'Come and sit near us. How is our brother Ramses?'

'He is in excellent health. May I say to the empress that her beauty illuminates this palace?'

Putuhepa smiled. 'Flattery is still one of your diplomatic weapons, I see.'

'We are at peace, and I no longer need to flatter you. My

declaration may perhaps be disrespectful, but it is sincere.'

The empress blushed slightly.

'If you are still a lover of beautiful women,' said the emperor, 'I shall have to be on my guard.'

'Yes, my tastes are unchanged, and fidelity is not one of my virtues.'

'Nevertheless, you saved Ramses from the traps which Hatti set him and dismantled our spy network.'

'I beg Your Majesty not to exaggerate anything. I put Pharaoh's plan into practice, and fate was kind, to me, that's all.'

'Well, all that belongs to the past. Now we must build the future.'

'Indeed,' said Ahsha earnestly, 'that is Ramses' opinion too. He attaches the greatest importance to reinforcing the peace with Hatti. On it the happiness of our two peoples depends.'

'We are pleased to hear these words,' said Putuhepa.

'Allow me to emphasize Pharaoh's wishes,' Ahsha went on. 'For him, the time of conflicts is over and nothing should be the cause of them flaring up again.'

Hattusilis's expression clouded over. 'What is the meaning of this emphasis?'

'Nothing, Majesty. Your brother Ramses wishes you to know his most intimate thoughts.'

'You will thank him for the trust he shows us, and you will explain that we are in perfect accord.'

'Our peoples and their allies will rejoice at this. Nevertheless . . .' Ahsha clasped his hands at chest level, in a pensive attitude, and rested his chin on them.

'What is it, Ahsha?' asked Hattusilis.

'Egypt is a rich country, Majesty. Will it never cease to be the object of covetousness?'

'Who is threatening Egypt?' put in the empress.

'Renewed unrest has broken out in Libya.'

'Surely Pharoah is capable of crushing this uprising?' she said.

'Ramses would like to act swiftly and have effective weaponry at his disposal.'

Hattusilis examined Ahsha curiously. 'Aren't his own weapons adequate?'

'Pharaoh would like his brother, the Emperor of Hatti, to supply him with a large quantity of iron, with which he will be able to manufacture weapons and crush the Libyan threat.'

There was a long silence. Then Hattusilis rose and began nervously pacing up and down the audience chamber.

'My brother Ramses is asking me for a veritable fortune! I have no iron, and if I did have some I'd keep it for my own army. Does Pharaoh, who is so rich, want to improverish me and ruin Hatti? My reserves are exhausted, and it isn't the right moment to manufacture iron.'

Ahsha kept his face expressionless. 'I understand.'

'Tell my brother,' Hattusilis went on, 'that he must get rid of the Libyans with his usual weapons. Later, if he still needs iron, I'll send him a reasonable quantity. Tell him, too, that this request surprises and shocks me.'

'I will tell him, Majesty.'

Hattusilis sat down again. 'Let us get to the main point: when must my daughter leave Hatti to become Ramses' Great Royal Wife?'

'Well . . . the date has not yet been settled.'

'Did you not come here to announce it?'

'A decision of this importance demands reflection and—'

'Enough of diplomatic talk,' interrupted the empress. 'Does Ramses agree to repudiate Iset the Fair and raise our daughter to the rank of Queen of Egypt?'

'The situation is delicate, Majesty. Egyptian justice does not accept repudiation.'

'Is a woman laying down the law?' asked Hattusilis drily. 'I'm not interested in this Iset and her wishes. Ramses only married her to replace Nefertari, a true queen who played an important role in building the peace. Iset doesn't count. To set the final seal on our alliance, Ramses must marry a Hittite.'

'Perhaps your daughter could become a secondary wife and—'

'She will become Queen of Egypt, or else—' Hattusilis broke off, as if he himself was afraid of the words he had almost uttered.

'Why does Ramses insist on refusing our suggestion?' asked the empress, in a conciliatory tone.

'Because, Majesty,' said Ahsha, 'a pharaoh does not repudiate a Great Royal Wife. To do so would be against the law of Ma'at.'

'Is this position unalterable?' she asked.

'I fear so, Majesty.'

'Is Ramses aware of the consequences of his intransigence?' demanded Hattusilis.

'Ramses has only one concern: to act righteously.'

The emperor rose. 'This audience is at an end. Tell my brother the pharaoh this: either he arranges a date as soon as possible for his marriage to my daughter, or it will be war.'

12

Ahmeni had chronic backache but he never had time to have a massage. As if his load of work weren't enough, he also had to lend Kha a hand in the preparations for the king's second regeneration festivities. Ramses protested that he was in excellent health, and wanted to postpone the event, but his son invoked the authority of the traditional texts. Ahmeni valued Kha's discipline, and enjoyed discussing literature with him, but was too overwhelmed with daily concerns to be able to savour the pleasures of fine prose.

The Great Council had just held a meeting, in the course of which Ramses had unveiled a vast plan to plant trees in the southern provinces, and had reprimanded the official responsible for repairing the dykes, who was behind schedule. After the meeting, Ahmeni and the king went for a stroll in the palace gardens.

'Has Your Majesty had any news of Ahsha?' asked Ahmeni.

'He has arrived safely in Hattusa.'

'It won't be easy to persuade Hattusilis to back down.'

'Ahsha has successfully carried out many difficult tasks,' said Ramses.

'This time his room for manoeuvre is rather limited.'

'What have you got to tell me that's too confidential to be heard by the members of the Great Council?'

'First, news of Moses,' said Ahmeni, 'then news of an . . . incident.'

'What about Moses?' asked Ramses quickly.

'He and his Hebrews are in a tight corner. Everyone's afraid of them, and they have to fight every inch of the way, just to survive. If we intervened, the problem would be solved quickly. But we are dealing with Moses, I know you will let fate take its course.'

'If you know the answer, why do you ask me?'

'The desert police are still watching him. If the Hebrews wanted to return to Egypt, what would you decide?'

'When they return, neither Moses nor I will still be in this world,' said Ramses shortly. 'Now, tell me, what is this "incident"?'

'The caravan-load of oliban we were expecting will not arrive.'

'Why not?'

'I've had a long report from the Phoenician merchant who deals with the producers. A violent hailstorm has damaged the trees, which were already diseased. This year there will be no crop.'

'Has such a disaster happened before?'

'I've consulted the archives and the answer is yes. Fortunately, the phenomenon is rare.'

'Have we enough in reserve?' asked Ramses.

'No restrictions will be imposed on the temples. I've already ordered the Phoenician merchants to deliver the next crop as soon as possible, so that we can build up our stocks again.'

Raia was celebrating. Though normally abstemious, he had indulged to the extent of drinking two cups of strong beer, one after the other. His head was spinning a little, but he thought his sequence of small successes – which would surely lead to the final victory – were worth his getting a bit drunk.

His contacts with his Syrian compatriots had surpassed all his hopes. The flame he had spread had revived the flagging energies of the defeated, the jealous and the envious. To the Syrians were added some Hittites, who, disappointed in Hattusilis's policies, accused him of weakness and of being incapable of setting out again to conquer Egypt. All these men had met Uri-Teshup in complete secrecy in one of Raia's warehouses, and there had been general enthusiasm for the prince. With a leader of his calibre, power would one day be within their grasp.

And there were other pieces of cheering news, which Raia would pass on to Uri-Teshup when the latter paused in his admiration of the three naked Nubian girls dancing in honour of the guests of the couple who were all the rage in fashionable Pi-Ramses: the Hittite prince and the Lady Tanit.

The wealthy Phoenician's life was simultaneously paradise and hell. Paradise, because her lover gratified her, at any hour of the day or night, with inexhaustible ardour and violence which made her delirious with pleasure. Hell, because she was afraid of being beaten by this monster, whose reactions were wholly unpredictable. Having previously lived exactly as she pleased, she had become a slave, both consenting and anguished.

Tanit and Uri-Teshup's hundred guests had eyes only for the three young dancers. Their firm, round breasts were not tossed about. Their long, slender legs titillated the most world-weary. But these delightful entertainers were untouchable: as soon as their performance was over, they disappeared without speaking to anyone. And the guests would have to wait for their next appearance, at a banquet as sumptuous as this one, to enjoy another spectacle of such quality.

Uri-Teshup moved away from his wife, who was deep in discussion with two businessmen, ready to sign any contract so as not to miss a second of the choreography. He seized a bunch of grapes and sat down on some cushions near a pillar decorated with painted vine leaves. Raia stood on the other side. The two men could talk softly without looking at each other, while the orchestra played.

'What's so urgent, Raia?'

'I've been talking to an elderly courtier to whom I sell my finest vases at reduced prices. The palace is in turmoil because of some rumour. I've been trying to get confirmation for the last two days. The matter seems serious to me.'

'What's it all about?'

'Emperor Hattusilis is insisting that, to consolidate the peace, his daughter must marry Ramses.'

'Another marriage of convenience. What does it matter?'

'No, no,' explained Raia. 'Hattusilis wants her to become the Great Royal Wife.'

'A Hittite on the throne of Egypt?'

'Exactly.'

'It's unthinkable!'

'They say that Ramses has refused to repudiate Iset the Fair and give in to Hattusilis's demands.'

Uri-Teshup said slowly, 'In other words . . .'

'Yes, my lord. There's hope of war!'

'That may upset our plans.'

'It's too early to tell. In my opinion, it would be better not to change anything until we've had some confirmation of the rumour. Ahsha is said to be in Hattusa to negotiate with the emperor. I've still got many friends there, and we shall soon be told what's happening. But that's not all. There's someone interesting I'd like you to meet.'

'Where is he?'

'Hidden in the garden. We could—'

'Take him to my room and wait for me. Go round behind the vine and enter the house through the linen room. As soon as this banquet is over, I'll join you.'

When the last guest had left, Tanit put her arms round Uri-

Teshup's neck and clung to him. Within her burned a fire that only her lover could extinguish. Almost affectionately, he dragged her to their bedchamber, a luxuriously furnished love-nest full of elaborate flower arrangements and perfume-burners. Before she had even crossed the threshold, she pulled off her gown.

Uri-Teshup pushed her into the room.

Tanit thought it was a new game, but she froze when she saw Raia there, accompanied by a strange, square-faced man with wavy hair and black eyes in which was a gleam of cruelty and madness.

'Who . . . who are you?' she asked.

'He is a friend of mine,' Uri-Teshup replied.

Terrified, Tanit seized a linen sheet and hid her generous curves. Raia was taken aback, unable to understand why the Hittite had brought his woman to this meeting. The man with the cruel eyes did not move.

'I want Tanit to understand everything that is said here,' declared Uri-Teshup. 'She has to become our accomplice and our ally. In future, her fortune will serve our cause. If she makes the slightest trouble, she will be killed. Are we all in agreement?'

'Yes. Oh yes!'

'Tanit, have we your unconditional support?'

'You have my word.'

'You won't regret it.'

With his right hand, the Hittite stroked his wife's breasts. At this simple gesture, the panic that had seized Tanit was dissipated.

Uri-Teshup turned to Raia. 'Introduce your guest.'

Reassured, the Syrian merchant said, 'We are lucky, very lucky. Our spy network was directed by a Libyan magus named Ofir. In spite of his exceptional powers and the blows he dealt the royal family, he was arrested and executed. For our group, this was a severe loss. But someone has decided to take up the torch and avenge Ofir: his brother Malfi.'

Uri-Teshup surveyed the Libyan from head to foot. 'A laudable plan. But what means has he at his disposal?'

'Malfi is the head of the best-armed tribe in Libya. Fighting Egypt is his sole reason for living.'

'Will he agree to obey me without argument?'

'He will put himself under your orders, providing that you destroy Ramses and his empire.'

'Very well, it's a bargain. You, Raia, will act as intermediary between me and our Libyan ally. His men must begin training and hold themselves in readiness to act.'

'Malfi will be patient, my lord,' said Raia. 'Libya has waited for many, many years, hoping to avenge the injuries inflicted by Pharaoh.'

'He is to await my instructions.'

The Libyan left, without having said a word.

13

Although the sun had risen long since, the Pi-Ramses palace was plunged in deep silence. True, people were going about their business, but they avoided making the slightest noise: from cooks to ladies of the bedchamber, each member of the household moved about like a shadow.

Pharaoh's rage had struck terror into the whole staff. Even the old servants, who had known him since his youth, had never seen him like this. He exhibited the might of Set with the violence of a storm, which left its victims numbed.

Ramses had toothache.

For the first time in his life, at fifty-five, he felt hampered by physical pain. Infuriated by the poor-quality treatment offered by the palace dentists, he had ordered them all out of his sight. With the exception of Ahmeni, nobody knew there was another reason for the pharaoh's wrath: Hattusilis had detained Ahsha in the Hittite capital on the pretext of continuing the negotiations. Ramses believed it was more a question of holding him hostage.

The hopes of the court now rested on one person: the head physician of the realm. If the physician did not succeed in relieving the king, there was a danger that the latter's mood might get even worse.

In spite of the pain, Ramses continued to work with the only person who could put up with him at such a time:

Ahmeni, who was also grumpy and who detested the courtiers' airs and graces. When you worked, you didn't need to be pleasant. The fact that the king was in a bad temper didn't stop them dealing with urgent dossiers.

'Hattusilis is playing games with us,' said Ramses.

'Perhaps he's looking for a way out,' suggested Ahmeni. 'Your refusal is an intolerable insult, but it's the Emperor of Hatti who will decide to start a new war.'

'That old fox will throw the blame on me.'

'Ahsha knows all the tricks of the game. I'm convinced Hattusilis is baffled.'

'You're wrong. He's bent on revenge.'

'As soon as Ahsha gets a message through to you, we'll know the truth,' said Ahmeni. 'From the code he uses, you'll know if he's free to negotiate or if he's a prisoner.'

'He's being kept against his will – it's obvious.'

There was a discreet knock at the door.

'I don't want to see anyone,' declared the king.

'Perhaps it's the physician,' said Ahmeni, as he went to open the door.

The head steward of the palace stood on the threshold, terrified at the idea of disturbing the monarch.

'The head physician has arrived,' he murmured. 'Will His Majesty receive her?'

He and Ahmeni made way for a young woman as beautiful as a spring dawn, as lovely as a budding lotus blossom, as fresh as a sparkling wave in the midst of the Nile. Her hair was verging on blonde, her face flawless, with soft contours, her gaze forthright and her eyes as blue as the summer sky. She wore a lapis-lazuli necklace round her slender neck, and bracelets of cornelian on her wrists and ankles. Her linen gown gave glimpses of her firm, high breasts, shapely, narrow hips and long, slender legs. Neferet, 'the Beautiful, the Perfect, the Accomplished' . . . What other name could she have had? Even Ahmeni, who scarcely had time to take an interest in women – fickle creatures, incapable of concentrating for hours on end on an abstruse papyrus – had to admit that this one could have vied with Nefertari in beauty.

'You took your time,' complained Ramses.

'I'm very sorry, Majesty. I was in the provinces, performing an operation which, I hope, will have saved the life of a little girl.'

'Your colleagues are imbeciles and ignoramuses!'

'Medicine is both an art and a science. Perhaps they lacked the right touch.'

'Fortunately, old Doctor Pariamaku has retired. All the people he used to treat have a chance of surviving.'

'But you are in pain.'

'I haven't time to be in pain, Neferet. Cure me as quickly as possible.'

Ahmeni rolled up the accounts papyrus he had just submitted to Ramses, greeted Neferet and went back to his office. He could not bear cries of pain or the sight of blood.

'Would Your Majesty be good enough to open your mouth?'

Neferet examined her illustrious patient. Before reaching the envied rank of general physician, she had studied and practised many specialities, from curing toothache to surgery and, at one stage, the treatment of eye diseases.

'A competent tooth-doctor will be able to give you relief, Majesty.'

'I'll have you, and no one else.'

'I can recommend an expert with a very steady hand.'

'You. Immediately. Your job is at stake.'

'Come with me, Majesty.'

The palace medical centre was airy and sunny; on the white walls were drawings of medicinal plants.

The king was installed in a comfortable armchair, his head tilted back, his neck resting on a cushion.

'To prevent any pain,' explained Neferet, 'I shall use one of the potions made by Setau. You will feel nothing.'

'What's wrong with me?'

'There are holes in two of your teeth, which have become infected. On one tooth this has caused an abscess, which I'm going to drain. It won't be necessary to pull the tooth out. I shall pack the hole with a mixture of resin and mineral substances. To treat the other tooth, I shall grind up some things to make a remedy which will "soon put you right", as we doctors say. The ingredients are medicinal ochre, honey, powdered quartzite, notched sycamore seeds, bean flour, cumin, colocynth, bryony, acacia gum and the sap of the grattilier tree.'

'How did you select them?'

'I have access to medical treatises written by the sages in the olden times, Majesty, and I check the composition with my favourite instrument.'

Between her thumb and forefinger Neferet held a linen thread, at the end of which swung a tiny piece of lozenge-shaped granite. It began to revolve very quickly above the appropriate remedy.

'You practise divining, as my father did,' said Ramses.

'And as you do yourself, Majesty – you found water in the desert, didn't you? But that's not all: after this little operation, you will have to look after your gums by chewing every day a paste made from bryony, juniper, wormwood, sycamore seeds, incense, and medicinal ochre. If you are in pain, you must drink a decoction made from willow bark.* It's very effective against pain.'

'Any more bad news?'

'My examination of your pulse and of the back of your eyes shows that you are endowed with exceptional energy, which will allow you to nip most diseases in the bud. But in

---

*The source of our modern aspirin.

your old age you will suffer from aching joints – and you'll have to put up with it.'

'I hope to die before that happens!'

'You are the embodiment of peace and happiness, Majesty. Egypt hopes to see you reach a great age. It's an urgent duty to look after you. The sages are said to live for over a hundred and ten years. Ptah-hotep waited till that age before he composed his *Maxims.*'

Ramses smiled. 'Just looking at you and listening to you relieves the pain.'

'It's the effect of Setau's potion, Majesty.'

'Tell me, are you satisfied with my policies for the people's health?'

'I shall soon be drawing up my annual report. On the whole the situation is satisfactory, though public and private health can never be developed too fast. Thanks to this, Egypt remains immune from epidemics. The head of your Double House of Gold and Silver must not skimp on the purchase of expensive and rare products which are used in the com-position of remedies. I have just heard that we shall not receive the usual delivery of oliban. Well, I can't manage without it.'

'Don't worry, we have ample reserves.'

'Are you ready, Majesty?'

Faced with thousands of war-crazed Hittites at Kadesh, Ramses had not flinched. But when he saw Neferet's instruments approach his mouth, he closed his eyes.

Ramses' chariot raced along so fast that Serramanna had difficulty keeping up with him. Since Neferet had treated him so remarkably effectively, the king's dynamism had intensified. Ahmeni, in spite of his backache, was the only one who managed to keep up with his pace of work.

A coded letter from Ahsha had reassured Ramses. His friend was not a prisoner, but was remaining in Hattusa to carry on the negotiations – they looked like continuing indefinitely. As Ahmeni had predicted, the emperor was reluctant to embark on a war whose outcome was so uncertain.

The Nile floodwaters were receding in Lower Egypt at the end of this month of September, whose gentle warmth was a physical comfort. The king drove his chariot alongside a canal which served several villages. Nobody, not even Ahmeni, knew the nature of the urgent mission which Ramses felt the need to carry out himself.

Since the death of Shaanar, the king's elder brother, and his accomplices, it was easier to ensure Ramses' safety. But Uri-Teshup's freedom of movement worried Serramanna. He deplored the monarch's impulsiveness, which had scarcely lessened with age.

Ramses came to a halt beside the canal, at the foot of a spreading tree with lovely tapering leaves.

'Come and look, Serramanna. According the archives of the House of Life, this is the oldest willow tree in Egypt. It's from willow bark that they extract the pain-relieving substance that helped me so much. That's why I've come to thank this tree. And I'll do more: with my own hands I shall plant willow branches in Pi-Ramses, near the ornamental pools, and I shall order the same to be done throughout the country. The gods and nature have given us everything: we must know how to make their treasures bear fruit.'

'No other land,' thought the former pirate, 'could have given birth to such a king.'

14

An icy wind blew over the high Anatolian plateau; in Hattusa autumn was sometimes little different from winter. Ahsha had no complaint about Hattusilis's hospitality. The food was acceptable, though plain, and the two Hittite girls responsible for entertaining him did their job with zeal and assurance.

But he missed Egypt. Egypt and Ramses. Ahsha wanted to grow old in the shadow of the monarch whom he had served throughout his life, and for whom he had consented, with secret enthusiasm, to face extreme dangers. Real power, which had fascinated Ahsha as an adolescent during their studies in Memphis, rested in Ramses' hands, not in Moses', as he had believed for a short period. Moses fought for the application of one categorical revealed truth; Ramses was responsible for fashioning, day by day, the truth of a civilization and a people, because he offered up his actions to Ma'at, to the Invisible and to the principle of life. Like his predecessors, Ramses knew that what was static led to death. He was therefore like a musician, able to play several instruments and endlessly create new melodies with the same notes of eternity. Of the power bequeathed to him by the gods, Ramses had made not a power over men but a duty to uprightness, and it was this devotion to Ma'at which prevented a pharaoh of Egypt from becoming a tyrant. His role was not to enslave men but to liberate them from themselves. Watching Ramses reign was like watching a stone-cutter carve the face of a deity.

Dressed in a black and red woollen cloak, similar to the one worn by his dead brother, Emperor Muwatallis, Hattusilis entered Ahsha's rooms.

'Are you satisfied with my hospitality, Ahsha?'

'It would be most satisfactory were it only half as generous, Majesty.'

'Doesn't winter's early arrival bother you?'

'I'd be lying if I said no; it's so mild on the banks of the Nile at this time of year.'

'Every country has its advantages . . . Don't you care for Hatti any more?'

'The older I get, Majesty, the more I like staying at home.'

'I've good news for you: I've finished reflecting on this matter. Tomorrow you will leave for Egypt again. But I also have bad news: I shall not compromise, and my demands remain unchanged. My daughter must become Ramses' Great Royal Wife.'

'And if Pharaoh continues to refuse?'

Hattusilis turned away from the Egyptian. 'Yesterday I summoned my generals and ordered them to prepare our troops for battle. Since my brother the pharaoh asks me for iron, I have had a unique weapon made especially for him.'

The emperor turned back again and drew from the inside pocket of his cloak an iron dagger, which he handed to Ahsha.

'A wonder, isn't it? As light and easy to handle as possible, but able to pierce any shield. I showed this dagger to my generals and promised them that I would recover it myself from the body of my brother Ramses, if he refuses my conditions.'

The sun was setting over the Temple of Set, the strangest building in Pi-Ramses. The sanctuary, which was the home of the master of celestial disturbances, had been built on the site of the capital of the Hyksos, those detested occupiers who had been driven out by the first kings of the eighteenth dynasty. Ramses had transformed this ill-fated place into a centre of positive energy; he had confronted Set here and appropriated his power. It was here, in a forbidden domain, where only the son of Seti dared enter, that Pharaoh derived the necessary strength to wage the next battle.

When Ramses left the temple, Meneptah approached him. 'My report is finished, father.'

'You've worked fast.'

'Not a single barracks in Pi-Ramses or Memphis has escaped my attention.'

'Didn't you believe the senior officers' reports?'

'Well . . .' Meneptah hesitated.

'Speak frankly.'

'Not a word of them, Majesty.'

'Why not?'

'I've been watching them. They're comfortably off and so confident in the peace you've established that they don't bother to conduct serious training. Confident in its strength, proud of its past victories, our army is asleep.'

'What about our weaponry?'

'The quantity is all right, but the quality is often dubious. The blacksmiths have been working too slowly for several years, and a number of chariots need to be completely overhauled.'

'See to it.'

'I may hurt people's feelings.'

'When the fate of Egypt is at stake, that is of no importance. Act like a real commander-in-chief. Retire the inefficient officers, appoint reliable men to the posts of responsibility, and provide our army with the weapons it needs. Don't appear before me again until you have carried out your mission.'

Meneptah bowed to Pharaoh and left for army head-quarters.

A father ought to have spoken differently to his son, but Ramses was Lord of the Two Lands and Meneptah was his possible successor.

Iset the Fair wasn't sleeping well.

She enjoyed much happiness: seeing Ramses every day, exchanging confidences with him, being at his side for the rituals and at official ceremonies. And her two sons, Kha and Meneptah, had brilliant careers.

But Iset was increasingly sad and lonely, as if this great happiness were wearing her down and sapping her strength. She knew the cause of her insomnia: Nefertari had been a creator of peace; she, Iset, was becoming synonymous with war. Just as Helen had been the cause of the terrible Trojan War, so Iset would be seen in the eyes of the people as the person responsible for starting a new war between Egypt and Hatti. Galvanized by Meneptah, whose authority no senior officer contested, Pi-Ramses was in the throes of military fever. Intensive training and arms production had been resumed.

Iset's hairdresser asked anxiously, 'When can I do your make-up, Majesty?'

'Is the king up?'

'A long time ago!'

'Are we to lunch together?'

'His Majesty told your steward that he would be working all day with the vizier and the heads of the Canaanite fortresses, who have been urgently recalled to Pi-Ramses.'

'Have my litter prepared for me.'

'Majesty! Your hair isn't done, I haven't put on your wig, or done your make-up, I—'

'Hurry!'

Iset the Fair was not a heavy burden for the twelve strapping fellows who carried her litter from the palace to Ahmeni's office. As the Great Royal Wife had told them to hurry, they would enjoy a bonus and an extra rest period.

The queen entered a veritable hive of activity. The score of scribes who made up Ahmeni's small staff were dealing with a huge number of dossiers and had not a second to spare for gossip. They had to read the dossiers, summarize them for the king's private secretary, sort and file them – and never get behind with their work.

Iset crossed the pillared hall; some of the officials didn't even look up. When she entered Ahmeni's office, he was chewing a slice of bread spread with goose fat and composing a letter of reprimand to the controller of one of the granaries.

He rose in astonishment. 'Majesty!'

'Sit down, Ahmeni. I need to talk to you.'

The queen closed the wooden door of the office and shot the bolt. The scribe felt ill at ease; he disliked Iset every bit as much as he had admired Nefertari, and had already clashed with her. Today, unusually for her, she had taken no trouble over her appearance. She looked washed-out and weary, and she wore no make-up to bring out the best of her features.

'It's vital that you help me, Ahmeni.'

'I don't understand, Majesty.'

'Don't play diplomatic games with me. I am well aware that the court would be relieved if Pharaoh repudiated me.'

'Majesty!'

'That's the way it is, and I can't change anything. You know everything, so tell me, what do the people think?'

'It's rather delicate . . .' said Ahmeni.

'I want to know the truth.'

'You are the Great Royal Wife. No criticism may be levelled at you.'

'The truth, Ahmeni!'

'You have to understand the people, Majesty. They've got used to peace.'

'The people loved Nefertari and they don't like me. That's the truth you want to hide from me, isn't it?'

'It's because of the circumstances, Majesty.'

'Speak to Ramses, tell him I know how serious the situation is and am prepared to sacrifice myself to prevent war.'

'Ramses has already made up his mind.'

'Make him listen, Ahmeni, I beg you.'

He was convinced of Iset's sincerity. For the first time, she seemed to him worthy of being Queen of Egypt.

15

'Why have you delayed your departure?' Hattusilis asked Ahsha.

'Because I still hope to make you reconsider your decision.'

The emperor, who detested the icy gusts of wind which swept the ramparts of his capital, was wrapped tightly in his long black and red woollen mantle and had a cap on his head. Even though he, too, was wrapped in a thick cloak, Ahsha felt the bite of the cold.

'That's impossible, Ahsha.'

'Will you really start a futile war because of a woman? Troy has shown us where that leads. Why make us slaves to a frenzy of killing? Queens should be a source of life, not of death.'

'Your arguments are excellent – but so Egyptian!' said the emperor. 'Hatti would never forgive me for losing face. If I back down from Ramses, my throne will totter.'

'But no one is threatening you.'

'If my actions humiliate the Hittite army, I shall not live long. We are a warlike people. And the tyrant who replaces me will be worse than I am – you can be sure of that.'

'Ramses hopes your reign will be a long one, Majesty.'

'Can I believe you?'

'I swear by what I hold most dear: the life of Ramses.'

The two men took a few steps on the covered way, bristling with watchtowers, which overlooked the capital. The army was present everywhere.

'Aren't you tired of waging war, Majesty?' asked Ahsha.

'Soldiers tire me. But without them, Hatti would disappear.'

'Egypt has no liking for war. We prefer to build temples. Surely the battle of Kadesh is now a thing of the past?'

'Don't try to make me say I'd like to have been born an Egyptian, Ahsha!'

'A new war between Egypt and Hatti would be a disaster which would weaken both our countries for the benefit of the Assyrians. I implore you, agree that your daughter shall be Ramses' diplomatic wife and that Iset the Fair shall remain the Great Royal Wife.'

'I can't back down now,' said the emperor.

Ahsha looked down on the lower town, at whose heart lay the temple of the God of Storms and the Sun Goddess. 'Men are perverse and dangerous animals,' he said. 'They end by defiling the earth and wiping out their own race. When they are trapped in a process of destruction which they have created themselves, no argument can release them. Why are they so stubbornly determined to cause their own ruin?'

'Because human beings are distancing themselves further and further from the gods,' replied Hattusilis. 'When every link has been cut, only fanatics will remain, manipulated by tyrants who will reign over an immense population of ants.'

'It's strange, Majesty. I have to admit to having spent my life fighting for Ma'at, for harmony between heaven and earth, as if everything else were simply pointless.'

'If you had done otherwise, would you have been Ramses' friend?'

The wind became stronger, the cold more intense.

'We had better go in,' said Hattusilis.

'It's all so *stupid*, Majesty.'

'I entirely agree, but neither you nor I can do anything, Let us hope that the gods of Hatti and Egypt bear witness to our good faith and bring about a miracle.'

On the wharf of the river port of Pi-Ramses, crowds were swarming in a state of great excitement. That day several boats from Memphis, Thebes and other southern cities had unloaded their goods. The local market, which was normally very busy, was doing business on an unprecedented scale. Those who had rented the best sites, among them many women who excelled in the art of trading, were determined to make substantial profits.

Uri-Teshup and Tanit wandered hand in hand among the onlookers, casting an eye over the fabrics, the sandals, the caskets of precious wood and many other marvels. All Pi-Ramses had turned up, and the lovely Phoenician found herself obliged to smile at her many women friends who were captivated by the lusty masculinity of the Hittite prince.

The latter had noted, not without great satisfaction, that Serramanna's henchmen were no longer following him. Since it was an offence to harass an honest citizen, Uri-Teshup would not have failed to lodge a complaint.

'May I . . . May I buy something?' begged Tanit.

'Come, come, my dear. You are a free woman.'

Tanit launched into a frenzy of buying, which calmed her nerves. As they wandered from stall to stall, the couple found themselves in front of Raia's display. The Syrian was offering pewter goblets, slender alabaster vases and coloured-glass perfume phials, over which fashionable ladies were fighting.

While Tanit was haggling fiercely over prices with one of Raia's assistants, the merchant said quietly to Uri-Teshup, 'Excellent news from Hattusa: Ahsha's negotiations have failed. The emperor refuses to moderate his demands.'

'Have the discussions been finally broken off?'

'Ahsha is on his way back to Egypt. Hattusilis's reply to Ramses is an iron dagger, which the emperor has vowed to recover from Pharaoh's body after defeating him.'

Uri-Teshup was silent for a long moment. Then he said, 'This evening, come yourself to deliver my wife's purchases.'

Setau, strapping fellow that he was, was filled every day with increasing wonder. How did Lotus manage never to age? Since she used neither salves nor pomades, it must be witch-craft alone that preserved her powers of seduction – which her husband could never resist. With her, lovemaking was a delightful game which never grew stale.

He kissed her breasts.

Suddenly she tensed. 'Did you hear a noise?'

'Only your heart, beating a little louder.'

Setau's ardour inflamed Lotus, who now had thought only for the intoxicating pleasure they shared.

The unexpected visitor froze. When she had found her way into the laboratory, she had hoped that the couple would not be there. But when Setau and Lotus stayed in Pi-Ramses, they didn't like being away too long from the vessels containing the venom of the royal cobra, the black cobra, the puff adder or the horned viper. In agreement with the head physician of the kingdom, they pursued their research in the hope of finding new cures or improving old ones. Banquets and social occasions bored them: how could anyone prefer spending endless hours in idle conversation to studying substances which could kill but could also save lives?

Sighs and gasps reassured the visitor; the two lovers were too busy to notice her presence. She must not make a mistake. She must obtain a flask of venom in complete silence. Which one should she choose? A stupid question. All these poisons were the same. In the raw state and before treatment, their effects were deadly.

One step, then another, then a third . . . Her bare feet glided over the paving-stones. One step more, and the intruder would be in the heart of this forbidden territory.

Suddenly a shape rose up.

The woman stood still, paralysed with fright. In the half-darkness she recognized a royal cobra, which was swaying backwards and forwards. The thief was so terrified that she could not even cry out. Her instinct bade her retreat very very slowly, moving almost imperceptibly.

She felt as if her flight took hours. When she was out of sight, the guardian cobra went back to sleep.

Ahmeni counted the papyri again. Forty-two: one for each province. The results would vary, according to the number of canals and lakes. Thanks to the great lake planned by the pharaohs of the Middle Kingdom, the Faiyum,* which was already planted with many species of trees, would fare particularly well. Following Ramses' orders, willow trees would be planted throughout Egypt, and the temple laboratories would extract from the bark the wonderful pain-killing substance, which would be made more widely available to the doctors.

This additional work had driven Ahmeni into a fury – his subordinates had borne the brunt of it – but there was no arguing with Pharaoh's instructions. Still, at least Ahmeni did not also have to worry about the preparations for war! Meneptah performed his duties perfectly and never came complaining to the scribe's office.

His arms loaded with papyri, Ahmeni stood in the path of the monarch as he was on his way to the Temple of Amon, to celebrate the evening rites.

---

* A fertile area to the west of the Nile Valley, south of the Delta, which was empty marshland during the Old Kingdom, but was drained and exploited in the Middle Kingdom. (Trans.)

'Could Your Majesty spare me a moment?'

'Only if it's urgent.'

'Very well, I won't insist,' said Ahmeni.

'You didn't just meet me by chance. What's on your mind?'

'Iset the Fair came to consult me.'

'Is she interested in affairs of state?'

'She doesn't want to be the cause of war with Hatti. I must admit that I was moved by her sincerity.'

'If Iset's charm acts on you, the kingdom *must* be in danger!'

'It's serious, Majesty. The Great Royal Wife really dreads being the cause of a new war.'

'That issue is settled, Ahmeni. If we concede a single inch of ground to the Hittites, the battles we have fought will have been fought in vain. To put aside a Great Royal Wife would be to open the door to barbarism. Iset is in no way responsible for this crisis. The only guilty person is Hattusilis.'

16

Icy rain was falling on Hattusa as Ahsha's convoy made ready to leave. Empress Putuhepa, looking elegant and of natural distinction in her fringed red gown – she seemed indifferent to the cold – came to bid him farewell.

'The emperor is confined to bed,' she told him.

'Nothing serious, I hope?'

'Just a slight fever, which will soon pass.'

'I wish him a speedy recovery, Majesty.'

'I'm sorry about the failure of the negotiations,' said Putuhepa.

'I am too, Majesty.'

'Perhaps Ramses will eventually give in?'

'We must have no illusions.'

'I have never seen you so pessimistic, Ahsha.'

'We have only two hopes left: a miracle and . . . you yourself. Could you not soften your husband's intransigence?'

'Up till now, I have had no success, but I shall keep trying.'

'Majesty,' said Ahsha hesitantly, 'I wanted to tell you . . . No, it's not important.'

'I'm listening.'

'No, it really isn't important.' How could he admit to the Empress of Hatti that, of all the women he had ever known, she was the only one whom he would willingly have made his wife? It would have been an unforgivable error of taste. He gazed intensely at Putuhepa, as if he wished to engrave on his mind the memory of an unattainable face. Then he bowed.

She said, 'Don't be sad at leaving, Ahsha. I shall do everything in my power to avoid the worst.'

'I shall, too, Majesty.'

When the convoy moved off to the south, Ahsha did not look back.

Setau felt in fine form. He left the bedchamber without waking Lotus, whose naked body never ceased to arouse his desire. He hesitated a moment, then made his way to his laboratory. The venom from the horned viper collected the previous night had to be treated that day. Despite his demanding job as a provincial administrator, he never forgot the rules of his calling as a snake-charmer.

A young serving-girl who was carrying a tray of fruit stood rooted to the spot. Setau's rough appearance scared her but she dared not run away. This man was a magician, who could grab hold of poisonous snakes without fear of being bitten.

'I'm hungry, my dear,' he told her. 'Go and fetch me some dried fish, milk and freshly baked bread.'

The servant obeyed, trembling. Setau went out into the garden and lay down in the grass to soak up the essence of the earth. He ate heartily then, humming a tune intended only for an informed ear, he returned to the wing of the palace set aside for experiments.

He couldn't find his usual garment, his antelope-skin tunic, saturated with all its antidotes to snakebite. It was necessary to use these products with caution, as it could be a case of kill or cure. Thanks to his travelling supply of medicines, Setau was able to combat many diseases.

Before taking Lotus in his arms, he had put his tunic down on a low chair. No, he was mistaken, it was in another room. Setau examined the antechamber, a small pillared hall, the shower-room, the water-closets. In vain.

The last possibility: the bedchamber. Yes, of course! That was where he had taken off his precious tunic. When he went in, Lotus was waking up.

Setau kissed her breasts affectionately. 'Tell me, darling, where did you put my tunic?'

'I haven't touched it.'

Setau searched the room, growing increasingly irritated. No success. 'It's disappeared,' he concluded.

Serramanna hoped that this time Ramses would take him with him to fight the Hittites. For several years he had wanted to slit those barbarians' throats and cut off the hands of the defeated, in order to keep count of the dead. When the king had fought the battle of Kadesh, the big Sardinian had been ordered to remain in Pi-Ramses to ensure the safety of the royal family. Ever since then he had been training men to carry out that task, and now he dreamt of nothing but doing battle.

Setau burst into the barracks where the Sardinian was exercising. Serramanna was surprised. The two men had not always been on the best of terms, but they had learnt to appreciate each other and knew they were linked by a common interest: their loyalty to Ramses.

Serramanna stopped lobbing punches at the wooden dummy which he was knocking to pieces. 'Trouble, Setau?'

'Someone's stolen my most precious possession: my medicinal tunic.'

'Who do you think has done it?'

'It's bound to be a doctor who's jealous of me – and he wouldn't even know how to use it!'

'Can you be more specific?'

'Unfortunately not,' admitted Setau.

'Someone probably wanted to play a trick on you because you've become too important in Nubia. You're not very popular at court.'

'Everywhere must be searched: the palace, the nobles' villas, the workshops, the—'

'Calm down,' said Serramanna. 'I'll put two men on the job, but we're getting close to the time for general mobilization and your tunic can't be considered a matter of priority.'

'Do you know how many lives it has saved?'

'I'm not unaware of that. But why not just get another one?'

'That's easy to say. I've got used to this one.'

'Come now, Setau, don't make such a fuss. Come and have a drink, and afterwards we'll go together to the best tanner in the city. Sooner or later one has to change one's skin!'

'I want to know who's responsible for this theft.'

Ramses read Meneptah's latest report, which was lucid and concise; his son was remarkably clear-headed. When Ahsha returned from Hatti, the pharaoh would engage in final negotiations with Hattusilis. But the emperor would not be deceived and, like the King of Egypt, would take advantage of this period to prepare his army for war.

The elite Egyptian troops were in better condition than Ramses had expected. It would be easy to engage hardened mercenaries and speed up the young recruits' training. As for the weaponry, it would soon be ready, thanks to intensive production by the armourers. The officers appointed by Meneptah, with Ramses' approval, would train and supervise soldiers capable of meeting the Hittites in battle and defeating them. When the army set out to march to the north, with Ramses at its head, the hearts of his regiments would be fired with the certainty of triumph.

Hattusilis was wrong to abandon the peace. Not only would Egypt fight passionately for her survival, but she would also make some unexpected moves, in order to take the enemy by surprise. This time, Ramses would seize the Kadesh fortress.

Nevertheless, the king's heart was filled with un-accustomed anxiety, as if he were unsure how to act. Now that Nefertari was no longer there to light up his path, he must consult a god. He ordered Serramanna to prepare a swift boat for a voyage to Khmun* in Middle Egypt.

When the king was already on the gangway, Iset the Fair begged him, 'May I come with you?'

'No, I need to be alone.'

'Have you had any news of Ahsha?'

'He will be back soon.'

'You know my feelings, Majesty. Give the order and I shall obey. Egypt's happiness counts for more than my own.'

'I am grateful to you, Iset, but that happiness would vanish if Egypt bowed down before injustice.'

The white sail moved off to the south.

On the edge of the desert, near the necropolis where the High Priests of Thoth were buried, there grew an immense doom-palm, much taller than any other. According to the legend, Thoth, heart of the divine light and master of sacred language, appeared here to those of his followers who had kept their mouths free from worthless words. Ramses knew that the god of the scribes was a fresh spring for those who kept silent, a spring which remained sealed for the talkative. So the king meditated for a day and a night at the foot of the doom-palm, in order to calm the turmoil of his thoughts.

At dawn a powerful shriek greeted the birth of the sun. Less than ten feet from Ramses stood an enormous ape, a dog-faced baboon with aggressive-looking jaws. The pharaoh withstood its gaze.

* Khmun, 'the City of the Eight [creative gods]', was called by the Greeks 'Hermopolis', 'the city of Hermes', Hermes being the Greek name for Thoth, who reigned over the city (present-day el-Ashmunein).

CITY OF LIMERICK PUBLIC LIBRARY

'Open the way for me, Thoth, thou who knowest the mysteries of the heavens and the earth. Thou hast revealed the Rule to gods and men, thou hast fashioned the words of power. Cause me to follow the right path, the one that will serve Egypt.'

The baboon reared up on its hind legs, standing taller than Ramses, and raised its front paws towards the sun, as a sign of worship. The king imitated its movements; he could look on the sun without his eyeballs being scorched.

The voice of Thoth sprang forth from the sky, from the doom-palm and from the throat of the baboon. Pharaoh received it in his heart.

17

It had been raining for several days and fog hampered the progress of Ahsha's convoy. He was full of admiration for the donkeys which, despite carrying big, heavy loads, advanced without faltering, indifferent to the bad weather. For Egypt, donkeys were an incarnation of the god Set, whose strength was inexhaustible; without donkeys there would be no prosperity.

Ahsha was in a hurry to leave northern Syria, to cross through Phoenicia, and enter the Egyptian protectorates. Usually he enjoyed travelling, but this journey was like a heavy burden he could barely lift. The scenery bored him, the mountains made him uneasy, the waters of the rivers carried black thoughts.

The soldier in charge of the convoy was an old campaigner. He had been part of the relief army which had come to Ramses' assistance when the king was fighting the Hittites single-handed. The man knew Ahsha well and held him in high regard; after his exploits as a secret agent and with his knowledge of the terrain, it was impossible not to respect him. The minister for foreign affairs also had the reputation of being a pleasant fellow, a brilliant conversationalist. But since their departure he had been gloomy and sad.

When they made a stop at a sheepfold, where both men and animals warmed themselves, the old campaigner came to sit beside Ahsha.

'Are you unwell?' he asked.

'Tired, that's all.'

'The news is bad, isn't it?'

'It could be better, but while Ramses reigns the situation will never be desperate.'

'I know the Hittites well. They're barbarians bent on conquest, and a few years of peace have made them more brutal than ever.'

'That's not what troubles me. Our world is facing destruction because of a woman. It is true she is not like other women, since she is the Great Royal Wife. Ramses is right: one must concede nothing when the fundamental values of our civilization are at stake.'

'That's hardly diplomatic language!'

'I'm nearing the age of retirement. I promised myself I'd hand in my resignation as soon as travelling became exhausting and uninteresting. That day has come.'

'The king will never agree to lose you.'

'I'm just as stubborn as he is and I shall try to win that argument. It will be easier than he imagines to find a successor to me. The Royal Sons aren't merely courtiers: some of them are excellent scrvants of Egypt. In my profession, when one's curiosity is extinguished, one must recognize that it's time to stop. The outside world no longer interests me. All I want is to sit in the shade of the palm trees and watch the Nile flow by.'

'Are you sure this isn't just because of a moment of weariness?' asked the soldier.

'Negotiating and endless talk no longer interest me. My decision is irrevocable.'

'It's my last journey, too. I'm going to enjoy peace and quiet at last!'

'Where do you live?'

'In a village near Karnak. My mother is getting on in years, and I shall be happy to help her spend a quiet old age.'

'Are you married?'

'I've never had the time.'

'Neither have I,' said Ahsha dreamily.

'You are still young.'

'I prefer to wait till old age has put out the fire of my passion for women. Until then I shall bravely accept the consequences of this foible. Let's hope the tribunal of the great god will pardon me for it.'

The veteran lit a fire with some flints and kindling. 'We have some excellent dried meat and a decent wine.'

'I'll be content with just a cup of wine.'

'Have you lost your appetite?'

'I've lost several appetites. Perhaps it's the beginning of wisdom.'

The rain had stopped at last.

'We should set out again,' said Ahsha.

'The men and animals are tired,' objected the soldier. 'When they've rested, they'll move faster.'

'I'll sleep for a little while,' said Ahsha, though he knew he would not be able to sleep.

The convoy travelled through a forest of green oaks, which overlooked a steep slope strewn with large fissured rocks. On the narrow path, they could move only in single file. Clouds massed in the unsettled sky.

Ahsha was haunted by a strange feeling which he could not identify. He tried in vain to drive it away by thinking of the banks of the Nile, the shady garden of the villa in Pi-Ramses where he would spend peaceful days, the dogs, monkeys and cats which he would at last have time to look after.

His right hand rested on the iron dagger that Hattusilis had entrusted to him in order to sow anxiety in Ramses' mind. To make Ramses anxious . . . How little did Hattusilis know the pharaoh! Never would he yield to threats. Ahsha felt inclined to throw the weapon into the river which flowed lower down the slope, but it was not this dagger that would start hostilities.

There had been a time when Ahsha thought it would be a good thing to unify customs and wipe out the differences between peoples. Now he was convinced of the opposite. Uniformity gave birth to monsters, states devoid of genius, in thrall to grasping powers and profiteers who would plead men's cause the better to stifle it and make them conform.

Only a Ramses could divert men from their natural bent – stupidity and laziness – and lead them towards the gods. And if life no longer offered the human race a single Ramses, it would disappear into chaos, drowned in the blood shed in fratricidal warfare.

How good it was to be able to rely on Ramses for vital decisions! Pharaoh, for his part, had no other guides than the Invisible and the hereafter. Alone, face to face with the Divine, in the heart of the temple, he was also face to face with his people, whom he had to serve without thought for his own reputation. And for centuries, the pharaonic institution had overcome obstacles and survived crises because it did not belong to this world.

When he returned home from his last journey as a roving ambassador, Ahsha would collect ancient texts on Pharaoh's double nature, celestial and terrestrial, and would offer the collection to Ramses. They would discuss them on mild evenings, under a vine arbour, or beside a pool covered with water-lilies.

Ahsha had been lucky, very lucky. To have been the friend of Ramses the Great, to have helped him demolish conspiracies and repel the Hittite peril – he could not have wished for a more exhilarating life. A hundred times he had despaired of the future, on account of men's pettiness, treachery and mediocrity; but a hundred times Ramses' presence had made the sun shine forth again.

A dead tree: huge, with an immense trunk, visible roots,

yet seeming indestructible.

Ahsha smiled. Wasn't this dead tree a source of life? Birds had found refuge in it, insects fed on it. It symbolized the mystery of invisible relationships between living creatures. What were the pharaohs if not immense trees, reaching up to the sky, offering nourishment and protection to a whole people? Ramses would never die, because his role had obliged him, during his lifetime, to pass through the gateways of the hereafter; and only knowledge of the supernatural enabled a monarch to give the right direction to daily existence.

Ahsha had not often been to temples; but he had been at Ramses' side and, by osmosis, had become initiated into certain secrets of which Pharaoh was the depository and keeper. Perhaps he was already bored with his peaceful retirement, even before he had experienced it. It might be more exalting to quit the external world and adopt the life of a recluse in order to experience a different adventure, that of the spirit.

The path grew steep, and Ahsha's horse climbed it with difficulty. One more pass, and then it would be the descent towards Canaan and the road to the north-eastern border of the Egyptian Delta. For a long time Ahsha had refused to believe that he would be satisfied with simple happiness in the land of his birth, sheltered from turmoil and passions. On the morning of his departure from Hattusa, on looking at himself in a mirror, he had seen his first white hair. The snow on the Anatolian mountains was early. It was a clear sign: the victory of old age which he had so feared.

Only he knew that his body was worn out by too many journeys, too many risks, too many dangers. Neferet would manage to relieve some of his pains and slow the deterioration, but Ahsha, unlike Ramses, did not have his energy renewed by rites. The diplomat had exceeded his strength; his life-span was almost exhausted.

Suddenly Ahsha heard the terrifying cry of a man mortally wounded. He halted his horse and looked round. More cries, coming from the rear. Lower down, there was fighting, and arrows were flying, shot from the tops of the oak trees.

Libyans and Hittites, armed with short swords and spears, leapt out from both sides of the path. Half of the Egyptian soldiers were wiped out in a few minutes; the survivors succeeded in shooting down a few of the attackers, but were greatly outnumbered.

'Run for it!' the old campaigner ordered Ahsha. 'Gallop straight ahead!'

Ahsha did not hesitate, Brandishing the iron dagger, he hurled himself on an archer – a Libyan, judging by the two feathers stuck in his hair which was held in a black and green head-band – and slit his throat with a sweeping gesture.

'Look out, look—.' The soldier's warning was lost in a death-rattle. A heavy sword, wielded by a long-haired devil whose bare chest was matted with red hair, had just split open his skull.

At the same moment, an arrow hit Ahsha in the back. He fell on the damp ground, his breath cut short.

All resistance had ceased.

The devil approached the wounded man.

'Uri-Teshup!' Ahsha managed to say,

'Yes, Ahsha, and I have beaten you! I'm finally getting my revenge on you, you cursed diplomat, you who contributed to my downfall! But you were only one obstacle in my path. Now it's Ramses' turn. He'll believe that the man behind this attack is the coward Hattusilis. What do you think of my plan?'

'That . . . the coward . . . is *you*.'

Uri-Teshup seized the iron dagger and plunged it into Ahsha's chest. Looting had already begun; if he didn't put a stop to it, the Libyans would kill each other.

Ahsha hadn't the strength to write Uri-Teshup's name in

full with his own blood. With his forefinger, drawing on every last vestige of his dying energy, he traced a single hieroglyph on his tunic, above his heart, then collapsed.

Ramses would understand his message.

18

On his return from Khmun, Ramses realized immediately that something dramatic had happened. The palace was plunged in silence. The courtiers slipped away, the administrative staff hid out of sight in their offices.

'Send for Ahmeni,' the king told Serramanna. 'Tell him to meet me on the roof terrace.'

From the highest point of the palace, Ramses gazed down on his capital, of which Moses had been one of the architects. The white houses, with their turquoise façades, dozed under the palm trees; strollers chatted in the gardens, near the ornamental ponds; tall flag-posts erected against the gateways proclaimed the divine presence.

Thoth had asked the monarch to preserve the peace, whatever sacrifices had to be made; in the maze of conflicting ambitions, it behove him to find the right path, which would avoid massacres and calamities. By expanding the king's heart, the god of knowledge had given him a new purpose: the son of Ra, the sun, the day-star which embodied the divine light, was also the son of Thoth, the night-star.

Ahmeni was even paler than usual. In his eyes there was an infinite sadness.

'You, at least,' said Ramses, 'will have the courage to tell me the truth.'

'Ahsha is dead, Majesty.'

Ramses remained impassive. 'How did he die?'

'His convoy was attacked. A shepherd discovered the bodies and informed the Canaanite police. They went to the place, and one of them recognized Ahsha.'

'Has his body been formally identified?'

'Yes, Majesty.'

'Where has it been taken?'

'To a fortress, with those of the other members of the convoy.'

'Were there any survivors?'

'None.'

'Any witnesses?'

'No, Majesty.'

'Serramanna must go to the site of the attack, collect even the slightest clue and bring back Ahsha's remains and those of his companions. They will rest in Egyptian soil.'

The Sardinian giant and a small group of mercenaries wore out several relays of horses in order to reach the fortress and return with all possible speed.

As soon as he arrived back in Pi-Ramses, Serramanna handed over Ahsha's body to an embalmer, who washed and perfumed it and prepared it to be presented to the pharaoh. Ramses took his friend in his arms and placed him on a bed in one of the rooms of the palace. Ahsha looked serene. Wrapped in a white shroud, he seemed to be sleeping.

Pharaoh stood before him, with Ahmeni and Setau at his side.

'Who killed him?' asked Setau, his eyes red with weeping.

'We shall find out,' promised the king. 'I am waiting for Serramanna's report.'

'His House of Eternity is completed,' said Ahmeni. 'Men's judgment of him has been favourable: the gods will cause him to be reborn.'

'My son Kha will direct the ritual and pronounce the

ancient incantations for resurrection. What has been bound together here below will be linked in the hereafter; Ahsha's loyalty to his country will protect him from the dangers of the Otherworld.'

'I shall kill the murderer with my own hands,' declared Setau. 'From now on this thought will not leave me, by day or night.'

Serramanna came into the room.

'What have you discovered?' asked Ramses.

'Ahsha was hit in his right shoulder-blade by an arrow, but that wound was not fatal. This is the weapon that killed him.' He handed Ramses the dagger.

'Iron!' exclaimed Ahmeni. 'The Emperor of Hatti's sinister gift! This is his message: the assassination of the Egyptian ambassador, Ramses' close friend!'

Serramanna had never seen Ahmeni in such a rage.

'So we know who the murderer is,' said Setau icily. 'It's no use Hattusilis hiding away in his citadel. I shall find my way into it and throw his body down from the top of the ramparts.'

'I must express a doubt,' remarked the Sardinian.

'You're wrong, I shall succeed!'

'I don't doubt your wish for revenge, Setau, but I do doubt this identification of the murderer.'

'This iron dagger's from Hatti, isn't it?'

'Of course it is, but I've found another clue.' Serramanna showed them a broken feather. 'This is a Libyan ornament of war.'

'Libyans, allies of the Hittites? Impossible!' said Setau.

'When the forces of evil decide to unite,' said Ahmeni, 'nothing is impossible. It's quite clear that Hattusilis has decided on a trial of strength. Like his predecessors, he thinks of nothing but destroying Egypt, and to do that he would be ready to ally himself with demons from hell!'

'There's something else we must take into account,' said

Serramanna. 'The convoy consisted of a small number of travellers. There must have been about forty attackers – fifty at the most. The ambush was set up by a band of plunderers, not a regular army.'

'That's only your opinion,' objected Ahmeni.

'No, those are the facts. I have examined the landscape, and the narrowness of the path and the traces left by the horsemen leave no room for doubt. I'm convinced there was not a single Hittite chariot in the area.'

'What difference does that make?' asked Setau. 'Hattusilis ordered a raiding-party to kill Ahsha with a fine gift for Ramses, this iron dagger! Since Pharaoh refuses to marry the emperor's daughter, the Emperor of Hatti assassinates one of his closest friends, a man of peace who believes in dialogue. No one can change the spirit of a people: the Hittites will always be barbarians, whose word can't be trusted.'

'Majesty,' declared Ahmeni seriously, 'I have a horror of violence and I detest war. But to let this crime go unpunished would be an intolerable injustice. As long as Hatti is not broken, Egypt will be in mortal danger. Ahsha gave his life to make us understand this.'

Ramses listened without showing the slightest emotion. He merely asked, 'What else, Serramanna?'

'Nothing, Majesty.'

'Did Ahsha write anything on the ground?'

'He didn't have time. The dagger-blow was extremely violent and he died very quickly.'

'What happened to his luggage?'

'It was stolen.'

'And his clothes?'

'The embalmer removed them.'

'Bring them to me.'

'But . . . he may have destroyed them.'

'Bring them to me, quickly.'

Serramanna had never in his life felt so afraid. Why should

Ramses be interested in a blood-stained tunic and cloak? He ran out of the palace, leapt on to his horse and galloped to the embalmers' village, on the outskirts of the city, where the head embalmer had prepared Ahsha's body for the last meeting on earth between Pharaoh and his friend.

'Where are Ahsha's clothes?' demanded the Sardinian.

'I haven't got them any more,' replied the embalmer.

'What have you done with them?'

'Well, as usual, I gave them to the laundryman in the northern suburb.'

'Where does he live?'

'In the last house in the street that curves round, at the edge of the canal.'

Serramanna sped off again. He forced his horse to jump over low walls, ride through gardens, race through narrow alleyways at the risk of running over passers-by, and he turned into the curving street without slowing down.

When he reached the last house, he hauled on the reins, pulled up his sweating horse and banged on the shutter. 'Laundryman!'

A woman opened. 'At the canal. He's working.'

Abandoning his mount, Seramanna ran to the canal reserved for washing clothes and soiled linen. He seized the laundryman by the hair just as he was about to soap Ahsha's tunic.

There were traces of blood on the cloak. On the tunic, too, but with an important difference: with a faltering finger, Ahsha had traced a sign.

'It's a hieroglyph,' said Ramses. 'How do you read it, Ahmeni?'

'Two outstretched arms, with the palms of the hands facing downwards. The sign of negation.'

'"No". I read it the same way as you.'

'The beginning of a name or a word, perhaps?' suggested

110

Ahmeni. 'What was Ahsha trying to tell us?'

Setau and Serramanna were equally puzzled.

'Ahsha only had a few seconds before he died,' said Ramses, 'and could only trace one single hieroglyph. He knew that we would think the author of this abominable attack must be Hattusilis and that I would be obliged to declare war on him immediately. So Ahsha uttered his last word to avoid a tragedy: "No." No, the real culprit is not Hattusilis.'

19

Ahsha's funeral had a grandeur befitting the head of the Egyptian diplomatic service. Clad in a panther skin, Kha performed the rite for the opening of the eyes, the ears and mouth, over the gilded acacia-wood sarcophagus containing Ahsha's mummified body. Then Ramses sealed up the entrance to the House of Eternity.

When silence fell once more on the necropolis, the king remained alone in the shrine, which was open to the outside. He was the first to carry out the priest's duties to his dead friend's *ka* by placing on the altar a lotus flower, irises, a fresh-baked loaf and a cup of wine. From now on, a priest paid by the palace would bring daily offerings and see to the upkeep of the place of Ahsha's funerary rites.

With Moses gone in search of his dream and Ahsha gone to the next world, the circle of childhood friends was shrinking. Sometimes Ramses found himself regretting this too-long reign, strewn as it was with shadows. Like Seti, Tuya and Nefertari, Ahsha was irreplaceable. Little inclined to confidences, he had passed through life with the grace of a panther. He and Ramses had not needed to talk much to know each other's most secret intentions.

Nefertari and Ahsha had built the peace; without their determination and courage, Hatti would not have agreed to abandon war. The man who had murdered Ahsha did not understand the indestructible ties of friendship. Even in death, Ahsha had found the strength to defeat lies.

Any man had the right to drown his sorrow in drink, to try to assuage his pain by giving free rein, with those close to him, to memories. Any man except Ramses.

To see Ramses the Great privately, even when one was both his younger son and the commander-in-chief of his army, was enough to take one's breath away. Meneptah tried to stay calm, knowing that his father would judge him, like Thoth weighing up men's actions.

'Father, I'd like to say—'

'Don't, Meneptah. Ahsha was my childhood friend, not yours. Expressions of sympathy will not lessen my sorrow. The only thing that counts is the perpetuity of the *ka*, beyond the death of the body. Is my army ready to fight?'

'Yes, Majesty.'

'From now on, there must be no slackness. The world is about to change greatly, Meneptah. We must be constantly prepared to defend ourselves, and you must be vigilant all the time.'

'Am I to I understand that war has been declared?'

'Ahsha tried to stop us falling into a trap and being the first to break the peace treaty. But, for all that, the peace has not been saved. To preserve his honour, which he thinks has been slighted, Hattusilis will be obliged to invade Canaan and launch an attack against the Delta.'

Meneptah was astonished. 'Do you mean, Majesty, that we should let him do so?'

'He will believe we are disorganized and unable to react. We shall attack him when he is foolish enough to enter the branches of the Nile and so divide his forces. The Hittites will not know how to manoeuvre on our ground.'

Meneptah seemed tense.

'What do you think of my plan, my son?' asked Ramses.

'It is . . . daring.'

'Don't you mean "dangerous"?' said Ramses.

'You are the pharaoh, and I must obey you.'

'You may speak frankly.'

'I am confident, Majesty. I have confidence in you, as do all Egyptians.'

'Hold yourself in readiness.'

Serramanna trusted in his pirate's instinct. He did not believe that Ahsha's death was the result of a normal attack by an officer obeying Emperor Hattusilis's orders. And this same instinct led him on to another track: that of a wild beast capable of killing to weaken Ramses and deprive him of precious, even indispensable, support. He therefore took up a position near Lady Tanit's villa and waited for Uri-Teshup to leave.

The Hittite left the house early in the afternoon and rode off on a black horse with white markings, having taken the precaution of checking that he was not being followed.

Serramanna identified himself to the doorkeeper and said, 'I want to see the Lady Tanit.'

She received the Sardinian in a magnificent two-pillared room, lit by four high windows arranged in such a way as to ensure a pleasant flow of fresh air. The lovely Phoenician had lost weight.

'Is this an official visit, Serramanna?' she asked.

'For the moment, just a friendly one. The rest will depend on your answers, Lady Tanit.'

'So it's an interrogation.'

'No,' said Serramanna, 'simply a conversation with a lady of quality who has gone astray by taking the wrong path.'

'I don't understand.'

'Of course you do. Something very serious has happened. Ahsha, the minister for foreign affairs, was murdered on his way back from Hatti.'

'Murdered!' Tanit turned pale. To get rid of Serramanna, she had only to call for help: the four Libyans hidden in her house would kill him instantly. But the disappearance of the head of Ramses' personal bodyguard would entail an inquiry and Tanit would be crushed in the judicial machine. No, she had to keep her head.

Serramanna went on, 'I want a detailed account of all your husband's activities over the past two months.'

'He spent most of his time here, in this house, as we are very much in love. When he goes out, he goes to a tavern or strolls about the town. We are very happy together.'

'When did he leave Pi-Ramses and when did he get back?'

'Since our marriage he hasn't left the city, whose attractions he greatly enjoys. So he's gradually forgetting his past. Our marriage has made him Pharaoh's subject, like you and me.'

'Uri-Teshup is a criminal,' said Serramanna. 'He threatens and terrorizes you. If you tell me the truth, I shall place you under my protection, and justice will see that you are rid of him.'

For a moment, Tanit was tempted to run out into the garden. Serramanna would follow her, she would warn him of the Libyans' presence, and she would be free again. But then she would never see Uri-Teshup again . . . To give up such a lover was more than she could bear. While he was away, she had been ill; she needed him like a drug. Thanks to Uri-Teshup, she was satiated with real pleasure, inexhaustible pleasure, which was worth every sacrifice.

'Even if you dragged me before a judge,' she said, 'I wouldn't change a word of my statement.'

'Uri-Teshup will destroy you, my lady.'

She smiled, thinking of the frantic lovemaking she had been enjoying just a few minutes before the Sardinian's arrival. 'If your list of stupid grievances is ended, leave.'

'I'd like to save you, Lady Tanit.'

115

'I'm not in danger.'

'If you change your mind, get in touch with me.'

She mischievously stroked the Sardinian giant's forearm with her soft hand. 'You're a fine man. But, unfortunately for you, I'm satisfied.'

Iset the Fair, the Great Royal Wife, drove slowly in her chariot through the avenues of Pi-Ramses. She was dressed in a pleated gown of royal linen, a pink cape and a crown topped with two tall feathers, and wore a gold necklace from which hung a lapis-lazuli scarab, and turquoise bracelets on her wrists and ankles. The charioteer had chosen two quiet horses. They were draped in multicoloured caparisons and their heads were adorned with ostrich plumes dyed blue, red and yellow. It was a magnificent spectacle.

News of the queen's passage spread quickly, and soon the crowds gathered to admire her. Children scattered lotus petals in front of the horses, while cheers rang out. The sight of the Great Royal Wife, so close to them, was a promise of happiness. It made them forget the rumours of war, and everyone approved of Ramses' decision: he must not repudiate Iset, no matter what the consequences of his decision might be.

Brought up in aristocratic circles, Iset the Fair enjoyed this contact with her people, where different social classes and cultures mingled. All the inhabitants of Pi-Ramses showed their attachment to her. In spite of the charioteer's reluctance, the queen insisted on visiting the poorest districts, where she received a warm welcome. How good it was to be loved!

On her return to the palace, Iset lay down on her bed, as if intoxicated. There was nothing more moving than this trust shown by the people, full of hope, certain of happy days ahead. She had emerged from her cocoon, and discovered the country of which she was queen.

That night, at a banquet to which the governors of the

provinces had been invited, Ramses announced the impending war. Everyone noted how radiant Iset the Fair was. Though she could not rival Nefertari, she was becoming worthy of her role and inspired the old courtiers' respect. To each and every one she addressed words of comfort: Egypt had nothing to fear from Hatti; their country would survive the ordeal, thanks to Ramses. The governors were impressed by the queen's certainty.

When Ramses and Iset were alone, on the terrace overlooking the town, Ramses took her affectionately in his arms. 'You have shown yourself worthy of your position, Iset.'

'Are you proud of me, at last?'

'I chose you as Great Royal Wife and I wasn't wrong.'

'Have the negotiations with Hatti been definitely broken off?'

'We are ready to fight.'

Iset rested her head on Ramses' shoulder. 'Come what may, you will be victorious.'

20

Kha could not hide his distress. 'War! Why war?'

'To save Egypt and allow you to find your book of knowledge,' replied Ramses.

'Is there really no way of reaching an understanding with Hatti?'

'Their troops are advancing towards provinces under our control. It is time to put our plan into action. I am going with Meneptah and I leave you in charge of the administration of the realm.'

'Father, I can't replace you, even for a short time!'

'Yes you can. With Ahmeni's help, you will carry out the mission I entrust you with.'

'What if I make mistakes?' asked Kha.

'Concern yourself with the people's happiness, and you won't.'

Ramses climbed into his chariot. He would drive it himself at the head of the regiments he intended to deploy at strategic points on the Delta and the north-eastern border. Behind him came Meneptah and the generals of the four army corps.

Just as he was preparing to give the signal to move off, a horseman rode at full speed into the courtyard of the barracks. He leapt down and ran to Ramses' chariot. It was Serramanna.

'Majesty, I must speak to you!' he said.

The pharaoh had ordered him to remain behind to ensure the safety of the palace. Ramses knew that he had disappointed the Sardinian, who longed to slaughter a few Hittites; but who else could he choose to keep an eye on Kha and Iset the Fair?

'I shall not change my mind,' said Ramses. 'You are to stay in Pi-Ramses.'

'It's nothing to do with me, Majesty. Come, I beg you!' Serramanna seemed extremely upset.

'What has happened?'

'Come, Majesty. Please come.'

Ramses told Meneptah to inform the generals that their departure was delayed.

Pharaoh's chariot followed Serramanna's horse, which led the way to the palace.

The lady of the bedchamber, the linen maid and the maidservants were all crouched down in the corridors, weeping.

Serramanna halted in the doorway of Iset the Fair's bedchamber. His eyes were full of bewilderment and helplessness.

Ramses went in.

An intoxicating scent of lilies filled the room, which was lit by the midday sun. Iset the Fair, dressed in a white ceremonial gown and wearing a turquoise coronet, lay on her bed, her arms stretched out by her sides, her eyes wide open. On a sycamore table by the bedside lay Setau's antelope-skin tunic, which she had stolen from his laboratory.

'Iset!'

Iset the Fair, Ramses' first love, the mother of Kha and Meneptah, the Great Royal Wife on whose account he was about to wage war . . . Iset the Fair was gazing on the Other-world.

'The queen chose death to prevent war,' explained Serramanna. 'She poisoned herself with one of the substances from Setau's tunic, so that she would no longer be an obstacle to peace.'

'Don't talk nonsense!'

Ahmeni intervened. 'The queen left a message. I read it and asked Serramanna to inform you.'

According to tradition, Ramses did not close the eyes of the deceased; it was necessary to confront the afterlife with a frank gaze and open countenance.

Iset the Fair was buried in the Valley of the Queens, in a tomb more modest than Nefertari's. Ramses had himself performed the resurrection rites on the mummy. A college of priests and priestesses would be responsible for worshipping the queen's *ka* and for keeping her memory alive. The pharaoh had placed in the Great Royal Wife's sarcophagus a branch of the sycamore he had planted in the garden of his Memphis home when he was seventeen years old. This youthful souvenir would cause Iset's soul to quicken again.

At the end of the ceremony Ahmeni and Setau asked Ramses for an audience. Without answering, he turned and began to climb the steep side of the valley. Setau followed him and Ahmeni did the same, despite the effort demanded of his frail strength.

The sand, the stony slope, Ramses' fast pace, which set his lungs on fire . . . Ahmeni cursed all the way up the hill, but managed to reach the summit, where the king stood looking down on the Valley of the Queens and the dwellings of Nefertari and Iset the Fair. Setau silently surveyed the magnificent site below him. Ahmeni sat down on a rock, completely winded, and wiped his brow with the back of his hand.

Then Ahmeni took courage and interrupted the king's thoughts. 'Majesty, there are urgent decisions to be made.'

'Nothing is more urgent than to look on this country beloved of the gods. They have spoken, and their voice has become sky, mountain, water and earth. We have dug out burial places in Set's red earth, with chambers of rebirth washed by the primordial waters that surround the world. Through our rites we preserve the energy of the first morning, and our country is reborn every day. The rest is beneath contempt.'

'To be reborn, one must first survive,' said Setau bluntly. 'If Pharaoh forgets men, the gods will withdraw for ever into the Invisible.' He expected his critical tone would earn a stinging retort from Ramses. But the king simply stared at the rough dividing line between the cultivated land and the desert, between the everyday and the eternal.

'What ruse have you devised, Ahmeni?' asked Setau.

'I have written to Hattusilis, informing him of Iset's death. During the period of mourning, there can be no question of starting the war.'

'No one could have saved Iset,' declared Setau. 'She had taken too large a dose of substances whose mixture was fatal. I've burnt that cursed tunic, Ramses.'

'I do not hold you responsible. Iset thought she was acting in the interests of Egypt.'

Ahmeni stood up. 'She was right, Majesty.'

The king turned on him furiously. 'How dare you say that?'

'I'm sorry if it angers you, but I must tell you what I think. Iset departed this world in order to save the peace.'

'What do you think, Setau?'

Like Ahmeni, Setau was upset by Ramses' furious expression, but it was his duty to speak frankly. 'If you refuse to understand Iset the Fair's message, Ramses, you will kill her a second time. Act in such a way that her sacrifice is not in vain.'

'And what way is that?'

'Marry the Hittite princess,' declared Ahmeni seriously.

'There is nothing to prevent it now,' added Setau.

Ramses clenched his fists. 'Are your hearts as hard as granite? Iset is scarcely laid to rest in her sarcophagus and you dare to speak to me of marriage!'

'You are not a widower mourning his wife,' argued Setau, 'but the Pharaoh of Egypt, who must preserve the peace and save his people. The people don't care about your feelings, your joy or sorrow. What they want is to be governed and led along the right path.'

'A pharaoh married to a Hittite Great Royal Wife. It's a monstrous idea!'

'On the contrary,' said Ahmeni. 'How better to seal the final reconciliation between the two peoples? If you agree to this marriage, the spectre of war will retreat for many years. Can you imagine the celebrations that Seti and Tuya will hold among the stars? Not to mention Ahsha, who gave his life to build a lasting peace.'

'You are becoming a formidable debater, Ahmeni.'

'I am just a sickly scribe who's not very clever. But I have the honour of bearing the sandals of the Lord of the Two Lands, and I don't want those sandals to be stained with blood.'

'The Rule obliges you to govern with a Great Royal Wife,' Setau reminded Ramses. 'And by marrying this foreigner you will win the greatest of all your battles.'

'I hate the woman already!'

'Your life does not belong to you, Ramses,' said Setau. 'Egypt demands this sacrifice of you.'

'And you, my friends, you too demand it of me!'

Ahmeni and Setau nodded.

'Leave me alone,' said Ramses. 'I need to think.'

Ramses spent the night at the top of the hill. After drawing nourishment from the rising sun, he went down again into the Valley of the Queens, where he lingered a while; then he joined his escort. Without a word, he mounted his chariot and sped to his House of Ramses, his Temple of a Million Years. After celebrating the dawn rites and meditating in Nefertari's shrine, the pharaoh withdrew to his palace, where he performed his ablutions, drank some milk and ate some figs and fresh-baked bread.

His face as calm as if he had slept for several hours, the monarch opened the door of Ahmeni's office, where the scribe, looking harassed, was dealing with administrative correspondence

'Select a high-quality virgin papyrus and write to my brother, the Emperor of Hatti.'

'What is the letter to say?'

'Tell him I have decided to make his daughter my Great Royal Wife.'

21

Uri-Teshup drained a third cup of mulled oasis wine. Sweet and syrupy, infused with herbs and resin, it was used by embalmers for preserving the intestines, and also by doctors for its medicinal properties.

'You drink too much,' remarked Raia.

'One must make the most of the pleasures Egypt offers – and this wine is a miracle! Are you sure you weren't followed?'

'Don't worry.' Raia had waited till midnight to slip into Lady Tanit's house. He seen nothing suspicious.

'Why this unexpected visit?' asked Uri-Teshup.

'Important news, my lord, very important.'

'Is it war, at last?'

'No, my lord, no. There will be no war between Egypt and Hatti.'

Uri-Teshup hurled his cup away and seized the Syrian by his tunic collar. 'What do you mean? The trap I laid was perfect!'

'Iset the Fair is dead and Ramses is preparing to marry Emperor Hattusilis's daughter.'

The prince let go of his ally. 'A Hittite Queen of Egypt? It's unthinkable – you must be mistaken!'

'No, my lord. The information is official. You killed Ahsha for nothing.'

'I had to get rid of that spy. Now our hands are free. None of Ramses' advisers is as quick-witted as Ahsha.'

'We've lost, my lord. It's peace, a peace that no one will manage to destroy.'

'You fool! Do you know the woman who is going to become Pharaoh's Great Royal Wife? A Hittite, Raia, a genuine Hittite, proud, cunning and uncontrollable.'

'But she's the daughter of your enemy Hattusilis.'

'She's first and foremost a Hittite! And she'll never submit to an Egyptian, even if he is the pharaoh! This is our chance.'

Raia sighed. The mulled oasis wine had gone to Uri-Teshup's head: with all hope lost, the prince was living in an unreal world. 'Leave Egypt,' he recommended.

'Suppose this Hittite princess were on our side, Raia. We'd have an ally in the heart of the palace!'

'That's just an illusion, my lord.'

'No, it's a sign sent us by fate, a sign that I shall be able to use to my advantage.'

'You'll be very disappointed.'

Uri-Teshup took a fresh cup, poured himself more wine and drank it down. 'We have forgotten one detail, Raia. There's still time to act – you must use the Libyans.'

Raia pointed at one of the curtains, which was stirring suspiciously. Uri-Teshup moved as silently as a cat towards the curtain, flung it open violently and dragged out a trembling Tanit.

'Were you were listening to us?' he demanded.

'No, no! I came to look for you.'

'We have no secrets from you, my dear, since you can't betray us.'

'You have my word!'

'Go to bed. I'll join you soon.'

Tanit's infatuated look promised the Hittite a lively end to the night. In a few curt words he gave Raia his instructions.

*

The principal Pi-Ramses armoury continued to manufacture swords, spears and shields at a hectic pace. Until Ramses' marriage to the Hittite princess had been celebrated, the preparations for war would continue.

The weapons taken from the Hittites were kept in a workshop close to the forges. The Egyptian craftsmen had studied them closely to discover the secrets of their manufacture.

One of the metalworkers, a very inventive young man, was studying the iron dagger, which the palace had just entrusted to him. The quality of the metal, the weight and width of the blade, the hilt shaped for ease of handling: everything about it was remarkable. It wouldn't be easy to copy it. He'd probably have to make several fruitless attempts before he succeeded. Intrigued by the challenge, the young man stared at the dagger.

'Someone to see you,' announced an orderly.

The visitor was a coarse-featured mercenary.

'What do you want?' asked the metalworker.

'The palace wants the dagger back.'

'Have you got a written order?'

'Of course.'

'Show it to me.'

The mercenary took a wooden tablet out of a bag hanging from his belt, and handed it to the young man.

'But these aren't hieroglyphs!'

Raia's Libyan knocked him senseless with a violent blow on the head. Then he picked up the tablet and dagger, which his victim had dropped, and ran out of the workshop.

After questioning him many times, Serramanna was convinced that the metalworker was not in collusion with the man who had stolen the dagger. The latter was probably a mercenary eager for profit – there were many such in the Egyptian army.

'He's a ruffian in Uri-Teshup's pay,' he told Ahmeni.

The scribe went on writing. 'Have you any proof?'

'My instinct is enough.'

'Your determination to pursue Uri-Teshup is getting you nowhere. He's married a fortune and is enjoying a life of pleasure. Why would he get someone to steal Hattusilis's dagger?'

'Because he's devised a plan to harm Ramses,' said Serramanna.

'At present, war with the Hittites is out of the question. Your inquiry into Ahsha's murder is the most important thing. Have you made any progress?'

'Not yet.'

'Ramses insists that the murderer's identity must be proved.'

'That crime and the theft of this dagger – it's all linked. If anything happens to me, see that you concentrate on the Uri-Teshup lead.'

'If anything happens to you?' asked Ahmeni. 'What are you going to do?'

'To make progress I must infiltrate Libyan circles. It'll be very risky. If I get near the truth, they'll try to kill me.'

'You're the head of Ramses' personal bodyguard! No one would dare attack you.'

'They didn't hesitate to kill his minister for foreign affairs, his childhood friend,' retorted Serramanna.

'Isn't there a less dangerous way?'

'I'm afraid not.'

Malfi's tent in the heart of the Libyan desert, far from any oasis, was a stronghold guarded by reliable men. The tribal chief lived on milk and dates. He touched neither beer nor wine, considering these drinks diabolical because they confused one's thoughts.

Malfi's personal guard was composed exclusively of

natives of his own village who, but for him, would have remained poor peasants. Now they had enough to eat, decent clothes, were armed with spears, swords, bows and slings, and had their choice of any women who pleased them. They literally worshipped Malfi, believing him the embodiment of the spirit of the desert. He was as swift as a panther, his fingers were as sharp as knives and nothing could be hidden from his gaze.

'My lord, there's been a scuffle,' a water-carrier informed him.

Malfi rose slowly and emerged from his tent. He was square-headed, his broad brow hidden under a white turban.

The training camp sheltered some fifty warriors, who fought each other with knives or bare fists in the full midday sun. Malfi liked the severe conditions of the heat and the desert. Only those who had the real warrior's temperament would emerge victorious from the ordeals he imposed on them. Those ordeals were indispensable in view of the task which awaited the Libyan army being formed: to crush Ramses' forces. Malfi thought constantly of the generations of Libyan chiefs humiliated by the pharaohs. The hostilities had lasted for centuries, punctuated by defeats inflicted by the Egyptians on the brave but badly organized desert tribes.

Ofir, Malfi's elder brother, had used a weapon he had thought decisive: black magic, used in the service of the pro-Hittite spy ring he led. He had paid with his life for his failure, and Malfi had vowed to avenge him. Gradually he would form the Libyan tribes into a federation, of which he would sooner or later become the undisputed leader. The pact with Uri-Teshup gave him an extra chance of success. With an ally of this calibre, victory would no longer be an idle dream. Malfi would wipe out centuries of shame and frustration.

A heavily built warrior of uncommon aggressiveness, forgetting he was only in training, had got carried away and had knocked out two opponents who were bigger than himself and armed with spears. When Malfi approached, the warrior was strutting about, occasionally stamping on the head of one of the men he had defeated.

Malfi took out a dagger hidden in his tunic and plunged it into the burly soldier's neck. The fighting stopped immediately, and all faces were turned towards Malfi.

'Go on with your training, but keep control over yourselves,' he ordered, 'and remember: the enemy can appear from anywhere.'

22

The great Pi-Ramses audience chamber was a wonder to behold. Even the courtiers accustomed to climbing the monumental staircase, which was adorned with figures of defeated enemies subjected by Pharaoh to the Rule of Ma'at, felt deep emotion as they ascended. The entrance door was surrounded by oval cartouches, on which Ramses' coronation names were painted in blue on a white ground, their shape symbolizing the cycles of the cosmos over which the Lord of the Two Lands reigned.

Plenary audiences, to which the whole court was summoned, were infrequent. Only exceptional events, when the future of Egypt was at stake, caused Ramses to address the entire higher administration. The prevalent feeling was one of anxiety. Rumour had it that the Hittite emperor was still angry. Ramses had insulted him by refusing, at first, to marry his daughter. The pharaoh's belated acceptance had not effaced the affront.

The floor of the great hall was covered with coloured glazed terracotta tiles decorated with images of fountains, flower gardens, ducks swimming on a blue-green pond and fish gliding among water-lilies. Ritualists, scribes, ministers, governors of provinces, those in charge of the offerings, Keepers of the Secrets and fine ladies, all delighted in the enchanting scenes that covered the walls, coloured in pale green, deep red, light blue, golden yellow and off-white, where hoopoes, humming-birds, swallows, bluetits, nightingales and kingfishers flitted. Looking up, the eye was charmed by beautiful friezes where poppies, water-lilies, daisies and cornflowers bloomed.

Silence fell as Ramses mounted the steps leading to his golden throne. On the top step was depicted a lion closing its jaws on the enemy emerging from the shadows – disorder, which endlessly attempted to destroy the harmony of Ma'at.

Wearing the two crowns, the White Crown of Lower Egypt framed by the Red Crown of Upper Egypt, Ramses bore on his head 'the Two Powers', charged with magic. On his brow was the golden uraeus, the female cobra spitting the fire which dispersed darkness. In his right hand the king held the sceptre named 'Magic', shaped like a shepherd's crook. Just as the shepherd mustered his flock, bringing back the sheep that strayed, so Pharaoh had to gather together all scattered energies. From Ramses' golden apron, beams of light seemed to shine out.

For a few seconds, the king's gaze lingered on a sublime painting of the face of a young woman lost in thought before a clump of hollyhocks. She resembled Nefertari whose beauty, even after her death, illuminated the reign of Ramses the Great. But Pharaoh had no time for nostalgia. The ship of state sailed on; he had to keep his hand on the helm.

'I have called you together,' he said, 'so that the whole country, through you, may be informed of major facts. Foolish rumours are circulating here and there, and I wish to establish the truth, which you will then spread.'

Ahmeni stood at the back with the other scribes, as if he occupied only a minor post; in this way, he would get a better idea of the audience's reactions. Serramanna, on the other hand, had chosen to keep an eye on the first row. At the slightest show of hostility, he would act. As for Setau, he occupied the place due to his rank, on the left of the Viceroy of Nubia, among the most important dignitaries – many of whom frequently eyed Lotus, who was dressed in a gown whose shoulder straps left her breasts bare.

The governor of Crown Prince province, in Lower Egypt, came forward and bowed low. 'May I speak, Majesty?'

'I am listening.'

'Is it true that Ahsha, the minister for foreign affairs, is being held prisoner in Hattusa and that the peace treaty with the Hittites has been broken?'

'My friend Ahsha was murdered while on his way back to Pi-Ramses. He rests for ever in Egyptian soil. The inquiry is proceeding; those guilty will be identified and punished. The peace with Hatti is largely Ahsha's work, and we shall continue that work. The treaty with the Hittites is still in force and will long remain so.'

'Majesty, may we know who will be the next Great Royal Wife?'

'The daughter of Hattusilis, Emperor of Hatti.'

A murmur ran through the audience.

A general asked permission to speak 'Majesty, isn't that giving too much to a people that used to be our enemy?'

'For as long as Iset the Fair reigned, I rejected Hattusilis's proposal. Today, this marriage is the only way to consolidate the peace the people of Egypt desire.'

'Will it be necessary to tolerate the presence of a Hittite army on our soil?'

'No, general, merely the presence of one woman.'

'Forgive my impertinence, Majesty,' the general went on, 'but isn't a Hittite on the throne of the Two Lands an affront to those who fought the Hittites? Thanks to Prince Meneptah, our troops are ready and well equipped. What have we to fear from fighting the Hittites again? Instead of giving in to their intolerable demands, would it not be better to oppose them?'

The officer's arrogance risked costing him his post.

'There is something in what you say,' observed Ramses,

'but you are seeing only one side of the question. If Egypt started a war, she would break the peace treaty and betray her word. Do you imagine that a pharaoh could behave in that way?'

The general stepped back and disappeared into the crowd of courtiers, whom the monarch's arguments had convinced.

The supervisor of the canals asked permission to speak. 'Suppose the Emperor of Hatti changed his mind and refused to send his daughter to Egypt? Would that not be an intolerable insult, Majesty?'

Kha, the High Priest of Memphis, came forward, dressed in a panther-skin. 'Will Pharaoh allow me to reply?'

Ramses agreed.

'In my view,' declared Kha, 'politics and diplomacy do not offer enough safeguards to allow us to make this vital decision. Respect for one's word and the Rule of Ma'at take precedence over everything; but it is also necessary to apply the magic laws of state which our ancestors taught us. In the thirtieth year of his reign, Ramses the Great participated in his first regeneration celebration; in future it will be necessary to let our sovereign build up more frequently the invisible forces that he needs in order to govern. Therefore the most urgent matter, in this thirty-third year, is to prepare his second regeneration feast. Then the horizon will become clearer, and our questions will be answered.'

'That will need long and costly organization,' protested the director of the House of Gold and Silver. 'Would it not be better to postpone the festival?'

'That's not possible,' retorted Kha. 'Study of the texts and the astrologers' calculations point to the same conclusion: Ramses the Great's second regeneration feast must be celebrated in less than two months. The whole realm must strive to bring together the gods and goddesses, and all our thoughts must be devoted to safeguarding Pharaoh.'

The commander of the fortresses along the north-eastern

CITY OF LIMERICK PUBLIC LIBRARY

border asked permission to speak. A career soldier and a man of great experience, he had the ear of many notables.

'I respect the High Priest's opinion,' he said, 'but what shall we do if the Hittites attack? When Hattusilis learns that Egypt is preparing this great celebration, instead of arranging his daughter's marriage, he may feel humiliated again and attack. While Pharaoh is performing the rites, who will be in command?'

'The performance of the rites will itself protect us,' declared Kha in his fine, deep, melodious voice. 'It has always been so.'

'That is the belief of an initiate into the secrets of the temples. An experienced soldier sees things differently. Hattusilis hesitates to attack us because he fears Ramses, the victor of Kadesh, who, he knows, can perform superhuman feats. If Pharaoh is not at the head of his troops, the Emperor of Hatti will throw all his forces into battle.'

'Egypt's best protection lies in magic,' declared Kha. 'The destroyers, whether Hittite or not, are simply the instruments of the forces of darkness – which no human army can halt. It was Amon himself who made Ramses' arm stronger than thousands of attackers, at Kadesh.'

The argument hit home. No other officer expressed any objection.

'I would have liked to be present at the performance of the ritual,' said Meneptah, 'but does Pharaoh not agree that it is my place to guard our borders?'

'With ten Royal Sons, you will ensure the safety of the realm during the festivities.'

Ramses' decision reassured the gathering, but the head of the ritualists, visibly annoyed, pushed his way to the front. He had a shaven head and a long, thin face, and was a rather ascetic figure.

'With Your Majesty's permission,' he said, 'I have a few questions to put to the High Priest.'

134

The king expressed no opposition. Kha was expecting this test, but he had hoped it would take place outside the court.

'Where does the High Priest of Memphis intend to celebrate the second regeneration festivities?' asked the ritualist.

'In the Temple of Ramses, which was built for this purpose.'

'Does the king indeed possess the legacy of the gods?'

'He does.'

'Who will preside over the ritual?'

'The immortal soul of Seti,' said Kha.

'What is the source of the light that will provide Pharaoh with the celestial energy?'

'This light is born of itself and is reborn every instant in Pharaoh's heart.'

The head of the ritualists asked no further questions. He would never manage to catch Kha out. He turned to Ramses, and said seriously, 'In spite of the High Priest's competence, I consider it impossible to celebrate this feast of regeneration.'

'Why?' asked Kha in astonishment.

'Because the Great Royal Wife must play an essential part in it. Now, Pharaoh is a widower and has not yet taken this Hittite princess for his wife. But no foreigner has ever had access to the mysteries of regeneration.'

Ramses rose. 'Did you think that Pharaoh was unaware of this difficulty?'

23

Teshonq had worked with leather since his childhood. The son of a Libyan who had been arrested by the Egyptian police following the theft of some sheep and sentenced to several years' hard labour, he had not accompanied his father when the latter returned home to preach armed struggle against Pharaoh. Teshonq had found work, first in Bubastis, then in Pi-Ramses, and gradually had even made a name for himself in his speciality.

As he neared his fiftieth year, he had had fits of remorse. He of the pot-belly and beaming countenance, he had betrayed the country of his birth, in too easily forgetting the military defeats of his people and the humiliations inflicted on them by Egypt. Now that he was a wealthy artisan, the head of a company with thirty employees, his door was always open to Libyans in difficulty. As the months went by he had become known as the saviour of his exiled compatriots. Some of them had quickly integrated with Egyptian society, while others still wanted revenge. But now another movement was growing. It frightened Teshonq, who no longer wished to see the Two Lands disappear. Suppose Libya were finally victorious, and a Libyan mounted the throne of Egypt? But first it would be necessary to get rid of Ramses.

To dispel this wild dream, Teshonq concentrated on his

work. He checked the quality of the goatskins, the skins of sheep, deer and other desert animals which had just been delivered to him. When they had been dried, salted and smoked, a team of specialists would treat them with ochre clay and soften them with urine, bird droppings and dung. This was the most evil-smelling operation carried out in his workshop, which regularly received visits from the public health service.

A temporary tanning with oil and alum was followed by the real tanning with a substance rich in tannic acid, extracted from the seedpods of the Nile acacia. If necessary, the skins were soaked again in oil, then pounded and stretched to make them supple. Teshonq was one of the best leather-workers in Egypt, for he was not satisfied with a crude tanning with fat. Moreover, he was particularly skilled at folding the skins on the trestle and cutting them, one reason why he had a large and varied clientele. His workshop made bags, dog collars and leashes, ropes, sandals, cases and sheaths for daggers and swords, helmets, quivers, shields and even writing-stands.

Using a leather-knife with a semi-circular blade, Teshonq was cutting a strap out of a prime-quality deerskin, when a moustachioed giant entered his workshop. Serramanna, the head of Ramses' personal bodyguard – the knife slipped, skidded across the deerskin and gashed the middle finger of the craftsman's left hand. He could not suppress a cry of pain. The blood flowed fast. Teshonq ordered an assistant to clean the leather, while he washed the wound and covered it with honey.

The huge Sardinian watched the scene without moving.

Teshonq bowed to him. 'Forgive me for keeping you waiting. A stupid accident.'

'And a strange one. You are said to have a very steady hand.'

Teshonq trembled with fear. He, a descendant of Libyan warriors, ought to have felled his opponent just with a look. But Serramanna was a mercenary, a Sardinian and a giant.

'Are you in need of my services?' asked Teshonq.

'I need a support-cuff in the finest leather. Recently, when I handle my battle-axe I've been feeling a slight weakness.'

'I'll show you several that you can choose from.'

'I'm pretty certain you keep the toughest ones hidden behind your workshop.'

'No, I—'

'Oh, yes you do,' interrupted Serramanna. 'I tell you, I know it.'

'Yes, yes, I remember.'

'Well then, let's go.'

Teshonq was sweating profusely. What had Serramanna discovered? Nothing – he couldn't know anything. Teshonq must get a grip on himself, not show any unfounded fear. Egypt was a country built on law; the Sardinian dared not use violence, for fear of being severely condemned by a court.

The Libyan led Serramanna into a small room where he kept his finest creations, those he had no intention of selling. Among them was a splendid support-cuff in red leather.

'Are you trying to corrupt me,' asked Serramanna.

'Certainly not!'

'Such a valuable piece! It's fit for a king.'

'You flatter me.'

'You are an outstanding craftsman, Teshonq. You have a brilliant career, a remarkable clientele, a promising future . . . What a pity!'

The Libyan turned ashen. 'I don't understand.'

'Why were you led astray, when your life was so bright?'

'Led astray? Me?'

Serramanna fingered a magnificent brown leather shield, fit for a commander-in-chief. 'I'm very sorry, Teshonq, but you may be in serious trouble.'

'Me? But why?'

Serramanna showed him a roll of leather to be used as a papyrus case. 'Do you recognize this?'

'Yes, but—'

'Yes or no?'

'Yes, I do.'

'Who was it intended for?'

'A ritualist in charge of the secrets of the temple.'

The Sardinian smiled. 'You're a sincere, honest man, Teshonq. I was sure of it.'

'I've nothing to hide, my lord!'

'Nevertheless, you've made a bad mistake.'

'What have I done?'

'Used this leather case to transmit a subversive message.'

The Libyan almost choked. His tongue swelled up in his mouth, and his temples throbbed. 'It's . . . it's . . .'

'It's an operational error,' explained Serramanna. 'The ritualist was utterly astonished to find in this case a call to the Libyans of Egypt, enjoining them to prepare an armed rebellion against Ramses.'

'No! *No!* That's impossible!'

'This case comes from your workshop, Teshonq, and it was you who wrote the message.'

'No, my lord, I swear I didn't!'

'I like your work very much, Teshonq. You're stupid to get mixed up in a plot which is beyond you. At your age, and in your circumstances, it's an unforgivable mistake. You have nothing to gain and everything to lose. What madness came over you?'

'My lord, I swear—'

'Don't swear any false oaths: you'd be condemned by the court of the hereafter. You've chosen the wrong path, but I'd like to believe that you've been made use of. From time to time we get muddled in our thinking.'

'It's a misunderstanding,' said Teshonq. 'I—'

'Don't waste time lying. My men have been watching you for a long time and know you are protecting the Libyan rebels.'

'Not rebels, my lord, only men in difficulties whom I, as a compatriot, try to help. That's only natural.'

'Oh, you're much more important than that,' said Serramanna. 'Without you, the underground network couldn't have been formed.'

'I'm an honest trader, I—'

'Let's face facts, my friend. I have proof against you which will send you to your death, or, at best, to prison for the rest of your life. I only have to take this document to the vizier for him to give me the order to imprison you. You're facing a trial that will make an example of you, and a punishment to fit your crime.'

'But I'm innocent!'

'Come, come, Teshonq, not to me! With proof like this, the judges won't hesitate. You have no chance of being found not guilty, none at all. Unless I take a hand.'

A heavy silence reigned in the room.

Then Teshonq asked nervously, 'What might that hand be, my lord?'

Serramanna fingered the leather shield. 'Whatever his position, every man has some unfulfilled wishes. I'm like everyone else. I'm well paid, I live in a pleasant official dwelling, and I have all the women I want. But I'd like to be richer and to have no worries about my old age. I could keep quiet and forget about this proof . . . but everything has its price.'

'A high price?'

'Don't forget that I must also buy the ritualist's silence. A fair shair of your profits would satisfy me.'

'If we can come to an agreement, will you leave me in peace?'

'I still have to do my job, my friend,' said the Sardinian.

'What do you want?'

'The names of the Libyans who murdered Ahsha.'

'My lord, I don't know who they are!'

140

'Either you're not telling the truth, or you will soon find out who they are. Be my special investigator, Teshonq, and you'll have nothing to complain about.'

'But what if I can't find out?'

'That would be a pity, my friend. But I'm sure you'll manage to avoid that disaster. Officially, I'm ordering a hundred shields and sword-scabbards for my men. When you come to the palace, ask for me.'

Leaving behind him a distraught Teshonq, Serramanna left the workshop. Ahmeni had persuaded him to pass himself off as a man open to bribery, ready to betray his king in order to get rich. If Teshonq took the bait, he'd be less afraid to speak and would put Serramanna on the right track.

24

In this thirty-third year of the reign of Ramses the Great, the Theban winter, which sometimes brought icy winds, was mild. The sky was a cloudless blue expanse, the Nile flowed calmly, the cultivated fields grew green following good floodwaters, donkeys laden with forage trotted from village to village, cows with well-filled udders went out to pasture, flanked by cowherds and dogs, little girls played with their dolls in the doorways of white houses, while little boys ran after balls made of cloth . . . The life of Egypt continued at its eternal pace as if nothing would ever change.

Ramses enjoyed this quiet moment, inscribed in everyday existence. How right his ancestors had been to choose to build their Houses of Eternity on the West bank, and to hollow out here the dwelling-places of life where, every morning, the bodies of light of the kings and queens were regenerated by the rising sun. Here, there was no borderline between earthly life and the hereafter; here, the human element was absorbed by the mysterious.

After celebrating the dawn ritual in the temple of Seti's *ka* in Gurnah, Ramses remained to meditate in the shrine, where his father's essence was expressed in the hieroglyphs engraved on the walls. In the depths of the silence, he heard the voice of the pharaoh who had become a star. Leaving the shrine, he advanced across the great courtyard, which was bathed in soft light. A procession of female singers and musicians was emerging from the Hall of Pillars. Among them was Meritamon. When she caught sight of her father, she left the procession, came towards him and bowed low, her arms crossed on her chest.

Every day she looked more and more like Nefertari. Her beauty, bright as a spring morning, seemed sustained by the wisdom of the temple. Ramses took his daughter's arm and the two of them walked slowly down the avenue of sphinxes, which was lined with acacias and tamarisks.

'Do you keep in touch with events in the outside world?' asked Ramses.

'No, father. You cause Ma'at to reign, you fight against disorder and darkness. That's all I need to know. Noises from the secular world do not pass the walls of the sanctuary, and it is right that they do not.'

'Your mother wanted this life, but fate decreed a very different one for her.'

'Weren't you the master of that fate?'

'Pharaoh has a duty to act in this world, although his thoughts remain among the secrets of the temple. Today I must preserve the peace, Meritamon. To do so, I shall marry the Emperor of Hatti's daughter.'

'Will she become the Great Royal Wife?'

'Yes, indeed, but I must celebrate my second feast of regeneration before the marriage. But I am faced with a decision which cannot take effect without your help.'

'I do not wish to play any part in the affairs of state, you know that.'

'The ritual cannot be accomplished without the active participation of an Egyptian Great Royal Wife. Is it too much to ask you to play that symbolic part?'

'That means leaving Thebes and going to Pi-Ramses,' said Meritamon. 'And what then?'

'Although Queen of Egypt, you will return here to live the

life you have chosen.'

'Will you not assign me secular tasks more and more frequently?'

'I shall call on you only for my regeneration feasts,' said Ramses. 'According to Kha, they will have to be celebrated every three or four years, until my span of life is finished. You are free to accept or to refuse.'

'Why have you chosen me?'

'Because years of meditation have given you the spiritual and magical capacity to play a crushing ritual part.'

Meritamon stood still and looked back towards the temple. 'You ask too much of me, father, but you are Pharaoh.'

Setau was in a bad mood. Far from his beloved Nubia, the snakes' paradise, he felt almost like an exile; he kept busy, though. With the help of Lotus, who every night tracked down some good-sized snakes, he had infused new energy into the laboratory responsible for preparing remedies based on snake venom. And, acting on Ahmeni's advice, he was taking advantage of his stay in Pi-Ramses to improve his ability as an administrator. As he grew older, Setau had had to admit that enthusiasm was not enough to persuade senior officials to grant him the funds and materials he needed for his Nubian province. Though he was far from becoming a courtier, he was learning to present his requests better and he was obtaining positive results.

As he left the office of the controller of the trading-fleet, who had agreed to the construction of three cargo boats earmarked for Nubia, Setau met Kha, who looked less serene than usual.

'Problems?' asked Setau.

'The preparations for the feast are taking every minute of my time. And I've just had a very nasty surprise. The manager of the sacred warehouses of the Delta, which I was counting on to supply many pairs of sandals, lengths of linen and alabaster goblets, has sent me practically nothing. That makes my task all the more difficult.'

'What reason did he give?'

'He's away. His wife answered my letter.'

'That's very offhand behaviour! I'm only a beginner at this administration business, but I don't like that attitude. Let's go and see Ahmeni.'

They found him enjoying a roast goose-leg dipped in red wine sauce, while rapidly reading a report from the Delta warehouses supervisor, whose offices were north of Memphis.

'Something's wrong,' Ahmeni said bluntly. 'Kha wasn't wrong to apply to this official, and there should have been no difficulty over supplying what is needed for the regeneration feast. I don't like it. I don't like it at all!'

'Could there be some mistake in the supervisor's dossiers?' asked Kha.

'Possibly, but not in *my* dossiers.'

'The celebrations are in danger of being partially compromised,' said the High Priest. 'To welcome the gods and goddesses, we need the finest lengths of linen, the best sandals, the—'

'I'll set up a detailed inquiry,' declared Ahmeni.

'Trust a scribe to suggest that!' Setau said scornfully. 'It will be long and complicated, and Kha's in a hurry. We must be more subtle. Make me a special supervisor and I'll soon learn the truth.'

Ahmeni was reluctant. 'We're barely within the law. And suppose it's dangerous?'

'I've got reliable and efficient assistants. Don't let's waste any more time talking. Give me written orders.'

In the heart of the warehouse district to the north of Memphis, Lady Sherit ran operations with the authority of an experienced general. Small, dark, pretty and imperious, she directed the drivers of the teams of donkeys laden with different produce, allocated tasks to the packers, checked the lists and did not hesitate to brandish her stick at the head of any protester. A woman of character, such as Setau liked.

With his hair all dishevelled, several days' growth of beard and his new antelope-skin tunic, which was even shabbier then the old one, Setau was quickly spotted.

'What are you doing loitering about here?' demanded Lady Sherit.

'I'd like to talk to you.'

'We don't talk here. We work.'

'It's about your work that I want to talk to you.'

Lady Sherit gave a nasty smile. 'You don't like the way I give orders, perhaps?'

'I'm concerned about your exact qualifications.'

The little brunette was astonished: no vagabond would talk like that. 'Who are you?' she asked.

'The special supervisor appointed by the central administration.'

'Forgive me . . . But the way you're dressed . . .'

'My superiors don't like it either, but they put up with this whim of mine because I get excellent results.'

'As a matter of form, can you show me your orders?'

'Here they are.'

The papyrus was furnished with all the necessary seals, including that of the vizier, who had approved Ahmeni and Setau's plan. Lady Sherit read and re-read the document, which gave the supervisor the power to inspect the warehouses as and when he pleased.

'I ought to show this document to your husband,' said Setau.

'He's away.'

'Shouldn't he be at his post?'

'His mother is very old and she needed him.'

'So you have taken your husband's place.'

'I know this work and I do it well.'

'We have a serious problem, Lady Sherit. You don't seem to be in a position to deliver what the palace needs for the king's regeneration celebrations.'

'Well, the order was unexpected and . . . Yes, at present that is unfortunately the case.'

'I need a full explanation.'

'I don't know everything, but I do know that an important transfer of material was made to another site.'

'Which one?'

'I don't know.'

'On whose orders was it done?'

'I don't know that either. But when my husband comes back he'll be able to answer you, and everything will be straightened out, I'm sure.'

'Tomorrow morning I shall inspect your records and the contents of the warehouses.'

'Tomorrow I was intending to clean out the warehouse and—'

'I'm in a hurry, my lady,' interrupted Setau. 'My superiors insist on a report immediately. So you will put your archives at my disposal.'

'There are so many of them!'

'I'll manage. See you tomorrow, Lady Sherit.'

25

Lady Sherit had no time to waste. Her husband had acted like a fool – again! – in answering the government's questions so quickly. When he showed her the copy of his letter she had flown into a rage. It was too late to intecept the courier . . . She had immediately dispatched her husband to a village south of Thebes, hoping that the incident would be lost in the sand and that the palace would apply to other warehouses.

Unfortunately the authorities had reacted quite differently. In spite of his strange appearance, this supervisor seemed determined and uncompromising. For a moment she had thought of trying to bribe him, but that was too risky. Her only option was to put the urgent contingency plan into practice. It was going to cost her a great deal: it would be a painful sacrifice, which would deprive her of considerable profits on the goods she had patiently diverted. But it was the only way of escaping the law.

When the warehouses were about to close, she took four packers aside. 'In the middle of the night,' she told them, 'you will enter the building on the right of the central warehouse.'

'It's always kept locked,' objected one of the packers.

'I shall open it for you. You will move all its contents to the main warehouse – as quickly as possible, and in silence.'

'It's outside our normal working hours, missus.'

'I shall pay you the equivalent of a week's wages. And if

I'm really pleased, I'll add a bonus.'

The four men smiled broadly.

'Then you'll forget all about the night's work. Are we agreed?' There was a scarcely veiled threat in Sherit's sharp voice.

'Agreed, missus.'

The warehouse district was deserted. At regular intervals, the police, accompanied by dogs, made their rounds.

The four men were hidden in a vast building in which were kept the wooden sleds used to transport heavy materials. They had had a drink of beer, eaten some fresh bread and then taken it in turns to sleep.

At midnight Lady Sherit's imperious voice rang out: 'Come.'

She had drawn the wooden bolts and broken the seals of dried mud which prevented entry to the building where, officially, her husband kept copper ingots intended for the temple workshops. Without asking any questions, the packers transferred a hundred jars of finest-quality wine, four hundred and fifty lengths of fine linen, six hundred pairs of leather sandals, spare parts for chariots, thirteen hundred small blocks of copper ore, three hundred bales of wool and a hundred alabaster goblets.

Just as they were depositing the last goblets, Setau emerged from the depths of the warehouse, where he had been hiding to watch the proceedings.

'Nice work, Lady Sherit,' he remarked. 'So you're returning what you stole, in order to pre-empt my investigation. Nice work, but too late.'

The little brunette did not panic. 'What do you want in exchange for your silence?'

'The names of your accomplices. Who do you sell the stolen objects to?'

'That's not important.'

'You'd better tell me, Lady Sherit.'

'So you won't negotiate?'

'It's not in my nature.'

'So much the worse for you. You shouldn't have come alone.'

'Don't worry, I have an ally.'

Lotus appeared in the doorway of the warehouse. The slender Nubian wore only a short papyrus kilt, leaving her breasts bare, and carried a wicker basket fitted with a leather lid.

Lady Sherit felt like laughing. 'That's a really powerful ally,' she declared ironically.

'Tell your bully-boys to clear off,' Setau said calmly.

'Grab those two,' Lady Sherit curtly ordered the packers.

Lotus put her basket down on the ground and opened it. From it emerged four very angry puff adders, recognizable by the three blue and green stripes on their neck. They expelled the air contained in their lungs to emit a terrifying hiss. The four packers leapt over the piles of material and made off as fast as their legs could carry them.

The adders surrounded Lady Sherit, who nearly fainted.

'You'd better talk,' advised Setau. 'These snakes' venom is very toxic. You may not die but it will cause irreparable damage to your system.'

'I'll tell you everything,' she promised.

'Whose idea was it to divert the goods intended for the temples?'

'It was . . . my husband's.'

'Are you quite sure?'

'My husband's and mine.'

'How long has your trafficking been going on?'

'A bit more than two years. If it hadn't been for this feast of regeneration, no one would have asked us any questions and everything would have continued—'

'You must have had to bribe the scribes.'

'No, there was no need to. My husband falsified the inventories, and we sold off the objects in batches of varying sizes, as opportunities occurred. I was just preparing to sell a very large batch.'

'Who's the buyer?' demanded Setau.

'The captain of a barge.'

'What's his name?'

'I don't know.'

'What does he look like?'

'He's tall and bearded, with a scar on his left forearm and brown eyes.'

'Is he the one who pays you?'

'Yes, with precious stones and some gold.'

'When is the next transaction?'

'The day after tomorrow.'

'Well,' concluded Setau with delight, 'we shall have the pleasure of meeting him.'

The barge drew alongside at the end of an uneventful day's sailing. It transported huge terracotta jars which potters manufactured in Arabia, using a secret formula which enabled the jars to keep water fresh and fit for drinking for a year. But these jars were empty, as they would be used to hide the objects bought from Lady Sherit.

The captain had worked all his life in the trading-fleet, and his colleagues thought him very professional: no serious accidents, his authority accepted by his crew, his deliveries almost never late. But his mistresses cost him dear and his outlays increased faster than his salary. After some reluctance he had agreed to the proposition put to him: transporting stolen goods. The extra money was enough for him to go on living the grand life he was so keen on.

Lady Sherit was as conscientious as himself. He knew that, as usual, the cargo would be ready, and it wouldn't take long to transfer it from the warehouse to the barge. This normal activity would surprise nobody, especially since the labels on the wooden chests and baskets showed that they contained foodstuffs.

But first of all, the captain would have to fight a hard battle. On one hand, Lady Sherit was becoming more and more greedy; on the other hand, the person masterminding the operation wanted to pay less and less for the stolen goods. The haggling might be long-drawn-out, but the parties would eventually have to reach a compromise.

The captain made his way towards Lady Sherit's official residence. As agreed, she waved from the top of her terrace. So everything was in order. He crossed the little garden and entered the reception hall with its two blue-painted pillars. There were benches along the walls.

Lady Sherit came softly down the stairs, followed by a beautiful Nubian.

'Who's that woman?' asked the captain.

'Don't turn round,' said Setau in his deep voice. 'There's a cobra behind you.'

'It's true,' confirmed Lady Sherit.

'Who are you?' asked the sailor.

'A messenger from Pharaoh,' said Setau. 'It's my job to put an end to your thefts. But I also want to know the name of the man you're working for.'

The captain thought he was living a nightmare. His world was collapsing around him.

'Who are you working for?' repeated Setau.

The captain knew his sentence would be heavy. He was determined not to be the only one punished. 'I only saw him once,' he said.

'Did he give his name?'

'Yes. It's Ahmeni.'

Setau was dumbfounded. He took a few steps and came to a halt in front of the captain. 'Describe him!'

The captain at last saw the man who wanted to arrest him.

152

He was the cobra! Convinced that Setau had only pretended the snake was there, in order to frighten him, he turned and tried to run. The cobra struck, biting him on the neck. The sailor lost consciousness and collapsed from pain and fear.

Believing that the way was clear, Lady Sherit ran towards the little garden.

'No!' shrieked Lotus, caught unawares.

The seond cobra, a female, bit the pretty brunette in the back as she ran through the door. Unable to breathe, her heart caught in a vice, she crawled away, clawing at the earth, then was still. The snake slowly joined its mate.

'There's no hope of saving them,' said Lotus regretfully.

'They robbed their country,' Setau reminded her, 'and the judges of the hereafter will not be lenient.'

He sat down, still overwhelmed. 'Ahmeni . . . Ahmeni corrupt!'

26

Emperor Hattusilis's latest letter was a masterpiece of diplomacy. Ramses had read it attentively at least a dozen times and still could not make up his mind. Did the emperor want peace or war? Did he still want to marry his daughter to Ramses or was he standing on his outraged dignity?

'What do you think, Ahmeni?'

The king's sandal-bearer seemed to have lost even more weight, in spite of all the food he ate in the course of a day. He had consulted Dr Neferet, who said that he was not suffering from any serious illness but that he should avoid overworking.

'If only Ahsha were here,' said Ahmeni. 'He'd have been able to decode this flowery epistle.'

'What's your opinion?'

'Although I'm pessimistic by nature, I have the feeling that Hattusilis is leaving a door open for you. Your regeneration celebrations begin tomorrow; the magic will give you the answer.'

'I'm glad to be meeting the community of gods and goddesses.'

'Kha has done some remarkable work; nothing will be lacking. And Setau has just put an end to some organized theft. The things he has recovered are already in Pi-Ramses.'

'Who are the culprits?' asked Ramses.

'They died in an accident. Their case will be put before the vizier's court and he will pronounce on the probable erasure of their names from all official documents.'

'I shall go to bed until dawn.'

'May the *ka* illuminate you, Majesty, and may you bring light to Egypt.'

The late summer night was warm and clear. Like most of his compatriots, Ramses had decided to sleep in the open air, on the roof terrace of the palace. Lying on a simple mat, he gazed up at the sky, where the souls of the pharaohs shone after they had been turned into light. The axis of the universe passed through the polar star, around which the court of the eternal stars was ranged. Since the time of the pyramids, the thoughts of the sages had been inscribed in the heavens.

Ramses made time stand still and looked back over all he had done in the thirty-three years of his reign. Up to now he had ceaselessly moved forward, overcoming obstacles, pushing back the limits of the impossible. But now, although his energy was undiminished, his view of the world was no longer that of a ram charging headlong, without caring who followed him. Reigning over Egypt was a matter not of imposing one man's law but of making the land breathe the breath of Ma'at, whose first servant Pharaoh was. As a young king, Ramses had hoped to change men's ways of thinking, carrying a whole society along with him, delivering them for ever from pettiness and meanness, enlarging men's hearts. With experience, the dream had vanished. Human beings would always be themselves, attracted by lies and evil; no doctrine, no religion, no politics would ever change their nature. Only the practice of justice, the permanent application of the Rule of Ma'at would keep chaos at bay.

Ramses had made every effort to respect what his father had taught him. His wish to be a great pharaoh, setting his seal on the destiny of the Two Lands, was no longer what counted. After having known every happiness, after having reached the height of his power, he had now only one ambition: to serve.

Setau was drunk, but carried on swigging mulled oasis wine. He paced stiff-legged up and down the bedchamber. 'Don't fall asleep, Lotus! This is no time for resting. We must think and come to a decision.'

'You've been saying the same thing for hours!'

'You'd do well to listen to me: I'm not speaking lightly. We know, you and I. We know that Ahmeni is a corrupt traitor. I hate that little scribe, I curse him, I'd like to boil him in the cauldrons where they boil souls. But he's my friend and Ramses' friend. And as long as we keep silent, he won't be condemned for theft.'

'This theft's linked to a plot against Ramses, isn't it?'

'We must think and come to a decision. If I go to the king . . . No, I can't. He's preparing for his regeneration celebrations. I can't spoil that moment. Suppose I go to see the vizier? He'll have Ahmeni arrested! And you . . . why don't you say something?'

'Sleep for a bit. You'll think more clearly afterwards.'

'It's not enough just to think. I must make a decision. And I can't do that if I'm asleep. Ahmeni . . . Oh, Ahmeni, what have you done?'

'At last you're asking the right question,' remarked Lotus.

Setau stood still as a statue, although his hands still trembled, and stared at his wife. 'What do you mean?'

'Instead of torturing yourself, ask yourself what Ahmeni has really done.'

'But it's quite clear, because the captain of the barge confessed. There was some trafficking and the mind behind the trafficking was Ahmeni. My friend Ahmeni.'

Serramanna was sleeping alone. At the end of an exhausting day, in the course of which he had thoroughly checked the security around the temple of the regeneration, he had slumped on to his bed, not even thinking of taking advantage of the delightful body of his most recent official mistress, a young Syrian as supple as a reed.

He was awakened by shouts. Struggling to clear his head of his deep sleep, the big Sardinian shook himself, stretched, and dashed out into the corridor, where his steward was trying to restrain Setau, who was visibly the worse for drink.

'You must set up an inquiry, immediately!' shouted Setau.

Serramanna pushed the steward aside, seized Setau by the collar of his tunic, dragged him into his room and emptied the contents of a jar of cold water over his head.

'What's all this?' spluttered Setau.

'Water. You must have forgotten the taste of it long ago.'

Setau fell back on the bed. 'I need you.'

'Who've your damned snakes bitten now?'

'You must set up an inquiry.'

'What about?'

Setau hesitated one last time, then blurted out, 'About Ahmeni's fortune.'

'What?'

'Ahmeni has amassed a secret fortune,'

'What on earth have you been drinking, Setau? It must be worse than snake venom!'

'Ahmeni has an illegal fortune – and it could even be more serious. There may be a threat to Ramses.'

'What do you mean?'

Without omitting any details, Setau gave a rambling account of how he and Lotus had put an end to Lady Sherit's trafficking.

'The confession of a bandit like that captain isn't worth much,' said Serramanna. 'He'd have said the first name that came into his head.'

'He seemed sincere,' objected Setau.

Serramanna was stunned. 'Ahmeni . . . The last person I'd

have suspected of betraying the king and his country.'

'Because you'd sooner have suspected me?'

'Stop being so touchy! It's Ahmeni we have to think about.'

'You must set up an inquiry, Serramanna.'

'Inquiry, inquiry! That's easy for you to to say. During the regeneration celebrations I have to see to Ramses' safety. And, besides, Ahmeni has locked everything up! If he's been guilty of any dishonesty, we must avoid alerting him and allowing him to obliterate any proof. Did you imagine we would accuse him lightly?'

Setau buried his head in his hands. 'Lotus and I are witnesses. The captain accused Ahmeni.'

The Sardinian felt sick. That a man like Ahmeni, the most loyal of the loyal, should have dreamt only of getting rich – the thought sickened him. Worst of all was Ahmeni's possible complicity with other conspirators: was his secret fortune being used to arm Ramses' enemies?

'I'm drunk,' admitted Setau, 'but I've told you everything. Now there are three of us who know.'

'I'd have preferred a different type of confidence.'

'What are you going to do about it?'

'Ahmeni has an official residence in the palace, but he nearly always sleeps in his office. We'll have to lure him outside and then organize a discreet search. If he's hidden gold or precious stones, we'll find them. Whenever he goes out he must be constantly followed, and all the people he receives must be identified. He must have contact with other members of his network. Let's hope my men don't make any mistakes. If the vizier's police get wind of this inquiry, I shall be in deep trouble.'

'We must think of Ramses, Serramanna.'

'I am.'

27

That morning the whole of Egypt prayed for Ramses. After such a long reign, how would he absorb the tremendous energy given off from the community of gods and goddesses? If his physical body was not in a fit state to serve as a receptacle for the *ka,* he would be destroyed, like a too-fragile vessel. The fire of Ramses' reign would return to the celestial fire, and his mummified body to the earth. But if the king were regenerated, new blood would circulate in the veins of the country.

Statues of the deities from the North and the South were gathered in Pi-Ramses, in the regeneration temple, where Kha received them. For the whole duration of the celebrations Pharaoh would be their host, remaining in the heart of the Supernatural, in a sacred space apart from the secular world.

At dawn, as he dressed, Ramses thought of Ahmeni, who must find these days interminable. As long as the ceremonies lasted, he would not be able to ask the king for advice and would have to file as 'waiting' a number of dossiers he considered urgent. According to Ahmeni, Egypt was never adequately administered, and no official took his job seriously enough.

Ramses appeared in the doorway of the palace, wearing the double crown, a pleated linen gown, a gilded kilt and golden sandals.

Two Royal Sons bowed before the monarch. They wore
wigs with long-side pieces, shirts with loose pleated sleeves
and long skirts; each carried a staff, the top of which was
carved in the form of a ram, one of the incarnations of Amon,
the hidden god.

The two standard-bearers walked slowly in front of the
pharaoh as far as the granite gateway to the regeneration
temple. This was twenty-four cubits high with obelisks and
gigantic statues in front of it, symbolizing the royal *ka*, like
those at Abu Simbel. When he began the construction of his
capital, Ramses had made provision for the site of this
temple, as if he had believed in his ability to reign for more
than thirty years.

Two priests wearing jackal masks welcomed the monarch;
one was the Opener of the Ways to the North, the other to the
South. They led Ramses through the Hall of Pillars, where
each pillar was twenty cubits high, and into the Hall of
Fabrics. The king removed his garments and put on a linen
tunic which reached just above his knees and resembled a
shroud. In his left hand he grasped the shepherd's-crook
sceptre; in his right hand the flail-like sceptre with three
thongs, which stood for Pharaoh's three births: in the realm
beneath the earth, on earth and in the sky.

Ramses had already undergone physical ordeals, both in
his fight with a wild bull and at the battle of Kadesh where,
isolated in the fray, he had had to face thousands of battle-
crazed Hittites. But the regeneration celebrations summoned
him to a different battle, this time against invisible powers.
Dying as himself, returning to the Uncreated from which he
came, Ramses had to be reborn from the love of the gods and
goddesses and so become his own successor. By this act of
magic, he wove permanent links between his symbolic person
and his people, between his people and the community of
creative powers.

The two priests in jackal masks led the sovereign into a

160

vast courtyard open to the sky, similar to that of the pharaoh Djoser in Saqqara. This was the work of Kha, who so admired the ancient architecture that he had had this replica built inside the outer walls of Ramses' regeneration temple.

She came to meet him.

Meritamon, the daughter of Nefertari, Nefertari herself resurrected in order to resurrect Ramses. Dressed in a long white gown, with a simple gold necklace, and two tall plumes in her hair which symbolized Life and the Rule, the dazzling Great Royal Wife came to stand behind the monarch. During every stage of the ritual, she would protect him by the magic of the word and the song.

Kha lit the flame which illuminated the statues of the deities, the shrines where they had been placed and the royal throne where Ramses would take his place if he emerged victorious from the ordeals. The High Priest would be assisted by a council of dignitaries from Upper and Lower Egypt, including Setau, Ahmeni, the High Priest of Karnak, the vizier, Neferet and Royal Sons and Daughters. Setau had sobered up and no longer wanted to think about Ahmeni's despicable behaviour; the only thing that mattered was the ritual, which he had to perform perfectly in order to renew Ramses' vital strength.

The dignitaries prostrated themselves before Pharaoh. Then Setau and Ahmeni, in their capacity as 'Special Friends', washed the king's feet, which, thus purified, would enable him to travel through the length and breadth of the earth, through water and fire. The vessel from which the two men poured the water was in the shape of the hieroglyphic sign *sema*, representing the whole formed by the heart and its main artery, and signifying 'to unite'. This sacred liquid made Pharaoh into a consistent being, the unifier of his people.

Walking slowly, because of his close-fitting tunic, Ramses caused the food offerings placed on the altars of the deities to become efficacious: by his gaze and by pronouncing the formula 'offerings made by Pharaoh', he caused the intangible *ka* of the food to emerge. The queen played the part of the celestial cow, responsible for feeding the king with the milk of the stars, to drive weakness and sickness out of his body.

Ramses paid homage to each of the divine powers, to preserve the multiplicity of creation, which sustained its unity. This was the necessary step to release the permanent unity hidden in every form, and to transmit a supernatural life to each statue.

For three days, processions, litanies and offerings succeeded each other in the great courtyard where the deities were present. They were sheltered in shrines, which were reached by little stairways, defining the sacred space and distributing their energy. The music of drums, harps, lutes and oboes, now lively, now contemplative, accompanied the episodes described on the papyrus unfolded by the leader of the ritual.

By absorbing the souls of the deities, by conversing with the bull Apis and the crocodile Sobek, by wielding the harpoon to prevent the hippopotamus from doing harm, Pharaoh wove links between the hereafter and the people of Egypt. The king's actions made the Invisible became Visible and built a harmonious relationship between nature and man.

In an adjoining courtyard a platform had been erected on which two thrones had been placed side by side. To reach them, Ramses had to climb a few steps. When he sat down on the throne of Upper Egypt, he wore the white crown; the red crown was for the throne of Lower Egypt. And every phase of the ritual was performed by both aspects of the royal person in turn, his dual function in motion, the apparently insurmountable opposition reconciled in the person of Pharaoh. Thus the Two Lands became one without either losing its identity. Seated alternately on one or other of the thrones,

Ramses was now Horus, with his piercing gaze, now Set, with his incomparable power, and always the third element which reconciled the two brothers.

On the last day but one of the celebrations, the king took off his white tunic and dressed in the traditional kilt of the monarchs of the time of the pyramids, to which was attached a bull's tail. The time had come to confirm whether the reigning pharaoh had correctly absorbed the energy of the gods and whether he was able to take possession of the heavens and the earth.

Since he had become privy to the secret of the two enemy brothers, Horus and Set, Pharaoh was qualified to receive once more the legacy of the gods which made him the heir to Egypt. When Ramses' fingers closed round the little leather case, in the shape of a swallow's tail, containing the precious document, everyone felt a pang of anxiety. Would the hand of a human being, even if he were the Lord of the Two Lands, be strong enough to grasp a supernatural object?

Firmly gripping the testament of the gods, Ramses grasped a steering-oar, which symbolized his ability to steer the ship of state in the right direction. Then he strode around the great courtyard, which stood for the whole of Egypt, just as the earth is the reflection of the sky. Four times the King of Lower Egypt ran the ritual course towards each point of the compass, and four times it was run by the King of Upper Egypt. The provinces of the Two Lands were thus trans-figured by Pharaoh's steps, which assured the reign of the gods and the presence of the celestial hierarchy; through him, the dead pharaohs were restored to life and Egypt became the fruitful field of the Divine.

'I have run,' proclaimed Ramses. 'I have held in my hand the testament of the gods. I have travelled the whole earth and touched its four sides. My heart has guided me through it. I have run, I have crossed the primeval ocean, I have touched the four sides of the sky, I have travelled as far as light and I have offered up the fertile earth to its sovereign, the Rule of Life.'

On this last day of the celebrations, towns and villages prepared to rejoice. It was known that Ramses had triumphed and that his energy for reigning had been renewed. But there could be no jubilation until the regenerated monarch showed his people the testament of the gods.

At dawn, Ramses took his place in a litter carried by the dignitaries of Upper and Lower Egypt. Ahmeni's weak back was painful, but he insisted on performing his share of the work. The pharaoh was carried to the four points of the compass, and at each one he bent his bow and shot an arrow to announce to the whole universe that Pharaoh continued to reign. Then he mounted a throne whose base was adorned with twelve lion's heads and he proclaimed on all sides that the Rule of Ma'at would silence the forces of evil.

Crowned once again, as on his first regeneration, Ramses paid homage to his ancestors. They who had opened paths into the Invisible formed the foundation of the kingdom. Setau, who prided himself on his toughness, could not hold back his tears; never had Ramses been so great, never had Pharaoh so fully embodied the light of Egypt.

The king left the great courtyard where time had stood still. He crossed the Hall of Pillars and climbed the steps leading to the top of the gateway. He appeared between the two high towers, like the sun at noon, and showed his people the testament of the gods.

A great shout went up from the crowd. Their acclamation acknowledged Ramses as worthy to govern; his words would be life, his deeds would link the earth to the heavens. The Nile would be fertile, it would reach to the foot of the hills, it would deposit fertile silt over the land, give men pure water and countless fish. As the deities were feasting, all hearts were filled with happiness. Thanks to the king, food would be

164

as abundant as the grains of sand on the banks of the Nile. It was true what people said of Ramses the Great: that he kneaded prosperity with his hands.

28

Two months and a day. A stormy day, after two months of discreet and painstaking inquiries. Serramanna had used his best, most experienced men to follow Ahmeni and to search his home and office without attracting attention. The Sardinian had warned them that, if they were caught, he would disown them; and if they incriminated him, he would strangle them with his own hands. But he also promised rewards: extra leave and finest-quality wine.

It had been difficult to get Ahmeni out of his office. A tour of inspection he made to Faiyum had given Serramanna an unexpected opportunity, but the search revealed nothing. Ahmeni hid nothing illicit, either in his official lodgings, which he hardly ever used, or in his chests, his library or behind his shelves. He continued to work day and night, ate much and slept little. As for his visitors, they were senior officials whom the scribe was in the habit of meeting to ask for accounts and to galvanize their zeal in the service of Egypt.

When he heard Serramanna's negative reports, Setau began to wonder if he had been dreaming. But Lotus, like himself, had definitely heard the captain of the barge mention Ahmeni's name. He could not wipe this stain from his memory.

Serramanna was thinking of ending the arrangements he

had set up. His men were getting fed up, and it wouldn't be long before they made a mistake. And on this stormy day, what he had feared duly occurred.

Early in the afternoon, while alone in his office, Ahmeni received a very unusual visitor: unshaven, one-eyed, coarse-looking and with a deeply wrinkled face. When the man left, Serramanna's agent followed him to the port of Pi-Ramses and had no difficulty in identifying him: he was the captain of a barge.

'Are you sure?' Setau asked Serramanna.

'The fellow left for the South with a cargo of jars. You can draw your own conclusions.'

Ahmeni at the head of a gang of thieves, Ahmeni, who knew the administration better than anyone and was exploiting it for his personal gain – and perhaps even worse.

'Ahmeni has been biding his time,' observed the Sardinian, 'but he was forced to make contact with his accomplices.'

'I don't want to believe it.'

'I'm sorry, Setau. I've got to tell Ramses what I know.'

Emperor Hattusilis had written to the Pharaoh of Egypt.

Forget your grievances. Restrain your arm and breathe the breath of life. In truth you are the son of the god Set! He has promised you the land of the Hittites, and they will bring you all the tribute you desired. Are they not at your feet?

Ramses showed the tablet to Ahmeni. 'Read it yourself. An astonishing change of tone!'

'Those in favour of peace have won the day. Queen Putuhepa's influence prevailed. Majesty, it remains only for you to draw up an official invitation for a Hittite princess to become the Queen of Egypt.'

'Prepare something suitably flowery, and I'll put my seal

on the document. Ahsha did not die in vain. With this, his life's work is crowned.'

'I'll go back to my office and draw up the letter.'

'No, Ahmeni, write it here. Sit in my chair – you'll get the benefit of the last of the sunshine.'

Ahmeni's jaw dropped. 'Me? Sit in Pharaoh's chair? Never!'

'Are you afraid?'

'Of course I'm afraid! People have been struck dead for doing something so mad!'

'Let's go up to the roof-terrace.'

'What about this letter?'

'It can wait.'

The view was spellbinding. Magnificent and peaceful, Ramses the Great's capital was abandoning itself to the night.

'This peace we want so much,' said Ramses, 'is here before our eyes. At every moment, we must be prepared to enjoy it like a rare fruit and give it its true value. But men think of nothing but disrupting the harmony, as if they can't bear it. Why is that?'

'I . . . I don't know, Majesty.'

'Have you never asked yourself this question?'

'I've never had the time. And Pharaoh is there to answer questions.'

'Serramanna has spoken to me,' Ramses revealed.

'Spoken to you? What about?'

'A surprising visitor to your office.'

Ahmeni did not seem worried. 'Who was it?'

'Can't you tell me yourself?'

The scribe thought for a few moments. 'I think it must have been that barge captain who hadn't got an appointment and forced his way in. I'm certainly not in the habit of receiving that sort of person! He rambled on and on about dockers and cargoes that were late. In the end I had to get the guards to throw him out.'

'Was it the first time you'd seen him?'

'And the last! But why all these questions?'

Ramses' gaze became as piercing as Set's; his eyes blazed, probing his friend's face in the twilight. 'Have you ever lied to me, Ahmeni?'

'Never, Majesty! And I never shall. May my words have all the weight of an oath, sworn on Pharaoh's life!'

For long moments, Ahmeni held his breath. He knew Ramses was judging him and was about to pronounce his verdict.

Pharaoh placed his right hand on the scribe's shoulder, and the latter immediately felt the effect of his magnetism.

'I trust you, Ahmeni.'

'What am I accused of?'

'Of organizing the theft of goods intended for the temples and making your fortune.'

Ahmeni nearly fainted. 'Me? Make my fortune?'

'We have work to do. Peace seems within our reach, but nevertheless we must immediately convene a war council.'

Setau fell into Ahmeni's arms.

Serramanna mumbled excuses. 'Obviously, if Pharaoh himself has cleared your name . . .'

'You . . . you actually believed me guilty?' Ahmeni asked incredulously.

'I betrayed our friendship,' acknowledged Setau, 'but I was only thinking of Ramses' safety.'

'In that case,' said Ahmeni, 'you did the right thing. And if you have any other suspicions, you must do it again. Safeguarding the person of Pharaoh is our most vital duty.'

'Someone has tried to discredit Ahmeni in His Majesty's eyes,' Serramanna reminded them. 'Someone whose trafficking Setau put an end to.'

'I want to know all the details,' demanded Ahmeni.

Setau and Serramanna told him every stage of their inquiry.

'The head of this network passed himself off as me,' the scribe concluded, 'and used the barge-captain, whom Setau's cobra dispatched to the hell reserved for thieves. By spreading this false information, he cast suspicion on me and my service. It only needed the visit of another captain to convince you of my guilt. Once I was out of the way, the administration of the country would have fallen apart.'

Ramses found his voice again. 'To sully those near to me is to defile the government of the country for which I am responsible. Someone is trying to weaken Egypt just when we are playing a difficult game with Hatti. It's not merely a matter of theft, even on a grand scale, but a gangrene which must be arrested urgently.'

'We must find the sailor who visited me,' suggested Ahmeni.

'I'll see to that,' said Serramanna. 'The fellow will lead us to his real master.'

'I'll help Serramanna,' Setau offered. 'I owe that at least to Ahmeni.'

'There must be no mistakes,' said Ramses. 'I want the mastermind behind all this.'

'What if it's Uri-Teshup?' put in Serramanna. 'I'm convinced he only wants one thing: to have his revenge.'

'It can't be him,' objected Ahmeni. 'He doesn't know enough about the way the Egyptian administration works to have organized the thefts.'

Uri-Teshup was determined to prevent Ramses' marriage to the daughter of Hattusilis, the tyrant who had removed him from power . . . The king did not reject Serramanna's suggestion.

'An underling could have acted on Uri-Teshup's orders,' said Serramanna.

'That's enough talk,' decided Ramses. 'Follow up the trail, urgently. You, Ahmeni, will work in a room adjoining the palace.'

'Why?'

'Because you are suspected of corruption and are being kept apart from other people. Our enemy must think his plan has succeeded.'

29

A fierce, icy wind swept through the ramparts of Hattusa. On the high Anatolian plateau, autumn had suddenly turned to winter. Torrential rains turned the roads into quagmires and made travelling difficult, if not impossible, for the merchants.

Emperor Hattusilis felt the cold and sat near the fire, drinking mulled wine. The letter he had just received from Ramses gladdened his heart. Hatti and Egypt would never again be at war. Although it was occasionally necessary to use violence, Hattusilis preferred diplomacy. Hatti was an ageing empire, weary of too much fighting. Since the treaty with Egypt, the people were growing accustomed to peace.

At last, Putuhepa arrived. The empress had spent several hours in the temple of the God of Storms, consulting the oracles. The beautiful, majestic High Priestess was respected as a sovereign, even by the generals.

'What news?' asked Hattusilis anxiously.

'Bad. The weather will get worse – and colder, too.'

'Well, I have a miracle to announce to you!' The emperor waved the papyrus from Pi-Ramses.

'Has Ramses given his final agreement?'

'Now that he has celebrated his regeneration feast and has symbolically married his daughter to celebrate the rites, the Pharaoh of Egypt agrees to wed our daughter. A Hittite Lady of the Two Lands . . . I would never have believed that this dream would come true!'

Putuhepa smiled. 'You were able to humble yourself before Ramses.'

'On your advice, my dear, on your wise advice. The words are unimportant; the main thing was to attain our goal.'

'Unfortunately, the skies are unleashing their fury against us.'

'The weather will get better eventually,' said Hattusilis hopefully.

'The oracles are not encouraging.'

'If we wait too long before we send him our daughter, Ramses will believe it is a trick.'

'What shall we do?' asked Putuhepa.

'Tell him the truth and ask for his help. The Egyptian magicians' knowledge is unequalled; let them appease the elements and clear the roads. We must write immediately to our beloved brother.'

With his stern, angular face and shaven head, his painful joints sometimes making it difficult to walk, Kha roamed through the necropolis of Saqqara; he felt more at home there than in the world of the living. He rarely left the ancient city of Memphis. He was fascinated by the era of the pyramids and spent long hours gazing at the three stone giants on the Giza plateau, the pyramids built by Khufu, Khafra and Menkaura.* When the sun reached its zenith, their white limestone-faced sides reflected the light and illuminated the funerary temples, the gardens and the desert. The pyramids were the embodiment of the primordial stone which arose out of the primeval ocean on the first morning of the world, and they were also petrified sun's rays which retained unchanging energy. Kha had perceived one of their truths: each pyramid

* Khufu and Khafra are also known by the names Cheops and Chefren respectively.

was one letter out of the great book of wisdom which he was seeking in the archives of the ancients.

But he was worried; near Djoser's immense architectural complex, which was dominated by the step pyramid, the pyramid of King Unas needed restoration. Dating from the end of the fifth dynasty, more than a thousand years before, the venerable monument had suffered serious damage. It was essential to replace several blocks on the facing.

Here in Saqqara, Kha conversed with the souls of the ancients. He stayed in the shrines of the Houses of Eternity, and read the columns of hieroglyphs which told of the fine highways of the Otherworld and the happy fates of those who possessed a 'righteous voice' because they had lived according to the Rule of Ma'at. As he deciphered the inscriptions, Kha restored life to the owners of the tombs, who had remained in the land of silence.

He was walking round the pyramid of Unas when he saw his father coming towards him. Ramses looked like one of those luminous spirits who, at certain hours of the day, appeared to clairvoyants.

'What are your plans, Kha?'

'In the first place, to speed up the restoration of those pyramids of the Ancient Empire which are in need of urgent repair.'

'Have you found the *Book of Thoth*?'

'Scraps of it. But I'm persistent. There are so many treasures in Saqqara that I shall probably need to have a very long life.'

'You're only thirty-eight. Didn't Ptah-hotep wait till he was a hundred and ten before he composed his *Maxims*?'

'In these places, father, eternity fed on men's time and transformed it into living stones. These shrines, these hieroglyphs, these people, who revered the secret of life and made offerings to it, are the best of our civilization.'

'Do you ever think about affairs of state?' asked Ramses.

'There's no need, while you reign.'

'The years are passing, Kha, and I, too, shall pass into the land that loves silence.'

'Your Majesty has just been regenerated, and in three years' time I shall organize your next regeneration celebrations – they'll be even better.'

'You know nothing about government, the economy, the army . . .'

'I have no taste for such things. In any case, the strict performance of the rites is the basis of our society. Our people's happiness depends on that, and I intend to devote myself to it more and more every day. Do you think I'm on the wrong path?'

Ramses looked up to the top of the pyramid of Unas. 'To look for the highest, the most vital, is always to follow the right path. But Pharaoh is obliged to descend into the world below and face the monster which tries to dry up the Nile and destroy the ship of light. If he did not wage this daily battle, what rite would one celebrate?'

'How can I serve Pharaoh?'

'The Emperor of Hatti wishes to send his daughter to Egypt for me to wed; but the weather is so bad in Anatolia that no convoy can make the journey. Hattusilis asks for one of our magicians to intervene and ask the gods for an improvement in the weather. Find the text that will enable me to meet his request as quickly as possible.'

No one could track down the barge-captain Rerek in his hiding-place. After he had paid a visit to a pale-faced scribe to tell him some cock and bull story, his boss had advised him to find a place to live in the Asiatic district of Pi-Ramses. The job had been well paid – much better paid than three months' work on the Nile. Rerek had again seen his employer, who was very pleased with him and told him that they had achieved the desired results. There was just one small snag:

175

his employer insisted that Rerek change his appearance. The sailor was proud of his beard and his whiskers and had tried to argue, but, as it was a question of his safety, he had let himself be persuaded. Once he was clean-shaven, he would resume his service in the South under another name and the police would never find him.

Rerek spent his days sleeping in the upper storey of a little white house. Today, his landlady woke him when the water-carrier passed. She had brought him pancakes stuffed with garlic and onion, a special treat.

'The barber is down in the square,' she told him.

Rerek looked out of the window. In the square, the barber had set up four posts supporting a canvas awning as protection from the sun. There were two stools under the awning, the higher one for the barber, the other for his client. As a dozen men had turned up, there would be a long wait. Three of the men were playing dice, the others sat down leaning against the wall of a house. Rerek went back to bed and to sleep.

He woke again to find his landlady shaking him: 'Wake up and go down! You're the last.'

This time, there was no escape. Rerek went down the stairs with his eyes still half shut, left the modest house and sat down on the three-legged stool, which creaked under his weight.

'What do you want me to do?' asked the barber.

'Shave off my beard and whiskers.'

'A fine beard like that?'

'That's my business.'

'As you wish, my friend. How will you pay me?'

'With a pair of sandals made of papyrus.'

The barber frowned. 'It's a lot of work . . .'

'If it doesn't suit you, I'll go somewhere else.'

'All right, all right.'

The barber wet the sailor's skin with soapy water, slid the

razor along his left cheek to test its sharpness, then, with a sudden movement, pressed it against his neck.

'If you try to run away, Rerek, or if you lie, I'll slit your throat.'

'Who . . . who are you?'

Setau nicked the skin, and blood trickled down on to Rerek's chest. 'Someone who'll kill you if you don't answer.'

'Ask me anything!'

'Do you know a barge-captain with a scar on his left forearm and brown eyes?'

'Yes.'

'Do you know Lady Sherit?'

'Yes, I've worked for her.'

'As a thief?'

'We did business.'

'Who's your boss?'

'His name's . . . Ahmeni.'

'Take me to him.'

30

Ramses was seated in his office, when Kha came in, a slight smile lighting up his stern face.

'I searched for three days and three nights in the library of the Heliopolis House of Life, Majesty,' said Kha, 'and I found the book of conjurations that will clear the bad weather in Hatti. The goddess Sekhmet's messengers are spreading noxious vapours into the atmosphere and preventing the sun from breaking through the clouds.'

'What must be done?'

'The litanies intended for appeasing Sekhmet must be recited continuously and for as long as necessary. When the goddess recalls her emissaries from Asia, the skies will clear. The priests and priestesses of Sekhmet are already at work. Thanks to the resonances set up by their chanting and the invisible effects of the rites, we can expect a swift result.'

Just as Kha withdrew, Meneptah came running in. The two brothers exchanged congratulations. The king watched them, so different, and yet complementing each other so well. Neither of them disappointed him. In his own way, Kha had just acted like a true statesman. He had the loftiness of thought essential for governing, while Meneptah had the necessary strength to command. As for Meritamon, she had returned to Thebes, where she directed the rites for animating the royal statues, both in Seti's shrine and in Ramses' Temple of a Million Years.

The pharaoh thanked the gods for giving him three exceptional children who, each in their own way, passed on the spirit of Egypt's civilization, to which they attached more importance than to their own person. Nefertari and Iset the Fair could rest in peace.

Meneptah bowed before Pharaoh. 'You summoned me, Majesty.'

'The daughter of Hattusilis and Putuhepa is preparing to leave the Hittite capital for Pi-Ramses. She will have the diplomatic title of Great Royal Wife, and this union will finally set the seal on the peace between Hatti and Egypt. This pact may displease certain groups of interests. Your mission will be to watch over the princess's safety from the moment she leaves the territories controlled by Hatti and enters our protectorates.'

'Your Majesty can rely on me. How many men shall I have at my disposal?'

'As many as you need.'

'An army would be useless – and anyway it would be too slow and too difficult to transfer the troops. I shall assemble a hundred experienced, well-armed soldiers who know those areas, and several messengers mounted on the finest horses. In case of attack, we shall be able to defend ourselves. I shall keep in regular touch with Your Majesty. If a courier is delayed, the nearest fortress will immediately send help.'

'Your mission is of the utmost importance, Meneptah.'

'I won't let you down, father.'

Since early morning a rainstorm had been beating down on Hattusa, threatening to flood the Lower Town; panic was beginning to spread. Empress Putuhepa addressed the people. Not only were the priests of Hatti continuously beseeching the God of Storms to show mercy, she told them, but an appeal had also been made to the magicians of Egypt.

Putuhepa's words were reassuring. A few hours later the rain stopped; heavy black clouds still hung in the sky, but a break in them appeared in the south. The princess's departure was becoming possible.

The empress made her way to her daughter's apartments. The twenty-five-year-old princess had all the untamed beauty of Anatolian women. She had fair hair, almond-shaped black eyes, a thin, slightly pointed nose and a wonderful complexion. Tall, with delicate wrists and ankles, and with a truly noble carriage of her head, she was the very essence of sensuality. A slight languidness in her movements betrayed a woman at once ready to offer herself and yet shying away. Every courtier in Hattusa had dreamt of marrying her.

'The weather is improving,' said Putuhepa.

The princess was dressing her long hair herself before scenting it. 'So I must get ready to leave.'

'Are you afraid?'

'Just the opposite. I'm going to be the first Hittite to wed a pharaoh – and what a pharaoh! Ramses the Great, whose glory has quenched the warlike fire of Hatti . . . Even in my wildest dreams, how could I have imagined a more fabulous destiny?'

Putuhepa was surprised. 'We are going to be parted for ever and you will never see your country again . . . Surely that must be a wrench?'

'I'm a woman and I'm going to wed Ramses and live in the land beloved of the gods, reign over a sumptuous court, enjoy unheard-of luxury, taste the delights of an incomparable climate, and many other things besides! But it isn't enough for me just to marry Ramses.'

'What do you mean?'

'I also want to captivate him. Pharaoh is thinking not of me but of diplomacy and peace, as if I were just a clause in a treaty. I shall make him think differently.'

'You may be disappointed,' warned Putuhepa.

180

'Am I ugly or stupid?'

'Ramses is no longer a young man. Perhaps he won't even set eyes on you.'

'My destiny is my own,' declared the princess, 'and no one can help me. If I can't win Ramses over, what use will this exile be?'

'Your marriage will guarantee the prosperity of two great peoples.'

'I shall be neither a servant nor a recluse but a Great Royal Wife. Ramses will soon forget my origins. I shall reign at his side, and every Egyptian will prostrate himself before me.'

'I hope so, daughter,' said Putuhepa.

'I hope so too, mother, no less than you do.'

A weak sun broke through. Winter was setting in, with its procession of winds and cold, but the route leading to the Egyptian protectorates would soon be passable. Putuhepa would have liked to exchange confidences with her daughter, but Ramses' future wife seemed to have become a stranger in her own home.

As he put away in his storeroom his most valuable vases, Raia was in a furious temper. A violent argument had broken out between him and Uri-Teshup, and the two men had parted without coming to an agreement. To the prince, the arrival of Hattusilis's daughter was something that could be turned to Ramses' disadvantage, and the princess should not be prevented from arriving in Egypt. Raia, on the other hand, believed that this marriage put an end to any lingering hope of war.

By relinquishing war, Hattusilis was playing into Ramses' hand. Raia was so tormented by this prospect that he felt like tearing out his little pointed beard and ripping up his coloured tunic. His hatred for Ramses had become his main reason for living, and he was ready to take any and every risk to overthrow this pharaoh, whose massive statues were enthroned in temples throughout the land. No! This monarch must not continue to succeed in all his undertakings.

Uri-Teshup was growing slack, sated with comfort and lechery. He, Raia, had not lost the will to fight. Ramses was only a man, and he would not survive a series of blows struck with force and precision. One thing was urgent: to prevent the Hittite princess reaching Pi-Ramses.

Raia decided that, without telling Uri-Teshup and his Hittite allies, he would organize an attack with Malfi's help. When Malfi knew that Meneptah was leading the Egyptian troops escorting the princess, he would lick his lips in anticipation: to kill both Ramses' future wife and his younger son – what a brilliant stroke!

Not one member of the convoy would survive. The pharaoh would believe it the work of a Hittite faction suffering from injured pride and hostile to the peace. It would be necessary to scatter some tell-tale weapons on the ground, together with the bodies of a few peasants dressed as Hittite soldiers. True, the battle would be fierce and there would be losses in the Libyan ranks, but Malfi would not be deterred by this detail. The prospect of violent action, bloody and victorious, would inflame the warlord.

Hattusilis would lose his daughter, Ramses his son. And the two sovereigns would avenge their losses in a war more bitter than any preceding one. Ahsha was no longer there to pour oil on troubled waters. As for Uri-Teshup, he would be faced with a fait accompli. He would either cooperate, while acknowledging he had been wrong, or he would be done away with. Raia was not short of ideas on how to erode the Egyptian state from within; Ramses would not be granted a single day's respite.

There was a knock at the door of the storeroom. At this late hour it could only be a customer.

'Who is it?' asked Raia.

'Captain Rerek.'

'You shouldn't have come here!'

'I've had a big problem. It's all right now, but I must talk to you.'

Raia opened the door halfway. He had barely glimpsed Rerek when the latter was pushed hard from behind. His hands were held in wooden handcuffs and his ankles tied with rope, preventing him from moving. He crashed into Raia, who fell head over heels, while Serramanna and Setau rushed into the storeroom.

The Sardinian pointed to Raia. 'What's this man's name?'

'Ahmeni', replied Rerek.

Taking advantage of the darkness that reigned in the depths of the storeroom, Raia wriggled away and climbed the ladder that led to the roof. With a little luck, he would shake off anyone following him.

A pretty Nubian woman was sitting on one corner of the roof, glaring at him. 'Don't go any further,' she said.

Raia drew a dagger out of the right sleeve of his tunic. 'Get out of my way, or I'll kill you!'

Just as he raised his arm to strike, a mottled adder bit his left heel. The pain was so intense that Raia dropped his weapon, bumped into a ledge, lost his balance and fell off the roof.

When Serramanna bent over the Syrian, he grimaced in annoyance. In his fall, Raia had broken his neck.

31

Lady Tanit had everything she could desire. Intoxicated by her lover's passion, she stretched herself out lazily across Uri-Teshup's powerful torso.

'Make love to me again, please.'

The Hittite would willingly have agreed, but his attention was caught by the sound of footsteps. He rose and drew a short sword from its scabbard. There was a knock on the door of the bedchamber.

'Who is it?' he asked.

'The steward.'

'I said we were not to be interrupted,' Tanit shouted angrily.

'It's a friend of your husband, my lady. He says it's very urgent.'

Tanit seized Uri-Teshup's wrist to hold him back. 'It may be a trap.'

'I can defend myself.'

Uri-Teshup called a Hittite who kept guard in the garden of the villa, proud to serve his former commander-in-chief. The man made his report in a low voice and vanished.

When her lover returned, Lady Tanit, naked, flung her arms round his neck and smothered him with kisses. But she sensed he was worried, so she drew away and gave him a cup of fresh wine to drink.

'What has happened?' she asked.

'Our friend Raia is dead.'

'How? An accident?'

'He fell from a roof while trying to escape from Serramanna.'

She turned pale. 'That damned Sardinian! But . . . will he be able to trace things back to you!'

'Possibly.'

'You must get away – at once!'

'Certainly not. Serramanna is watching out for the slightest slip. If Raia didn't have time to talk, I'm still safe. In fact, Raia's removal is quite good news. He was beginning to lose his head, and I don't need him any more, now that I'm in direct contact with the Libyans.'

'Why can we simply make the most of our happiness?'

Uri-Teshup squeezed her breasts roughly. 'You just be an obedient, silent wife, and I'll make you happy.'

When he devoured her like a ripe fruit, she swooned with pleasure.

The hunters showed Teshonq their skins. The Libyan chose his raw materials himself. He trusted no one's judgment but his own and was extremely strict, refusing three-quarters of the goods offered him. That morning he had turned away two hunters who offered him poor-quality skins.

Without warning, a tunic with coloured stripes was flung down at his feet.

'Do you recognize it?' asked Serramanna.

The Libyan clutched his pot-belly, suddenly suffering an attack of colic. 'It's . . . it's a quite common garment.'

'Examine it closely.'

'I assure you, I can't see anything unusual about it.'

'I'll help you, Teshonq, because I've a soft spot for you. This tunic belonged to the Syrian merchant Raia, a suspicious individual who had a lot on his conscience and who stupidly got killed while trying to make a run for it. It's said that he'd gone back to being a spy. For my part, I'm certain of one thing: you must have been friends or, rather, accomplices.'

'I didn't mix with that—'

'Don't interrupt me,' barked Serramanna. 'I've no proof, but I'm absolutely sure that the late Raia, you and Uri-Teshup have been plotting against Ramses. The Syrian's death is a warning: if your other allies keep trying to harm the king, they'll finish up like Raia. And now, I'd like what's owing to me.'

'I'll have a leather shield and a pair of finest-quality sandals delivered to your house.'

'That'll do to begin with. Have you any names for me?'

'Everything's quiet among the Libyans, Lord Serramanna. They recognize Ramses' authority.'

'See that they continue to do so. I'll see you again soon, Teshonq.'

As soon as Serramanna's horse was out of sight, the Libyan rushed to the privy, clutching his belly.

Emperor Hattusilis and his wife were arguing. Usually the empress valued her husband's wisdom and his sound views, but not this time.

'We *must* inform Ramses of our daughter's departure,' insisted Putuhepa.

'No!' retorted the emperor. 'It's better to use the situation to find out if seditious elements in the army are thinking of attacking us.'

'Attacking us? Attacking your daughter and her escort, you mean! Do you realize that you are thinking of using your own child as bait?'

'She will be in no danger, Putuhepa. If there is an attack, my finest troops will protect her and wipe out the rebels. In that way, we'll kill two birds with one stone: get rid of the last few elements of the military opposed to our policy, and seal the peace with Ramses.'

'My daughter must not be put in danger,' said Putuhepa angrily.

'I have made my decision: she will leave tomorrow. Ramses will not be informed of his future wife's arrival until she has passed through Hatti and reached the fringes of Egypt's zone of influence.'

How frail the young princess looked, surrounded by Hittite officers and soldiers in their heavy breastplates and threatening helmets. Armed with new weapons and mounted on mettlesome young horses, the elite escort detachment seemed invincible. Emperor Hattusilis knew that his daughter was at risk, but the occasion was too good to miss. A head of state had always to give priority to his power, sometimes to the detriment of his own family.

Several wagons carried the princess's dowry and gifts for Ramses the Great: gold, silver, bronze, fabrics, jewels. And there was one gift which the pharaoh would particularly appreciate: ten magnificent horses, which he would care for himself and which would take turns to draw his chariot.

The sky was quite clear, the heat astonishing. The soldiers were suffocating and sweating in their winter cloaks. February suddenly seemed like a summer month. This abnormal weather could not continue; in a few hours rain would certainly fall and fill the water-tanks.

The princess knelt before her father, who anointed her with the oil of betrothal.

'Ramses himself will celebrate the marriage unction,' he announced. 'Farewell, future Queen of Egypt.'

The convoy moved off. Behind the wagon in which the princess had taken her place, was another, of the same size and equally comfortable, in the back of which Empress Putuhepa was seated on a light wooden throne.

'I am going with my daughter,' she told the emperor as she

was driven past him, 'and I shall accompany her as far as the border.'

Menacing mountains, steep tracks, ominous gorges, dense woods where raiders could hide . . . Empress Putuhepa was afraid of her own country. True, the soldiers were on the alert, and their numbers should have discouraged any attacker. But Hatti had been for so long the scene of bloody internal struggles. Would Uri-Teshup, or one of his ilk, try to kill the princess, the symbol of peace?

The most disturbing thing was the absence of winter. Bodies prepared for the cold season had to suffer scorching sun and drought; unaccustomed fatigue built up, making the journey exhausting. Putuhepa noticed that the escort were less vigilant and their officers' authority had diminished. Would they be capable of meeting a large-scale attack?

The princess remained impassive, as if the ordeal had no effect on her. Her haughty appearance and fierce determination to reach her destination lit up the way.

When the pine trees rustled, when the rushing of a torrent sounded like the approach of armed men, Putuhepa started. Where were the rebels hiding? What would their strategy be? She frequently woke during the night, listening for the slightest suspicious sound, and all day she continually peered into the woods and along the steep slopes and the riverbanks.

The princess and her mother exchanged no words. Enclosed in her silence, Putuhepa's daughter refused all contact with her former life. Hatti was dead for her, and the name of the future was Ramses.

Hot, thirsty and exhausted, the convoy passed Kadesh and arrived at the border post of Aya, in southern Syria. There stood a Egyptian fortress, on the edge of the territory controlled by Pharaoh.

Bowmen took up their position on the battlements, and the great gate slammed shut: the garrison thought it was an attack. The princess alighted from her wagon and mounted one of the horses intended for Ramses. Under the astonished eyes of her mother and the Hittite soldiers, she galloped up to the fortress and halted at the foot of the ramparts. No Egyptian archer dared shoot.

'I am the daughter of the Emperor of Hatti, the future Queen of Egypt,' she announced. 'Ramses the Great is waiting for me to celebrate our wedding. Grant me a suitable welcome, otherwise Pharaoh's anger will burn like fire.'

The commander of the fortress appeared. 'There is an army behind you!'

'Not an army, my escort.'

'Those Hittite warriors look threatening.'

'You are wrong, Commander. I have told you the truth.'

'I have not had any orders from the capital.'

'Inform Ramses of my presence. Immediately.'

32

Ahmeni had caught a cold. His chest felt tight, he had difficulty breathing and his eyes were inflamed. The February nights were icy and the pale daytime sun was not strong enough to warm the air. Ahmeni had ordered a large quantity of wood for heating, but the delivery was late. He was about to vent his wrath on one of his subordinates when an army courier placed on his desk a message from the fortress of Aya, in southern Syria.

Between bouts of sneezing Ahmeni deciphered the message, threw a woollen mantle over his thick linen gown, wrapped a scarf round his throat and, with his lungs on fire, ran to Ramses' office.

At this late hour the king was working by the light of oil lamps, whose wicks produced no smoke. Placed on tall sycamore lampstands, they shed a soft light all around. A few braziers warmed the big room.

'Majesty, incredible news! Hattusilis's daughter has arrived at Aya. The commander of the fortress awaits your instructions.'

'It must be a mistake,' said Ramses. 'Hattusilis would have informed me of his daughter's departure.'

'The commander says he is faced with a Hittite army which claims to be . . . a wedding convoy!'

The king rose and took a few steps round his office.

'It's a trick, Ahmeni, a trick by the emperor to confirm the

190

extent of his power inside Hatti. The convoy could have been attacked by rebel soldiers.'

'You think he's capable of using his own daughter as bait?' said Ahmeni incredulously.

'For the moment, Hattusilis will have been reassured. Meneptah must leave immediately for Syria with the troops intended to protect the princess. Order the commander of the Aya fortress to open the gates and welcome the Hittites.'

'And what if—'

'I'll take the risk.'

Each side as surprised as the other, the Hittites and the Egyptians fraternized, celebrated, drank and ate together like old comrades in arms. Putuhepa could return to Hattusa reassured, while her daughter, accompanied by high officials and some Hittite soldiers, would continue on her way to Pi-Ramses, protected by Meneptah.

Tomorrow would come the final parting. Her eyes wet with tears, the empress looked at her beautiful, commanding daughter.

'Have you no regrets at all?' asked Putuhepa.

'I have never been so happy!'

'We shall never see each other again.'

'That is the law of life. To each his destiny – and mine is fantastic!'

'Be happy, my child.'

'I am already!'

Putuhepa was deeply hurt, and did not even embrace her daughter. The final link had been broken.

'It's freakish,' said the commander of the Aya fortress, a veteran soldier with a square face and a rough voice. 'At this time of year, the mountains should be covered with snow and it should be raining every day. If this heatwave continues, the water-tanks won't fill.'

'We moved by forced marches,' Meneptah recalled, 'and I'm sorry to report several cases of illness. On the way, we found that a number of springs and wells had dried up. I fear I may be leading the princess into danger.'

'Freakish,' repeated the commander. 'Only a god could upset the weather like this.'

This opinion confirmed Meneptah's own forebodings. 'I'm afraid you're right. Have you got a protective statue in the fortress?'

'Yes, but it only drives away local evil spirits. It isn't powerful enough to affect the weather. You'd have to pray to a god whose energy is as great as that of the sky.'

'Have you enough reserves of water to supply us for our return journey?' asked Meneptah.

'I'm afraid not. You'll have to stay here and wait for the rains.'

'If this false summer lasts, there won't be enough water for both the Egyptians and the Hittites.'

'It's winter and this drought should soon end.'

'You said yourself, commander, that it isn't natural. To leave is risky. To remain looks no less so.'

The officer frowned. 'What are you going to do?'

'Inform Ramses. He's the only one who will know how to act.'

Kha unrolled on Ramses' desk three long papyri he had unearthed in the archives of the House of Light at Iunu.

'The texts are explicit, Majesty. Only one god, Set, reigns over the climate of Asia. But no college of magicians is qualified to enter into direct contact with him. It's for you, and you alone, to ask Set to restore the seasons to their rightful places. However . . .'

'What is it, my son?'

'However I am against that. Set's power is dangerous and uncontrollable.'

192

'Are you afraid I won't be strong enough?'

'You are the son of Set, but to modify the climate involves handling lightning, thunderbolts and storms. Now, Set is unpredictable, and Egypt needs you. Let us send several statues of deities and a convoy of food supplies to Syria.'

'Do you think that Set would allow them to pass?'

'No, Majesty.'

'So he leaves me no choice. Either I am victorious in the duel to which he challenges me, or else Meneptah, the Hittite princess and all their companions will die of thirst.'

Kha could not answer his father.

'If I don't return from the Temple of Set,' Ramses told him, 'you will be my successor and give life to Egypt.'

In her rooms, in the commander's apartments in the fortress, the Hittite princess demanded to speak to Meneptah. He found her restless and dictatorial, but treated her with the respect due to a great lady.

'Why do we not leave immediately for Egypt?' she asked him.

'Because it's impossible, princess.'

'The weather is magnificent.'

'There is a drought when it should be the rainy season, and we're short of water.'

'Do you mean we're stuck here in this horrible fortress?'

'Heaven is against us. We're held here by the will of a god.'

'Can't your magicians do something?'

'I have appealed to the greatest of them all: Ramses in person.'

The princess smiled. 'You're a clever man, Meneptah. I shall tell my husband so.'

'Let us hope, princess, that the gods hear our prayers.'

'I'm sure they will. I haven't come here to die of thirst. Heaven and earth are both in Pharaoh's hand, are they not?'

*

Neither Setau nor Ahmeni had succeeded in persuading the king to change his mind. At dinner, Ramses had eaten a piece of meat cut from the leg of an ox, the animal which embodied the power of Set, and drunk some strong oasis wine, placed under the protection of the same god. Then, after purifying his mouth with salt, the exudate of Set, bearer of the earthly fire essential for preserving food, he had stood in meditation before the statue of his father, Seti, he who had dared, by his name, proclaim himself the earthly representative of the lord of storms.

Without Seti's help, Ramses had no chance of defeating Set. One single error, one slightly inaccurate ritual gesture, one momentary lapse of concentration, and the thunderbolt would strike. Faced with power in its raw state, there was only one weapon: righteousness, the righteousness Seti had taught Ramses when initiating him into his role as pharaoh.

At midnight, the king entered the Temple of Set. It was built on the site of Avaris, the hated Hyksos invaders' capital, a place devoted to silence and solitude, a place which only Pharaoh could enter without fear of being destroyed.

When face to face with Set, he must conquer fear, then look on the world with blazing eyes, recognize its violence and convulsions, and become the primeval force in the heart of the cosmos, to which human intelligence could not penetrate.

Ramses placed a cup of wine and a miniature oryx made of acacia wood on the altar. The oryx, which could resist the extreme heat of the desert and survive in that hostile environment, was filled with Set's fire.

'Thou bearest the sky in thy hands,' the king said to the god, 'the earth on thy feet. What thou commandest comes to pass. Thou hast caused the heat and the drought. Give us back the winter rains.'

The statue of Set did not react; its eyes remained cold.

'It is I, Ramses, the son of Seti, who addresses thee. No

god has the right to upset the order of the world, and the course of the seasons. Every deity must submit to the Rule, thou like all the others.'

The statue's eyes glowed; the shrine was suddenly filled with heat.

'Do not direct thy power against Pharaoh; in him are united Horus and Set. Thou art within me, and I use thy strength to combat darkness and repel disorder. Obey me, Set, cause rain to fall on the lands of the North!'

Lightning flashed across the sky and thunder crashed around Ramses. A night of battle was beginning.

33

The princess confronted Meneptah. 'This waiting is intolerable! Take me to Egypt immediately,'

"I am under orders to guarantee your safety. As long as this strange drought continues, it would be unwise to set out.'

'Why doesn't Pharaoh act?'

A drop of water fell on the princess's left shoulder, a second one on her right hand. She and Meneptah looked up simultaneously at the sky which had grown dark, covered with black clouds. A flash of lightning pierced the clouds, followed by a rumble of thunder, and heavy rain began to fall. In a few minutes it had grown cold: a winter in accordance with the law of the seasons had driven away the heat and the drought.

'Here is Ramses' reply,' said Meneptah.

The princess threw her head back, opened her mouth and greedily drank the water from heaven. 'We must leave,' she said. 'We must leave immediately.'

Ahmeni paced up and down in front of the door of the king's bedchamber. Setau sat with his arms folded, gloomily looking straight in front of him. Kha was reading a magic papyrus, whose contents he chanted to himself.

For the tenth time, Serramanna cleaned his short sword with a rag soaked in linseed oil. 'When did Pharaoh leave the

Temple of Set?' he asked.

'At dawn,' replied Ahmeni.

'Did he speak to anyone?'

'No, he didn't utter a single word,' said Kha, 'just shut himself up in his room. I sent for Neferet and he agreed to see her.'

'She's been examining him for the past hour and more!' Setau protested.

'Visible or not, Set's burns are fearsome,' the High Priest explained. 'We must trust in Neferet's skill.'

'I've given him several restoratives for his heart,' Setau recalled.

At last the door opened. The four men crowded round Neferet.

'Ramses is out of danger,' she confirmed. 'After a full day's rest, he will be able to resume his normal activities. Wrap up warm: it's going to become cold and damp.'

Rain was beginning to fall on Pi-Ramses.

United like brothers under Meneptah's command, Egyptians and Hittites travelled through Canaan, took the coast road overlooked by Sinai, and entered the Delta. Whenever they halted at small forts, there were celebrations; during the journey, several soldiers exchanged their weapons for trumpets, flutes and drums.

The princess couldn't take her eyes off the green countryside; she marvelled at the palm groves, the fertile fields, the irrigation canals, the papyrus forests. The world she was discovering could hardly have been more different from the harsh Anatolian plateau of her youth.

When the procession reached Pi-Ramses, the streets were black with crowds. No one could say how the information had spread, but everyone knew that the Emperor of Hatti's daughter would soon make her entrance into the capital of Ramses the Great. The wealthy mingled with humble folk, notables rubbed shoulders with labourers, and all hearts swelled with joy.

'Extraordinary,' commented Uri-Teshup, from where he sat in the front row of the spectators, accompanied by his wife. 'This pharaoh has achieved the impossible.'

'He made it rain after defeating Set,' observed Lady Tanit, equally dazzled. 'His power is infinite.'

'Ramses is water and air for his people,' added a stone-cutter. 'His love is like the bread we eat and the clothes we wear. He is the father and mother of the entire country!'

'His gaze fathoms minds and searches into souls,' added a priestess of the goddess Hathor.

Uri-Teshup was close to despair. How could he fight against a pharaoh who had supernatural powers? Ramses could command the elements, change the weather even in Asia, and reign over a legion of spirits capable of defeating any army in the world. And, as the Hittite sensed, nothing could have stopped the princess successfully completing her journey. Any attack against the convoy would have been doomed to failure.

The prince took a grip on himself. He wasn't going to succumb to Ramses' magic like everyone else! His aim, his sole aim, was to bring down this man who had ruined his career and reduced proud Hatti to the condition of a vassal. Whatever his powers, this pharaoh was not a god but a human being, with weaknesses and inadequacies. Intoxicated with his victories and his popularity, Ramses would eventually lose his ability to think clearly; time would tell against him. And he was going to wed a Hittite princess, in whose veins ran the blood of an indomitable, vengeful nation. In believing he was sealing the peace by this union, Ramses might be sadly mistaken.

'There she is!' shouted Lady Tanit, and her cry was taken up by thousands of enthusiastic throats.

The princess was seated in her wagon, finishing her make-up. She had painted her eyelids with a green cosmetic made from powdered copper mixed with water, and had traced a black oval round her eyes, using a little stick to apply a mixture of powdered black lead, silver and charcoal. She gazed at her work in a mirror and was satisfied. Her hand had not trembled.

Meneptah helped the young Hittite to alight from the wagon.

The crowd was struck dumb by her beauty. Dressed in a long green gown, which flattered her pearly complexion, she had indeed the bearing of a queen.

Suddenly all heads turned towards the main avenue of the city, from whence came the characteristic sound of horses galloping and chariot wheels rumbling. Ramses the Great was coming to meet his bride.

The two spirited young horses drawing his chariot were the offspring of the pair, who, with the lion, Invincible, had been Pharaoh's sole allies at Kadesh, when his soldiers had deserted him in the face of the Hittite charge. Each superb animal was adorned with a head-dress of red plumes, tipped with blue and had, on its back, red, blue and green cotton trappings. The reins were attached to the king's girdle and he held the sceptre of illumination in his right hand.

The gold-plated chariot advanced swiftly and smoothly. Ramses controlled his horses without needing to raise his voice. Wearing the Blue Crown, which recalled the celestial origin of the pharaonic monarchy, the sovereign seemed otherwise to be clad entirely in gold. Yes, he was the sun itself, running its course, lighting up his subjects with its beams. When the chariot came to a standstill, a few paces from the princess, the grey clouds broke and the sun reigned supreme in the sky, which was now blue. Was not Ramses, the Son of the Light, the author of this new miracle?

The young woman kept her eyes lowered. The king noted that she had decided on a simple appearance: a plain silver necklace, small bracelets of the same metal, a gown free of ornamentation. The lack of adornment showed her magnificent body to advantage.

Kha approached Ramses and handed him a blue earthenware vase. Ramses anointed the princess's forehead with fine oil.

'This is the marriage unction,' declared Pharaoh. 'It makes you the Great Royal Wife of the Lord of the Two Lands. May all evil forces keep far from you. On this day you are born to your role, according to the Rule of Ma'at, and you take the title of "The One who sees Horus and the Perfection of the Divine Light".* Look at me, Mat-Hor, my wife.'

Ramses stretched out his arms to the young woman who, very slowly, placed her hands in his. She, who had never known fear, was terrified. After hoping so much for this moment, when she had meant to use her thousand and one powers of seduction, she was afraid she might swoon like a scared little girl. Ramses gave off such magnetism that she felt as though she was touching the flesh of a god and was falling into another world where she had no landmarks. To seduce him . . . She now realized the vanity of her plans, but it was too late to retreat, although she felt like fleeing back to Hatti, far, far from Ramses.

With her hands imprisoned in his, she dared to raise her eyes and look at the king. She saw a superb figure of a man, of unique presence. With his broad open forehead, strongly marked eyebrows, thick eyelashes, piercing eyes, prominent cheekbones, long, thin, slightly hooked nose, round, delicately rimmed ears and broad chest, he was the ideal combination of strength and refinement. Mat-Hor, the Hittite who had become an Egyptian, immediately fell in love with him, with all the violent passion of the women of her race.

* In Egyptian 'Mat-Hor-neferu-Ra', which we abbreviate to 'Mat-Hor'.

Ramses invited her to climb into his chariot.

'In this thirty-fourth year of my reign, peace with Hatti is proclaimed for ever,' the pharaoh declared in a ringing voice which rose to the skies. 'Stelae devoted to this marriage will be erected in Karnak, Pi-Ramses, Elephantine, Abu Simbel and all the shrines in Nubia. There will be feasting in all the towns and villages and wine will be drunk, donated by the palace. As from this day, the borders between Egypt and Hatti are open; people and goods may circulate freely inside a vast area where war and hatred are banished.'

A tremendous cheer greeted Ramses' declaration.

Seized with excitement in spite of himself, Uri-Teshup raised his voice and joined in the rejoicing.

34

With the north wind swelling the rectangular linen sail, which stretched from the top of the double mast to the deck, the royal ship sailed swiftly upstream towards Thebes. The captain stood in the bows, regularly sounding the depth of the Nile with a long pole. He knew the currents and the sand-banks so well that no ill-advised moves would jeopardize the voyage of Ramses and Mat-Hor. Pharaoh himself had helped to hoist the sail, while his young bride rested in a cabin decorated with flowers, and the cook plucked a duck for their dinner. Three helmsmen held the steering-oar, on which were painted two magic eyes indicating the right course; a sailor held on to the guardrail with one hand and drew water from the river, while a cabinboy, nimble as a monkey, climbed to the top of the mast to look into the distance and warn the captain of any herds of hippopotami.

The crew had been favoured with an exceptionally fine vintage wine from the great vineyard of Pi-Ramses, dating from the twenty-second year of the king's reign, the memorable year in which the peace treaty with Hatti had been signed. The wine had been kept in conical pinkish-beige terracotta jars, whose straight spouts were closed by stoppers made of clay and straw. On their sides were depicted water-lilies and the god Bes, the master of initiation into the great mysteries, a thickset, broad-chested, short-legged individual, putting out a red tongue to express the omnipotence of the Word.

After stopping to enjoy the invigorating air blowing over the river, Ramses went back to the central cabin. Mat-Hor was awake. Scented with jasmin, bare breasted and wearing an extremely short kilt, she was seduction itself.

'Pharaoh is the master of radiance,' she said softly, 'the shooting-star in whose wake trail fiery rays, the sharp-horned bull that cannot be tamed, the crocodile in the midst of the waters which cannot be approached, the falcon which seizes its prey, the divine vulture that none can vanquish, the tempest which breaks out, the flame which pierces the densest darkness.'

'You know our traditional texts well, Mat-Hor.'

'Egyptian literature is one of the subjects I studied. Everything that is written about Pharaoh fascinates me, for he is the most powerful man in the world.'

'Then you must know that I detest flattery,' Ramses said drily.

'It wasn't flattery. I can imagine no greater happiness than this moment. I dreamt of you, Ramses, while my father was fighting against you. I was convinced that the sun of Egypt alone would give me life. Today I know that I was right.'

The young woman clung to Ramses, and he embraced her affectionately.

'Am I forbidden to love the Lord of the Two Lands?' she asked.

The love of a woman . . . Ramses had not thought of this for many long years. Nefertari had been love, Iset the Fair had been passion, and that happiness belonged to the past. This young Hittite awoke in him desire which he thought extinguished. Artfully perfumed, offering herself without obvious gestures, she had the gift of making herself alluring without losing her nobility.

Ramses was moved by her untamed beauty and the charm

of her almond-shaped black eyes. 'You're very young, Mat-Hor.'

'I am a woman, Majesty, and also your wife. It is my duty to win you.'

'Come to the bow of the ship and discover Egypt. I am Egypt's husband.'

The king wrapped a cloak round Mat-Hor's shoulders and led her to the bow. He told her the names of the provinces, towns and villages, described their riches, explained the irrigation systems, customs and celebrations.

And then they arrived at Thebes.

Mat-Hor gazed with wonder on the vast temple of Karnak on the east bank, and the shrine of the *ka* of the gods, Luxor, source of light. She stood speechless with admiration before the House of Ramses on the east bank, overlooked by the great peak where the goddess of silence dwelt, Ramses' Temple of a Million Years, and the gigantic statue depicting in stone the king's *ka*, likened to a divine power.

Mat-Hor noted that one of Pharaoh's names, 'He who Resembles a Bee', was fully justified, for Egypt was indeed a beehive where no idleness was permitted. Everyone had a part to play, while respecting the difference in rank of their duties. In the temple itself there was ceaseless activity: groups of tradesmen went about their business near the shrine, while the initiates celebrated the rites inside. During the night, those responsible for observing the heavens and the stars made their calculations.

Ramses gave the new Great Royal Wife no time to adapt. She was lodged in the palace of the House of Ramses and had to submit to the demands of her post and learn her duties as queen. She knew that obedience was essential in order to win over Ramses.

At the entrance to the village of Deir el-Medina, which was guarded by police and soldiers, the royal chariot halted.

Behind it came a convoy bringing the usual supply of food to the craftsmen charged with digging out and decorating the tombs in the Valleys of the Kings and the Queens: loaves of bread, sacks of beans, fresh vegetables, finest quality fish, pieces of dried and preserved meat. The government also provided sandals, lengths of cloth and ointments.

Ramses gave Mat-Hor his arm to help her alight from the chariot.

'Why have we come here?' she asked.

'For what is, for you, the most important thing of all.'

To the accompaniment of cheers from the artisans and their families, the royal couple made their way to a two-storeyed white house, the home of the village headman, a fifty-year-old whose genius as a sculptor commanded everyone's admiration.

'How can we thank Your Majesty for his generous gifts?' the headman asked as he bowed.

'I know the value of your hands, and I also know that you and your brothers ignore fatigue. I am your protector and I shall enrich your community, so that your work may be immortal.'

'Command us, Majesty, and we shall act.'

'Come with me and I will show you where two building-sites are to be opened up immediately.'

When the royal chariot entered the road leading to the Valley of the Kings, a feeling of anguish gripped Mat-Hor. The sight of the cliffs, on which the sun beat down and from which all life seemed to have fled, wrung her heart. Snatched away from the luxury and comfort of the palace, she was shocked by the stones and the desert.

At the entrance to the Valley of the Kings, which was guarded day and night, some sixty high officials of various ages awaited Ramses. Their heads were shaven, and they wore long, pleated kilts, wide collars and carried staffs of sycamore wood tipped with ostrich plumes.

'These are my Royal Sons,' explained Ramses.

They raised their staffs in a guard of honour, then formed a procession to follow the monarch.

Ramses halted not far from the entrance to his own tomb. 'Here,' he ordered the headman of Deir el-Medina, 'you will dig out a vast tomb with halls of pillars and as many funerary chambers as there are Royal Sons.* I shall protect them for ever, in the company of Osiris.'

He then handed the headman the plan of another tomb, which he had himself drawn on papyrus. 'This is the House of Eternity of the Great Royal Wife, Mat-Hor. You will dig out this tomb in the Valley of the Queens, a good distance from that of Iset the Fair and a long way from that of Nefertari.'

The young Hittite turned pale. 'My tomb? But . . .'

'Such is our tradition,' explained Ramses. 'As soon as anyone takes on heavy responsibilities, they must think of the hereafter. Death is our best counsellor, for she places our actions in their correct contexts, and allows us to distinguish the essential from what is of lesser importance.'

'But I don't want to be submerged in melancholy thoughts!'

'You are no longer a woman like others, Mat-Hor. You are no longer a Hittite princess concerned solely with her own pleasure; you are the Queen of Egypt. The only thing that matters now is your duty; in order to understand it, you must meet your own death.'

'I won't!'

Ramses' expression immediately made her sorry she had spoken.

She fell to her knees. 'Forgive me, Majesty.'

---

* This tomb, in the Valley of the Kings, bears the number 5. It was discovered in 1820 by James Burton. Excavations have recently been resumed by an American team. They were astonished by the size of the monument: it is the largest known Egyptian tomb.

'Rise, Mat-Hor. You are not my servant, but the servant of Ma'at, the Rule of the Universe which created Egypt and will survive her. And now, let us go to meet your destiny.'

Drawing on all her pride, the young queen succeeded in mastering her fear. She found the Valley of the Queens, despite its barren character, less austere than that of the Kings, for the site was not enclosed by high cliffs but open to the world of the living, which she felt to be quite near. Mat-Hor gazed up at the pure blue of the sky and recalled the beautiful countryside of the genuine valley, that of the Nile, where she hoped to experience countless hours of gaiety and pleasure.

Ramses thought of Nefertari, who rested here, in the gilded chamber of a magnificent House of Eternity, where she was reborn every moment in the form of a phoenix, a ray of light or a breath of wind, rising up to the ends of the earth; Nefertari, who sailed in a ship on the celestial waters, in the heart of the light.

Mat-Hor kept silent, not daring to interrupt the king's thoughts. In spite of the solemnity of the place and the moment, she was troubled in her innermost depths by his presence and his power. Whatever the ordeals to be faced, she would achieve her aim: to seduce Ramses.

35

Serramanna had run out of patience. He finished his meal of a rib of beef with chick-peas, and rode off to Teshonq's workshop. Since the softly softly approach wasn't working, he had decided to use more direct methods. This time the Libyan would tell him everything he knew and, most important of all, the name of Ahsha's murderer.

When he dismounted, Serramanna was surprised to see a crowd in front of the tanner's workshop. Women and children, old men and workmen, all chattering away nineteen to the dozen.

'Out of the way,' he shouted, 'and let me pass!'

He didn't have to repeat his order; there was immediate silence.

Inside the building the stench was as terrible as ever. The Sardinian, who had adopted the Egyptian custom of scenting himself, hesitated to go in. But the sight of the team of tanners congregating near the cured deerskins prompted him to venture into this foul-smelling place. He pushed aside some strings of acacia pods, rich in tannic acid, passed a trough of ochre clay and put his enormous hands on the shoulders of two apprentices.

'What's going on?'

The apprentices moved aside, to reveal Teshonq's body, the head lying in a basin full of urine and bird-droppings.

'An accident, a terrible accident,' explained the head of the workshop, a stocky Libyan.

'How did it happen?'

'No one knows. Teshonq must have come to work early – we found him like this when we arrived.'

'No witnesses?'

'None at all,' said the workman.

'It looks odd to me. Teshonq was experienced and expert in his work, not the kind to die stupidly. No, it's foul play and one of you must know something.'

'You're wrong,' the workman protested half-heartedly.

'I'll confirm that for myself,' promised Serramanna, with a hungry eye on his prey. 'We'll need to question everyone thoroughly.'

The youngest apprentice wriggled out of the workshop like an eel and made off as fast as his legs could carry him. But the good life had not blunted Serramanna's reflexes, and he set off in hot pursuit. The alleyways of the district held no secrets for the youngster but the Sardinian was strong enough to keep up with him. When the apprentice tried to climb a wall, a heavy hand grabbed him by the kilt. The fugitive was plucked into the air and fell heavily on the ground.

'My back! It's broken!'

'We'll see about that when you've told me the truth. Be quick about it, you rascal, or I'll break your wrists as well.'

The terrified apprentice spoke jerkily. 'It was a Libyan who killed Teshonq . . . a man with black eyes, a square face and curly hair . . . He called Teshonq a traitor . . . Teshonq protested, and swore he hadn't told you anything . . . but the other man didn't believe him . . . He strangled him and pushed his head into the basin of dung . . . Then he turned to us and threatened us: "As true as my name's Malfi and I'm the lord of Libya, I'll kill you if you talk to the police." And now that I've told you everything, I'm as good as dead!'

'Don't talk nonsense, boy,' growled Serramanna. 'You'll

never set foot in that workshop again. You'll work for the palace steward.'

'You . . . you won't send me to prison?'

'I've a soft spot for brave lads. Come on, on your feet.'

The apprentice hobbled along as well as he could and managed to follow the giant, who was extremely put out. Contrary to what he had hoped, it was not Uri-Teshup who had killed Teshonq.

The Hittite traitor Uri-Teshup allied with Malfi, a murdering Libyan, a hereditary enemy of Egypt . . . Yes, that was what was being plotted in the dark. But he still had to convince Ramses.

Setau washed the copper bowls, flasks and filters of different sizes while Lotus cleaned the shelves of the laboratory. Then he took off his antelope-skin tunic, soaked it in water and wrung it out to extract the potions with which it was saturated. It was Lotus's job to transform the tunic back into a veritable walking medicine store, by means of the treasures offered by the black cobra, the puff adder, the horned adder and the like. The lovely Nubian bent over a basin of thick brown liquid; when diluted it would be an effective remedy for thin blood and weak hearts.

When Ramses entered the laboratory, Lotus bowed, but Setau went on with his work.

'You're in a bad mood,' the king remarked.

'Right.'

'You don't approve of my marriage to this Hittite princess.'

'Right again.'

'Why not?'

'She'll bring you bad luck,' said Setau, with a scowl.

'Surely you're exaggerating.'

'Lotus and I know snakes well. To discover the life in the heart of their venom, you have to be an expert, and this Hittite viper is capable of attacking in a way that even the best expert couldn't predict.'

'Ah, but thanks to you, I'm immunized against snakebite.'

Setau muttered to himself. In fact, ever since Ramses' adolescence he had given him regular doses of a potion containing minute quantities of venom, enabling him to survive the bite of any snake.

'You are too confident in your power, Majesty. Lotus believes you are almost immortal, but I'm convinced that this Hittite will try to harm you.'

'The word is that she is very much in love,' Lotus murmured.

'So what?' exclaimed Setau. 'When love turns to hatred, it's a terrifying weapon. It's obvious that this woman will try to avenge her people. And she's got the use of an unexpected battlefield, the royal palace. Of course, Ramses won't listen to me.'

The pharaoh turned to Lotus. 'What do you think?'

'Mat-Hor is beautiful, intelligent, cunning, ambitious and . . . a Hittite.'

'I won't forget that,' Ramses promised.

Ahmeni, pale-faced, his hair thinner than ever, had transcribed, accurately and with a steady hand, Serramanna's passionate declarations. The king read the report attentively.

'Uri-Teshup is Ahsha's murderer, and Malfi, the Libyan, is his accomplice . . . But there's no proof.'

'No court would find them guilty,' Ahmeni acknowledged.

'This Malfi, have you heard of him?'

'I've consulted the archives at the Foreign Affairs secretariat and Ahsha's notes. I've also questioned experts on Libya. Malfi is the leader of a warlike tribe with a particular hatred of us.'

'Are they just a band of madmen or a real danger?'

Ahmeni thought for a moment before answering. 'I'd like

to give you a reassuring reply, but rumour has it that Malfi has succeeded in uniting several clans which, up till now, were at each other's throats.'

'Is that just rumour or is it true?'

'The desert police haven't managed to locate the site of his camp.'

'And yet this Malfi has entered Egypt, murdered a compatriot in his own workshop and got away unpunished.'

Ahmeni dreaded bearing the brunt of Ramses' anger, which was all the more violent for being rare.

'We didn't know how dangerous he is,' the scribe explained.

'If we cannot detect evil, how will we be able to govern the country?'

Ramses rose and walked over to the large window of his office, from where he could look on the sun without scorching his eyes. The sun, his protective star, gave him every day the energy to assume his burden, whatever the difficulties might be.

'We mustn't ignore Malfi,' the king declared.

'The Libyans couldn't possible attack us!'

'A handful of demons can sow misfortune, Ahmeni. This Libyan lives in the desert. He picks up destructive forces there and dreams of using them against us. It will not be a war like those we have waged against the Hittites. It will be war of a different kind, more underhand but no less savage. I sense Malfi's hatred. It is growing, and it is coming nearer.'

Formerly, Nefertari had used her powers of clairvoyance to direct the king's actions. Since she had become a star shining in the sky, Ramses had the feeling that her spirit lived on in him and that she continued to guide him.

'Serramanna will undertake a throrough investigation,' Ahmeni pointed out.

'Have you any other worries, my friend?'

'A hundred or so problems, as I have every day, all very

212

urgent.'

'It's useless to ask you to rest a little, I suppose?'

'The day when there are no more problems to resolve, I shall rest.'

36

The most skilled of the palace masseuses was rubbing natron into Mat-Hor's skin to cleanse it of impurities. Then she washed the young queen with a soap made from the bark and pith of the balanite tree, which is rich in saponin, and asked her to lie down on warm paving stones to be rubbed down. The fragrant salve relieved aches and pains, got rid of tension and perfumed the body.

Mat-Hor's life was bliss. Never at her father's court had anyone treated her with so much care and skill. Make-up artists, manicurists and chiropodists exercised their art to perfection, and the new queen of Egypt felt more beautiful every day – which was essential if she was to win Ramses' heart. Bursting with youth and happiness, Mat-Hor felt herself to be irresistible.

'Now,' decided the masseuse, 'the anti-wrinkle cream.'

The Hittite was appalled. 'At my age? You're mad!'

'It's at your age that one must begin to fight against ageing, not when it's too late.'

'But . . .'

'You must trust me, Majesty. For me, a Queen of Egypt's beauty is a matter of state.'

Mat-Hor gave in. She surrendered her face to the masseuse, who applied a costly cream made of honey, red natron, powdered alabaster, fenugreek seeds and ass's milk.

After the first sensation of coolness there followed a gentle warmth, which felt as though it would put off the onset of ugliness and old age until a long-distant future.

Mat-Hor went from banquets to receptions, was received by the nobility and the wealthy, visited harems where weaving, music and poetry were taught, and every day knew the exquisite delight of familiarizing herself with the art of living in the Egyptian way.

It was all so much finer than anything she had dreamt of! She no longer thought of Hattusa, the melancholy, grey capital of her childhood, devoted to asserting military power. Here, in Pi-Ramses, instead of high walls there were gardens, ornamental lakes and houses decorated with the glazed tiles which gave Ramses' capital the name of City of Turquoise, where the joy of living was accompanied by the songs of birds.

The Hittite princess had dreamt of Egypt, and Egypt belonged to her! She was Egypt's queen, respected by all.

But did she really reign? She knew that Nefertari had worked every day at Ramses' side, had taken a real part in the conduct of affairs of state, and had even been the principal architect of the peace treaty. Mat-Hor's life was a whirl of luxury and pleasure, but she saw so little of Ramses! True, he made love to her with desire and affection, but he remained distant and she exercised no power over him. And she had learnt nothing of the secrets of government.

This failure was only temporary. Mat-Hor would beguile Ramses, she would get the better of him. Intelligence, beauty and cunning would be her three weapons. The battle would be long and difficult, since he was a considerable opponent; nevertheless the young Hittite did not doubt her success. She had obtained what she had so ardently desired. And what she wished for now was to become so celebrated a queen that she would wipe out the very memory of Nefertari.

'Majesty,' her maid murmured, 'I think . . . I think that Pharaoh is in the garden.'

215

'Go and see if it really is him, and come back immediately.'

Why hadn't Ramses let her know he was there? He was not in the habit of taking a rest at this hour, in the late morning. What unexpected event had caused this departure from custom?

The maid returned in a fluster. 'It really is Pharaoh, Majesty.'

'Is he alone?'

'Yes, alone.'

'Give me my lightest, simplest gown.'

'You don't want the linen one, with the red embroidery and—'

'Hurry.'

'What jewels do you want?'

'No jewels.'

'And which wig?'

'No wig. Will you hurry now?'

Ramses was seated like a scribe at the foot of a sycamore tree with spreading branches and dazzling foliage, laden with green and red seeds. The king was dressed in the traditional kilt of the pharaohs of the Old Empire, the time when the pyramids were built. On his wrists were two gold bracelets.

The queen stood watching him. There was no doubt: he was talking to someone.

She approached, barefoot. A slight breeze rustled the leaves of the sycamore, whose song was sweet as honey. To her astonishment, the young woman discovered that the person the monarch was talking to was Wideawake, his dog, which lay on its back.

'Majesty.'

'Come, Mat-Hor.'

'You knew I was there?'

'Your scent gave you away.'

216

She sat down beside him. Wideawake rolled on to its side and lay down like a sphinx.

'You were talking to this animal?'

'All animals can talk. When they are close to us, as my lion was and this dog now, who is the heir to a dynasty of Wideawakes, they even have things to tell us, if we know how to listen.'

'What does he tell you?'

'He hands down loyalty, trust and uprightness, and he describes to me the fine paths of the hereafter, along which he will guide me.'

Mat-Hor grimaced. 'Death . . . Why speak of that horror?'

'Only humans commit horrors. Death is a simple physical law, and what comes after death can become fulfilment, if we have led just lives in accordance with the Rule of Ma'at.'

Mat-Hor moved closer to Ramses and gazed at him with her beautiful black almond-shaped eyes.

'Aren't you afraid to soil your gown?' he asked.

'I'm not dressed yet, Majesty.'

'You are dressed severely, no jewels, no wig. Why such simplicity?'

'Does Your Majesty think it wrong?'

'You have a rank to observe, Mat-Hor, and you cannot behave like other women.'

The Hittite said rebelliously, 'Have I ever done so? I am the daughter of an emperor and now the wife of the Pharaoh of Egypt! My life has always been subjected to the demands of protocol and power.'

'Protocol certainly, but why mention power? You exercised no power at your father's court.'

Mat-Hor felt trapped. 'I was too young. Besides, Hatti is a military state, where women are considered inferior beings. Here, everything's different! Doesn't the Queen of Egypt have a duty to serve her country?' She spread her hair over Ramses' lap.

'Do you feel really Egyptian?'

'I don't want to hear any more talk of Hatti!'

'Are you rejecting your father and mother as well?' asked Ramses.

'No, of course not, but they are so far away . . .'

'You are living through a difficult time of trial.'

'Trial? No, this is what I've always wanted. I don't want to talk about the past.'

'How can you prepare for tomorrow if you have not penetrated the secrets of yesterday? You are young, Mat-Hor, and you are restless, searching for your equilibrium. It will not be easy to discover it.'

'My future is all marked out: I am the Queen of Egypt.'

'The ability to reign is something which is built up day by day. It can never be acquired.'

The Hittite was taken aback. 'I don't understand.'

'You are the living emblem of the peace between Egypt and Hatti,' declared Ramses. 'Many dead have marked the route which led to the end of a long conflict. Thanks to you, joy has replaced suffering.'

'Am I only a symbol? Nothing more?'

'It will take you many years to penetrate Egypt's secrets. Learn to serve Ma'at, the goddess of truth and justice, and your life will be illumined.'

'I want to reign at your side, Ramses.'

'You are only a child, Mat-Hor. Abandon your whims, observe your rank, and let time do its work. And now, leave me alone; Wideawake has much he wants to confide to me.'

The Hittite was furious. She ran back to her rooms: she would not let Ramses see her weep with rage.

37

The months that followed this conversation with Ramses saw Mat-Hor at her most dazzlingly beautiful. In her most magnificent attire, she lit up the fashionable Theban evening gatherings with her beauty and charm, and acted to perfection her part as a queen devoted to the life of high society. Carefully following the king's counsels, she familiarized herself with the customs of the court and increased her knowledge of the culture of ancient Egypt, whose depth fascinated her.

She met no hostility, but failed to get Ahmeni to like her, Ahmeni, who everyone said was the king's closest friend. As for Setau, another confidant, he had left again for Nubia, accompanied by Lotus, to collect the venom of his beloved snakes and to put into application his ideas about the development of the region.

The young Hittite had everything and yet nothing. Power was so close, yet it eluded her, and bitterness began to creep into her heart. She sought in vain for the means of winning Ramses and, for the first time, doubted herself. But she would not give the king the opportunity of noticing this; so she gave herself over to the whirl of celebrations and festivities, of which she was the undisputed queen.

This autumn evening Mat-Hor felt tired. She dismissed her servants and lay down on her bed with her eyes open, the better to dream of Ramses, that all-powerful and elusive man. The linen curtain in front of the window billowed out. A gust of wind. At least, so she thought. But moments later a long-haired, broad-chested man suddenly appeared.

Mat-Hor sat up and crossed her arms over her chest. 'Who are you?'

'A compatriot.'

The moonlight enabled the queen to make out the face of her unexpected visitor. 'Uri-Teshup!'

'So you remember me, young lady.'

'How dare you enter my bedchamber!'

'It wasn't easy, and I've been watching you for hours. That devil Serramanna has me watched constantly. I've had to wait a long time before approaching you.'

'Uri-Teshup . . . You killed Emperor Muwattalis and you tried to kill my father and mother,' said Mat-Hor furiously.

'All that's in the distant past. Today we are two Hittites exiled in Egypt.'

'Aren't you forgetting who I am?'

'A pretty woman condemned to find excitement in an artificial world.'

'I am Ramses' wife and the queen of this country!'

Uri-Teshup sat down on the end of the bed. 'Stop dreaming, girl.'

'I'll call the guard!'

'Very well, call him.'

They exchanged defiant looks. The young woman got up and poured herself a cup of fresh water.

'You are nothing but a monster and a brute,' she said. 'Why should I listen to you, you traitor general?'

'Because we belong to the same people, who will always be the enemies of this damned Egypt!'

'Stop this crazy talk. The peace treaty has been signed.'

'Don't delude yourself, Mat-Hor. To Ramses you are only a foreigner, who will soon be shut up in a harem.'

'You're wrong.'

'Has he granted you the slightest scrap of power?'

The young woman was silent.

'In Ramses' eyes, you don't exist. You are simply a Hittite and the hostage for this peace – which the pharaoh will eventually break in order to crush a demobilized enemy. Ramses is deceitful and cruel. He laid a subtle trap and Hattusilis fell into it. And you, you were sacrificed by your own father! Forget your disappointments in a round of pleasure, Mat-Hor, enjoy yourself, for youth quickly passes, much faster than you imagine.'

The queen turned her back on him. 'Have you finished?'

'Think about what I've said, and you'll find I've told you the truth. If you want to see me again, be careful to let me know without alerting Serramanna.'

'What reason could I possibly have for wanting to see you again?'

'You love your country as much as I do. And you accept neither defeat nor humiliation.'

Mat-Hor hesitated a long time before turning round. A breeze blew up the linen curtain; Uri-Teshup had vanished. Was he just a demon of the night or had he reminded her of the true facts?

The six men were singing at the top of their voices, stamping their feet in time to their song. Working in an immense cask, they trampled with gusto on the ripe bunches of grapes, which would give an excellent wine. Half drunk with the grape-fumes, they held on to the branches of the vine with more or less unsteady hands. The most enthusiastic of all was Serramanna, who set the pace for his companions.

'Someone's asking for you,' said one of the vintagers.

'Carry on,' Serramanna ordered his men, 'and don't slacken off.'

The man was an officer from the desert police, with a

deeply lined square face, who was never separated from his bow and arrows or his short sword.

'I've come to report,' he told Serramanna. 'Our patrols have been covering the Libyan desert for several months, looking for Malfi and the rebels he's leading.'

'Have you finally found them?'

'Unfortunately, no. That desert is immense, and we only control the zone nearest to Egypt. It would be too risky to venture further. The Bedouin watch for us and warn Malfi of our approach. For us he's an elusive shadow.'

Serramanna was disappointed and angry. The competence of the desert police was beyond doubt. Their failure proved how formidable an opponent Malfi was.

'Is it true that Malfi has united several tribes?' he asked.

'I'm not certain,' replied the officer. 'It may be just a rumour like all the others.'

'Has Malfi ever boasted of owning an iron dagger?'

'Not that I've heard.'

'Leave some men in place to warn the palace of the slightest incident.'

'As you wish. But what do we have to fear from the Libyans?'

'We are convinced that Malfi will try to harm us in one way or another. And he's suspected of committing a crime.'

Ahmeni never threw any document away. As the years went by, his office in Pi-Ramses filled with archives in the form of papyri and wooden tablets. Three adjoining rooms held old dossiers. On several occasions his subordinates had suggested he get rid of unimportant documents, but Ahmeni wanted to keep his hands on as much information as possible, so that he wouldn't have to have obtain it from government departments whose slowness exasperated him.

The scribe worked fast. In his view, any problem whose solution dragged on tended to get worse. And usually it was better to depend only on himself and to ignore the innumerable functionaries – who were quick to disappear as soon as the difficulty seemed insuperable.

Ahmeni had just finished off a huge dish of boiled meat and was working by the light of oil lamps, when Serramanna came into his office.

'Still busy reading . . .'

'Someone must see to details in this country.'

'You'll wear yourself out, Ahmeni.'

'That happened a long time ago.'

'Can I sit down?'

'Providing you don't disturb anything.'

The Sardinian stayed standing. 'No news of Malfi,' he said regretfully. 'He's gone to earth in the Libyan desert.'

'And Uri-Teshup?'

'He's leading the good life with his rich wife. If I didn't know him like a hunter knows his prey, I'd swear he's become a respectable wealthy citizen, with no other ambitions than to enjoy a happy marriage and to eat well.'

'Well, why not? Other foreigners have been attracted by a quiet life.'

'Exactly.'

Serramanna's tone of voice intrigued Ahmeni. 'What are you suggesting?'

'You're an excellent scribe, but time is passing, and you're no longer young.'

Ahmeni put down his writing-brush and crossed his arms.

'I've met a charming woman who's very shy,' said the Sardinian. 'It's clear that she doesn't suit me. You, on the other hand, would appreciate her.'

'Are you trying to marry me off?'

'Me, I like plenty of variety, but you'd be faithful to a good wife.'

Ahmeni flew into a rage. 'My life is this office and the management of public affairs. Can you imagine a woman in here? She'd have ideas about tidiness and would mess everything up and create chaos everywhere!'

'I thought—'

'Well, don't think! Instead, try to find Ahsha's murderer.'

38

Ramses' Temple of a Million Years, on the west bank of Thebes, covered an immense area. In accordance with the pharaoh's wishes, the gateways seemed to soar up to the sky, trees shaded the ornamental lakes of clear water, the gates were of gilded bronze, the paving of silver, and living statues, animated by the presence of the *ka*, dwelt in its courtyards. Around the sanctuary were storehouses and a library. In the heart of the temple were shrines dedicated to Seti, Tuya and Nefertari.

The Lord of the Two Lands frequently went to this magical domain, home of the deities, to worship the memory of his loved ones, who were ever present in himself; but this journey was exceptional. Meritamon was to perform a rite which would make the reigning pharaoh immortal.

When he saw her, Ramses was once again struck by her likeness to her mother. In her close-fitting gown, adorned with two rosettes on her breast, Meritamon embodied Sekhet, the goddess of writing. Her delicate face, framed by a pair of disc-shaped earrings, was frail and luminous.

The king took her in his arms. 'How are you, my beloved daughter?'

'Thanks to you, I can meditate in this temple and play music here for the gods. At every moment I sense the presence of my mother.'

'It is at your request that I have come to Thebes. What mystery do you want to reveal to me, you who are the only Queen of Egypt recognized by the temples?'

Meritamon bowed low. 'Will His Majesty be good enough to follow me?'

The goddess she embodied guided Ramses to a shrine where a priest awaited them, wearing the ibis mask of Thoth. Watched by Ramses, Thoth and Sekhet inscribed the king's five names on the leaves of a great tree carved in relief in the stone.

'Thus,' said Meritamon, 'your annals are recorded millions of times, and so they will endure for ever.'

Ramses felt a curious emotion. He was just a man to whom fate had entrusted a heavy responsibility, but the divine couple evoked another reality, that of Pharaoh, whose soul had been transmitted from king to king since the beginning of the dynasties.

The two celebrants withdrew, leaving Ramses to contemplate the Tree of a Million Years, on which his eternity had just been inscribed.

Meritamon was on her way back to the temple musicians' house, when her path was barred by a young blonde woman, magnificently dressed.

'I am Mat-Hor,' she said aggressively. 'We have never met, but I had to speak to you.'

'You are my father's official wife. We have nothing to say to each other.'

'You are the real Queen of Egypt!'

'My role is strictly religious.'

'In other words, essential!' said Mat-Hor bitterly.

'Interpret the facts as you wish. For me there will never be any Great Royal Wife but Nefertari.'

'She is dead, and I am alive! Since you refuse to reign, why won't you let me do so?'

Meritamon smiled. 'You have too fertile an imagination. I

live here as a recluse and am not interested in affairs of the world.'

'You attend the state rites, in your capacity as Queen of Egypt.'

'That is Pharaoh's wish. Are you questioning it?'

'Speak to him. Persuade him to grant me my rightful place. Your influence would be decisive.'

'What do you really want, Mat-Hor?'

'I have the right to reign. My marriage permits it.'

'Egypt cannot be conquered by force; that takes love. On this earth, if you forget your duties and ignore the Rule of Ma'at, you will be painfully disillusioned.'

'I'm not interested in all that, Meritamon. I demand your help. *I* am not renouncing the world.'

'You are braver than I am. I wish you luck, Mat-Hor.'

Ramses spent a long time meditating in the vast Hall of Pillars of the temple of Karnak which Seti had begun and which, in his capacity as son and successor, he had completed. The light, filtered through the stone grilles of the windows, caught in turn the carved and painted scenes which depicted the pharaoh making offerings to the deities so that they would agree to dwell on earth.

Amon, the great soul of Egypt, who breathed life into every nostril, remained mysterious but everywhere present at work. In the words of a sacred song, '*He comes in the wind, but he is not seen. The night is filled with his presence. Whatever is high, whatever is low, it is he who fashions it.*' As it said in the *Book to Emerge into the Light,* to attempt to know Amon, while yet realizing that he would always escape human understanding, was to ward off evil and darkness, to penetrate the future and organize the country in such a way that it became the image of heaven.

A man came towards Ramses. He was dressed in an immaculate white robe, and had a shaven head and a square, unprepossessing face which age had not softened. A former supervisor of the royal stables, he had entered the service of Amon at Karnak, and risen rapidly through the priesthood to become the god's Second Prophet.

He halted a few paces from the king. 'Great is my joy at seeing you, Majesty.'

'Thanks to you, Bakhen, the temples at Karnak and Luxor are worthy of the deities who dwell there. How is High Priest Nebu?'

'He never leaves his little house near the great lake any more, and he is very old and frail; but he still gives orders.'

Ramses valued Bakhen's loyalty highly. He was one of those exceptional beings who were free of ambition and whose principal concern was to act righteously. The management of the largest sacred domain in Egypt was in good hands. However, Bakhen seemed less serene than usual.

'Are you worried about something serious?' asked Ramses.

'I've had complaints from the small sanctuaries in the Theban region. They are running short of oliban, incense and myrrh, which are essential for the daily performance of the rites. For the time being, we have enough reserves at Karnak to be able to send them what they need, but my own stocks will be exhausted in two or three months.'

'Deliveries are due be made to the temples before the beginning of winter.'

'True, majesty, but how much will we get? Last year's crops were so poor that we may run out of these essential substances altogether. If the rituals aren't performed properly, what will become of the harmony of the country?'

As soon as Ramses was back in the capital, Ahmeni presented himself at his office, his arms laden with papyri. Everyone wondered how a scribe who looked so frail could carry such heavy loads.

'Majesty, you must act urgently! The tax on the cargo boats is excessive and—' Ahmeni broke off: it was clear from Ramses' expression that this was no time to bother him with details.

'What is the state of our reserves of oliban, incense and myrrh?' asked the king.

'I can't tell you immediately; I'll have to check. But there's no cause for alarm.'

'How can you be so sure?'

'Because I've set up a system of control. If the stocks had fallen significantly, I'd have known.'

'In the Theban region, there will soon be a shortage,' said Ramses.

'We must use the reserves from the Pi-Ramses storehouses and hope that the next crops will be good.'

'Delegate all less important tasks and look into this problem at once.'

When Ramses had gone, Ahmeni sent for three officials: the man in charge of the stocks in the White Double House, the head of the Treasury and the head of the House of Pine, who was responsible for checking deliveries of imported goods. All three men were well past fifty.

'I've had to leave an important meeting,' complained the head of the Treasury. 'I hope you aren't disturbing us for nothing.'

'You three are responsible for our stocks of oliban, myrrh and incense,' Ahmeni reminded them. 'Since not one of you has warned me, I take it that the situation gives no cause for alarm.'

'I've almost no oliban left,' admitted the man from the White Double House, 'but I'm sure my colleagues have plenty.'

'I've only a little,' said the head of the Treasury, 'but we haven't yet reached the danger point, so I didn't think it necessary to report to my colleagues.'

'I'm in much the same position,' said the head of the House of Pine. 'If my stocks had continued to fall in the next few months, I'd have had to do something.'

Ahmeni was aghast. These three officials had obeyed the letter rather than the spirit of the law and, as so often happened, had not kept each other informed.

'Tell me the exact state of your stocks,' he said coldly.

He made some rapid calculations: by next spring, there would be not a single grain of incense in Egypt, and myrrh and oliban would have disappeared from the laboratories and the temples. Throughout the country, anger at Ramses' lack of foresight would grow and spread.

39

Neferet, looking as beautiful as a spring dawn, had just finished preparing a mixture of pistachio resin, honey, minute quantities of copper and a little myrrh, to treat one of her illustrious patient's teeth.

'There's no abscess,' she explained to Ramses, 'but your gums are unhealthy. Also, your tendency to swollen, painful joints has become more marked. Your Majesty must not forget the mouth-washes and the extracts of willow bark.'

'I've had thousands of willows planted along the banks of the lakes. You'll soon have plenty of this soothing bark.'

'Thank you, Majesty. I'm also giving you a paste to chew, made from bryony, juniper, sycamore seeds and incense. Talking of incense and myrrh, which are remarkably effective against pain, I have to inform you that we shall soon be short of them.'

'I know, Neferet, I know.'

'When will the doctors get their new supplies?'

'As soon as possible.'

Realizing the monarch's embarrassment, Neferet didn't dare ask the question on the tip of her tongue. The problem must be serious, but she trusted Ramses to get the country out of this awkward situation.

In his plain, white-walled office, Ramses meditated long

before the statue of his father, whose stone face the sculptor's art had brought vividly to life. Seti's presence linked the thoughts of the reigning pharaoh to those of his predecessor. When he had to make decisions involving the future of the kingdom, Ramses always consulted the soul of the king who had taught him his duties through a strict education, which few people would have borne.

Seti had been right. If Ramses was able to endure the burden of a long reign, it was because of this rigorous training. The fire that burned within him had not lessened in intensity as he grew older, but youthful passion had turned into an ardent desire to build up his country and people as his ancestors had done before him.

When Ramses' eyes lighted on the large map of the known world, which he frequently consulted, he thought of Moses, his childhood friend. In him, too, there burned a fierce fire, his true guide in the desert, in search of the Promised Land. There had been several times when, overruling his military advisers, Ramses had refused to take action against Moses and the Hebrews. They, too, had a destiny to fulfil.

Ramses called in Ahmeni and Serramanna, and told them, 'I have made several decisions. One of them should please you, Serramanna.'

When he heard what the king had to say, the Sardinian was delighted.

Tanit never tired of Uri-Teshup's body. Although he treated her roughly, she yielded to all his demands. Thanks to him, she rediscovered every day the pleasures of the carnal act and experienced a renewed youth. Uri-Teshup had become her god.

He kissed her passionately, rose, and stretched himself like a great cat, in all the splendour of his nakedness.

'You're a magnificent filly, Tanit! At times you almost make me forget my own country.'

Tanit rose from the bed, too, and crouched down to kiss her lover's legs. 'We are happy, so happy! We must think of nothing but ourselves and our pleasure.'

'We leave tomorrow for your house at Faiyum.'

'I don't like it there, my love. I prefer Pi-Ramses.'

'As soon as we get there, I shall leave again, but you will let it be known that we are both there in our love-nest.'

Tanit rose to her feet, pressed her heavy breasts against Uri-Teshup's chest and embraced him passionately. 'Where are you going and how long will you be away?'

'You don't need to know. When I return, if Serramanna questions you, you will say only that we weren't parted for a single instant.'

'Trust me, dearest, I—'

He slapped her so hard that she cried out with pain.

'You are a female, and a female must never interfere in men's affairs. Just obey, and everything will be all right.'

Uri-Teshup was leaving to meet Malfi to intercept the convoy of oliban, myrrh and incense and destroy the precious cargo. This disaster would seriously undermine Ramses' popularity and the country would be affected by unrest, creating ideal conditions for a surprise attack by the Libyans. In Hatti, the party hostile to the peace would drive Hattusilis from his throne and recall Uri-Teshup, the only warlord capable of defeating Pharaoh's armies.

A scared serving-maid appeared in the bedroom doorway. 'My lady, it's the police. A giant, armed, in a helmet . . .'

'Send him away,' ordered Tanit.

'No,' said Uri-Teshup. 'Let's see what our friend Serramanna wants. Tell him to wait. We're coming.'

'I won't talk to that oaf!'

'Oh yes you will, my girl! And don't forget that we're the most loving couple in the country. Put on a gown that leaves your breasts bare and sprinkle some perfume on yourself.'

'A little wine, Serramanna?' asked Uri-Teshup a few

minutes later, clasping a languishing Tanit in one arm.

'I'm on an official mission.'

'What has it got to do with us?' asked Tanit.

'Ramses granted Uri-Teshup the right to his protection in these difficult times. He's pleased with the way the prince has integrated into Egyptian society, and is therefore granting you a privilege that you can be proud of.'

Tanit was astonished. 'What is it?'

'The queen is undertaking a visit to all the harems in Egypt, where numerous festivities will be organized in her honour. I have the pleasure of announcing that you are to be among the guests and will accompany her for the duration of her journey.'

'That . . . that's wonderful!' exclaimed Tanit.

'You don't look pleased, Uri-Teshup,' observed the Sardinian.

'Of course I am. Me, a Hittite . . .'

'Queen Mat-Hor is of Hittite birth, and you are married to a Phoenician. Egypt is very hospitable when people respect her laws. Since you do respect them, you are considered a true subject of Pharaoh.'

'Why is it you who are telling us this news?' asked Uri-Teshup

'Because I'm responsible for the safety of distinguished guests,' replied Serramanna with a broad smile. 'And I shan't take my eyes off you for a single moment.'

There were only a hundred of them, but they were heavily armed and perfectly trained. Malfi's raiding-party was made up of his best men, a mixture of experienced warriors and young soldiers with inexhaustible energy.

After a final training session, which had seen the death of a dozen incompetents, the party had left the secret camp in the heart of the Libyan desert to set out on the road to the north, heading towards the western fringe of the Egyptian Delta.

They would cross the Delta from west to east, now by boat, now along muddy paths, then branch off towards the Arabian peninsula to attack the oliban convoy. Uri-Teshup and his followers would join them before the border to give them detailed information which would enable them to dodge the Egyptian patrols and avoid being seen by the lookouts.

The first stage of the conquest would be a triumph. The oppressed Libyans would regain hope, and Malfi would become the hero of an avenging people, eager for reprisals. Thanks to him, the Nile would be turned into a river of blood. But it was necessary first to strike Egypt in what she valued most: the performance of the rites and the worship of the gods, the expressions of the Rule of Ma'at. Without oliban, without myrrh and without incense, the priests would feel abandoned and would accuse Ramses of having broken the pact with heaven.

A scout returned from his patrol. 'We can't go any further,' he told Malfi.

'Have you gone out of your mind?'

'Come and see for yourself, my lord.'

Flat on his face on a mound of soft earth, hidden by thornbushes, Malfi stared unbelievingly. The Egyptian army was deployed on a wide strip of ground between the sea and the marshes, where archers in small boats were on guard. Wooden towers allowed lookouts to survey a vast horizon. There were several thousand men there. Their commander was Meneptah.

'We'd never get past,' said the scout. 'We'd be spotted and killed to a man.'

Malfi knew the scout was right. He could not drag his best men, the future spearhead of the Libyan army, to their deaths. To attack a caravan was easy, but to take on the Egyptian army would be suicidal. In his fury, the Libyan grasped a small branch of the thorn-bush and crushed it in his fists.

CITY LIMERICK PUBLIC LIBRARY

235

40

The owner of the caravans leaving for Egypt was stunned. He was an experienced trader, a fifty-eight-year-old Syrian, who had travelled every known road in the course of his business, but never had he seen such a treasure. He had asked the producers to meet him at the north-west point of the Arabian peninsula, in a barren, desolate region where the days were scorching and the nights often freezing – and then there were all those snakes and scorpions . . . It was an ideal hiding-place for a secret storehouse, and here, for the last three years, the Syrian had been accumulating wealth stolen from the Egyptian Treasury.

He had assured his accomplices, Malfi and Uri-Teshup, that his stocks of oliban, incense and myrrh, which had anyway been very small because of poor harvests, had been destroyed. Malfi and Uri-Teshup were warriors, not merchants; they didn't know that a good trader never throws away any valuable wares.

The Syrian had black hair plastered down on a round skull, a moonface, and a top-heavy torso planted on short legs. He had been lying and stealing since adolescence, always making sure to buy the silence of anyone who might have denounced him to the authorities. Like his friend the late Raia, the caravan-owner had secretly amassed a tidy fortune over the years. But it was nothing compared to the incredible gold mine which had just been deposited in his storehouse.

The Arabian incense trees had given three successive crops, which were so abundant that it had been necessary to engage twice as many seasonal workers than usual. The dark green leaves and the golden flowers with their crimson hearts were purely ornamental beside the magnificent brown bark. When the bark was scraped, it gave off droplets of resin which experts made into hard balls; when these were burnt, they gave off a wonderful scent.

And then there was the vast quantity of oliban! Its whitish resin, milky and fragrant, had flowed so generously that it was worthy of the golden age; the little pear-shaped tear-drops, white, grey or yellow, made the caravan-owner weep for joy. He was aware of the many medicinal virtues of this costly, much-sought-after substance. Egyptian physicians used it in ointments, plasters, powder, or even as a drink, as a remedy against tumours, ulcers, abscesses, and inflammation of the eyes and or ears. Oliban staunched bleeding and hastened the formation of scar tissue over wounds; it was even an antidote to some poisons. To any physician, oliban was worth its weight in gold.

There were also huge amounts of green resin-gum from the giant fennel, of dark rock-rose resin, of the thick, resinous oil of the balsam tree, and of myrrh . . . The Syrian was in ecstasies. What merchant could ever have dreamt of one day possessing such a treasure?

He had set up a decoy for his allies, by sending a caravan along the road where they were waiting for it. He wondered whether he had been wrong to send only a modest load. Unfortunately, rumours were already circulating of an exceptional crop and these rumours might already have reached Uri-Teshup and Malfi.

How could he gain time? In two days the Syrian was due to meet Greek, Cyprian and Canaanite merchants, to whom he would sell the contents of his storehouse. Then he would flee to Crete, where he would live out a happy retirement. Two interminable days, during which he was afraid his formidable allies might appear.

'A Hittite wishes to speak to you,' one of his servants informed him.

The Syrian's mouth went dry and his eyes burned. Catastrophe! Uri-Teshup had grown suspicious and was coming to demand an explanation. What if he forced him to open his storehouse? Should he run for it or try to talk Uri-Teshup round? The Syrian was speechless, unable to decide what to do.

The man who came towards him was not Uri-Teshup.

'You . . . you are a Hittite?'

'I am.'

'And you're a friend of—'

'No names! Yes, I'm a friend of the general, the only man capable of saving Hatti from dishonour.'

'Good, good. May the gods favour him! When shall I see him?'

'You will have to be patient.'

'There's nothing wrong, is there?'

'No, you've nothing to worry about – it's just that official ceremonies oblige him to remain in Egypt. But he counts on you to respect the terms of your contract to the letter.'

'He needn't worry. The contract has been fulfilled and everything has been done as he wished.'

'So I can put the general's mind at rest?'

'He can rejoice: his wishes have been granted. When I arrive in Egypt, I shall get in touch with him.'

As soon as the Hittite had left, the caravan-leader drank three cups of strong liquor without pausing for breath. Luck was serving him beyond his wildest hopes! Uri-Teshup was detained in Egypt . . . There was definitely a guardian spirit for thieves!

That left Malfi, a dangerous madman with occasional

gleams of lucidity. Usually the sight of blood was enough to intoxicate him. Murdering the merchants with the decoy convoy would have given him as much pleasure as lying with a woman, and he'd have neglected to examine the goods closely. If he became suspicious, though, he would hunt down the caravan-owner in an insane lust for revenge. The Syrian had many good qualities, but physical courage was not one of them; he could never face Malfi.

In the distance a cloud of dust appeared. The merchant was not expecting anyone – it could only be the Libyan and his band of assassins! He collapsed on his mat, overwhelmed with fear. His luck had run out. Malfi would delight in cutting his throat slowly and he would die in agony.

The cloud of dust seemed to be moving rather slowly. It couldn't be horses; they would have been faster. Donkeys? Yes, it must be donkeys. So it was a caravan. But wherever had it come from?

Relieved but curious, the merchant got up, his eyes fixed on the procession of heavily laden donkeys which came steadily on at their own pace. Then he recognized the donkey-drivers: they were the ones he had sent to their deaths, on the road where Malfi was waiting for them! Could it be a mirage? No, here was the leader of the convoy, a compatriot older than himself.

'Did you have a safe journey, my friend?' asked the merchant.

'No problems.'

The merchant hid his astonishment. 'Not even a small incident?'

'Nothing at all. We badly need a drink, something to eat, a wash and some sleep. You'll see to the load?'

'Of course, of course. Go and rest.'

The caravan was safe and sound, the load intact. There was only one possible explanation: Malfi and his Libyans had been intercepted. Perhaps the crazy warlord had been killed by the desert police. Good luck and a fortune . . . Life was showering the Syrian with every happiness. How right he had been to take risks!

A little tipsy, he hurried to the storehouse, to which only he had a key. The wooden bolt was broken. Infuriated, he pushed open the door.

Facing him, in front of the heap of treasures, stood a man with a shaven head, dressed in a panther-skin.

'Who . . . who are you?' asked the merchant.

'Kha, High Priest of Memphis, son of Pharaoh. I have come to look for what belongs to Egypt.'

The Syrian seized his dagger.

'Don't make any futile gestures. Pharaoh is watching you.'

The thief turned round. Egyptian archers suddenly appeared on all sides from behind every sand dune. And there, in his chariot in the sunlight, stood Ramses the Great, wearing the Blue Crown.

The merchant fell to his knees. 'Forgive me! I'm not guilty . . . I was forced—'

'You will be put on trial,' announced Kha.

At the thought of appearing before a court which would pronounce the supreme punishment, the Syrian lost his head. He rushed at one of the archers, who was approaching him with wooden handcuffs, and plunged his dagger into his arm. Thinking their comrade in danger, three other archers immediately loosed their arrows, piercing the body of the thief, who fell dead.

Although Ahmeni had been against it, Ramses had insisted on heading the expedition himself. With information provided by the desert police, and using his divining-rod, the king had located the clandestine destination of the stolen caravan cargos. And he had also sensed another anomaly, whose reality he wanted to verify.

The pharaoh's chariot, followed by a crowd of military ones, drove off into the desert. Ramses' two horses were so swift that they soon left the escort far behind.

The landscape was nothing but sand, rocks and dunes, right up to the horizon.

'Why is the king losing himself in these isolated wastes?' a lieutenant of the chariot corps asked the archer beside him.

'I took part in the battle of Kadesh. Ramses never acts at random. He's guided by a divine force.'

The king passed a dune and halted.

As far as the eye could see were magnificent trees with yellow and grey bark and soft, white wood: an extraordinary plantation of oliban trees which would provide Egypt with their precious resin for many long years.

41

Uri-Teshup's nerves were under severe strain. Neither the beauty of the gardens nor the quality of the food, nor even the attraction of the concerts, could let him forget Serramanna's constant presence and intolerable smile. Tanit, on the other hand, was enjoying this visit to the harems in the company of a dazzlingly beautiful queen who charmed the most sour-tempered of the administrators. Mat-Hor seemed delighted to be flattered by courtiers seeking her favour.

'Excellent news,' Serramanna announced to him. 'Ramses has just performed another miracle. He has discovered an enormous plantation of olibans, and the caravans have arrived safely in Pi-Ramses.'

The Hittite clenched his fists. Why had Malfi not acted? If the Libyan had been arrested or killed, Uri-Teshup no longer had any chance of sowing unrest in Egypt.

Tanit was talking to some business women invited by the queen to the harem of Mer-Ur, the very same of which Moses had once been a manager. Uri-Teshup sat a little apart, on a low dry-stone wall beside an ornamental lake.

'What are you thinking about, dear compatriot?'

He looked up and saw Mat-Hor, who was at the height of her beauty,

'I am sad,' he said.

'Why?'

'Because of you.'

'Me?' Mat-Hor was startled. 'But what have I done?'

'Do you still not understand Ramses' strategy?'

'Tell me what it is.'

'You are living through the last moments of a dream. Ramses has just led a military expedition to subjugate the people of his colonies even more. You must be blind not to realize that he is consolidating his bases for an attack on Hatti. Before he does so, he will have to deal with two embarrassing people: you and me. I'll be put under house arrest and will probably have a fatal "accident". You'll be shut up in one of these harems that you are so enjoying visiting.'

'The harems aren't prisons,' she protested.

'You will be given an honorary and meaningless title, and you will never see the king again.'

'How can you be so sure?'

'I have friends. They give me reliable information, to which you do not have access.'

The queen seemed perturbed. 'What do you suggest?'

'The king enjoys his food. He is particularly fond of a dish created for him, called Ramses' Delight: beef and fillets of Nile perch in a marinade of mild garlic, onions, and red oasis wine. It's a weakness that a Hittite should be able to exploit.'

'You dare to suggest. . .?'

'Don't act the innocent!' said Uri-Teshup scornfully. 'In Hattusa you learned to handle poisons.'

'You're a monster!'

'If you don't dispose of Ramses, he will destroy you.'

'Never speak to me again, Uri-Teshup!' And Mat-Hor stormed off.

The prince knew he was taking an enormous risk. If he hadn't succeeded in sowing doubt and anxiety in Mat-Hor's mind, she would denounce him to Serramanna. But if he *had* succeeded, he would have gone a long way towards his goal.

*

The restoration programme Kha had undertaken on the Saqqara site was already showing remarkable results. Djoser's step pyramid, and the one at Unas, inside which the first pyramid texts had been inscribed, revealing how royal souls were resuscitated, as well as the monuments of Pepy I, had all benefited from the craftsmen's care.

And the High Priest of Memphis had not stopped there. He had also asked his teams of master-builders and stone-cutters to repair the damage to the pyramids and temples of the Fifth Dynasty pharaohs at Abusir, north of Saqqara. In Memphis itself, Kha had had the Temple of Ptah enlarged; it would now shelter a shrine to the memory of Seti, to which would be added, in the near future, a shrine to the glory of Ramses.

Overcome by fatigue, Kha made his way to the spot where the tombs of the First Dynasty kings had been hollowed out, on the edge of the barren Saqqara plateau, overlooking the palm groves and cultivated fields. The burial place of King Djet, which was indicated by three hundred terracotta bull's heads projecting around the circumference and fitted with real horns, transmitted to him the necessary energy to consolidate the links between the present and the past.

Kha had not yet found the *Book of Thoth* and sometimes thought he never would. Could his failure be due to his lack of vigilance or some negligence in the worship of Apis? He promised himself to correct his mistakes, but first he had to complete his programme of restoration.

But Kha was anxious. Would he ever manage it?

For the third time this year, he had himself driven by chariot to the pyramid of Menkaura, on which, once the restoration was completed, he wished to carve a commemorative inscription. And for the third time, the site was empty, except for an old stone-cutter who was eating a piece of bread rubbed with garlic.

'Where are your colleagues?' asked Kha.

'Gone home.'

'Is it that ghost again?'

'Yes. It appeared again, and several people saw it. It was holding snakes in its hands and threatened to kill anyone who approached. Until it's driven away, no one will work here, not even for high wages.'

This was the disaster Kha feared: to be unable to restore the monuments on the Giza plateau. And this ghost dropped rocks and caused accidents. Everyone knew it was a soul in torment, returned to earth to wreak havoc among the living. In spite of all his knowledge, Kha had not managed to prevent it doing harm.

He had asked Ramses for help, and when he saw his chariot approaching, Kha's hopes revived. But if the king failed, it would be necessary to declare part of the Giza plateau a forbidden zone, and become resigned to seeing masterpieces decay.

When he had greeted his father, Kha said, 'The situation is getting worse, Majesty. No one will work here any more.'

'Have you pronounced the usual exorcisms?'

'They did no good.'

Ramses contemplated the pyramid of Menkaura with its powerful granite foundations. Every year, he came to Giza to draw energy from the stone in which the builders had embodied the rays of light uniting the earth and sky.

'Do you know where the ghost's hiding-place is?' he asked.

'None of the workmen has dared follow it.'

The king noticed the old stone-cutter, who was still eating his bread, and went up to him. In his surprise, the old man dropped his bread; he knelt down, with his arms stretched out in front of him and his forehead on the ground.

'Why didn't you run away with the others?' asked Ramses.

'I . . . I don't know, Majesty.'

'You know where the ghost hides, don't you?'

To lie to the king was to be damned for all eternity. The stone-cutter nodded.

'Take us there.'

Trembling, the old man guided Ramses and Kha along the passages in the tomb complex where Menkaura's loyal servants rested, those who, in the hereafter, would continue to form the royal court. Kha's experienced eye noted that some of these paths, which were more than a thousand years old, were in need of repair. They entered a little courtyard open to the sky, where the ground was littered with fragments of limestone. In one corner was a pile of small blocks of stone.

'It's here,' said the stone-cutter. 'Don't go any further.'

'Who is this ghost?' asked Kha.

'A sculptor whose memory has not been honoured and who takes his revenge by attacking other sculptors.'

According to the hieroglyphic inscriptions, the man in question had been in charge of a team of builders at the time of Menkaura.

'Remove those blocks of stone,' Ramses ordered.

'Majesty. . .'

'Get to work.'

After a while, the mouth of a rectangular well appeared, with a knotted rope hanging down one side-wall. Kha threw in a pebble; its fall seemed endless.

'More than thirty cubits,' the stone-cutter concluded when he heard the stone land at the bottom of the well. 'It's the jaws of hell down there, Majesty. Don't venture in.'

'Someone will have to go down,' declared Ramses.

'In that case, it's my job to take the risk,' said the workman.

'If you meet the ghost,' objected Kha, 'will you be able to recite the incantations to stop it harming you?'

The old man looked down.

'I am the High Priest of Ptah,' Kha went on. 'It is my duty to perform this task. Do not forbid it, father.'

246

Kha started on a descent which seemed interminable. The well was not dark; its limestone walls emitted a strange glow. At last he set foot on solid – though uneven – ground: he had reached the bottom. He saw an opening in the wall. It led to a narrow corridor which ended at a false door on which the dead man was portrayed, surrounded by columns of hieroglyphs.

Then Kha understood.

A wide crack ran from top to bottom of the carved stone, disfiguring the man who should have benefited from the resuscitation texts. Unable to be embodied in a living image, the spirit had been transformed into an angry ghost, tormenting the living for having scorned his memory.

Kha climbed back up the well, exhausted but happy. As soon as the false door was restored, and the dead man's face lovingly carved again, the evil spell would be broken.

42

Since his return to Pi-Ramses, Uri-Teshup had been in a permanent fury. To be continually watched by Serramanna during an interminable journey, to be reduced to inactivity and deprived of information – he felt like slaughtering the whole population of Egypt, beginning with Ramses. On top of all this, he had to put up with the amorous assaults of the besotted Tanit, who needed her daily ration of pleasure.

And here she came, half naked in a cloud of perfume.

'Dearest,' she said excitedly, 'the Hittites!'

'What about them?'

'Hundreds of them . . . hundreds of Hittites have invaded the centre of Pi-Ramses!'

Uri-Teshup seized her by the shoulders. 'Have you gone mad?'

'My servants assure me it's so!'

'The Hittites have attacked! They've struck at the heart of Ramses' kingdom . . . This is fantastic, Tanit!'

Uri-Teshup pushed his wife away and put on a short black and red striped tunic. Exulting as at the height of his glory, he ran to the stables and leapt on to his horse, ready to hurl himself into battle. Hattusilis must have been overthrown. The advocates of all-out war had triumphed, the Egyptian lines of defence had been broken by a surprise attack, and the fate of the world was in the balance.

Under the Western Acacia

In the grand avenue leading from the Temple of Ptah to the royal palace, a motley crowd was rejoicing. Not a soldier in sight, not the slightest trace of fighting. The wind was abruptly taken out of Uri-Teshup's sails.

He called to a policeman who was good-naturedly joining in the jubilation, 'I hear the Hittites have invaded Pi-Ramses.'

'That's right.'

'Well, where are they, then?'

'At the palace.'

'Have they killed Ramses?'

'What on earth are you talking about?' said the officer. 'They are the first Hittites to visit Egypt and they've brought gifts for our sovereign.'

Visitors . . . ? Uri-Teshup was dumbfounded. He pushed his way through the crowds and presented himself at the great gate of the palace.

'We've been waiting for you,' Serramanna thundered. 'Do you want to take part in the ceremony?'

Dazedly, the prince let the big Sardinian drag him into the audience chamber, which was crowded with courtiers. Right at the front stood the visitors' delegates, their arms loaded with gifts.

When Ramses appeared the chattering ceased. One by one, the Hittites presented Pharaoh with lapis-lazuli, turquoises, copper, iron, emeralds, amethysts, carnelian and jade. He lingered over several magnificent turquoises; they could only have come from Sinai, which he had visited in his youth, accompanied by Moses. He would never forget the red and yellow mountains, their fearsome crags and secret ravines.

'You who bring me these wonders,' said Ramses, 'have you met Moses and the Hebrew people on your travels?'

'No, Majesty.'

'Have you heard anything of them?'

'Everyone is afraid of them, because they are quick to wage war. But Moses still insists that one day they will reach their own land.'

So Moses was still pursuing his dream. Thinking of those long-ago years when their respective destinies were being formed, the monarch gave only half his attention to the presentation of the other gifts.

The leader of the delegation was the last to bow before Ramses.

'Are we free to come and go in the whole of Egypt, Majesty?' he asked.

'Such is the result of the peace.'

'Shall we be able to honour our gods in your capital?'

'In the east of the city stands the temple of the Syrian goddess Astarte, a companion of our god Set and the protector of my chariot and horses. She is the one I asked to watch over the safety of the port of Memphis. The God of Storms and the Sun Goddess, whom you worship in Hattusa, are also welcome in Pi-Ramses.'

When the Hittite delegation left the palace, Uri-Teshup followed them out and went up to one of them.

'Do you recognize me?' he asked.

'No.'

'I am Uri-Teshup, the son of Emperor Muwattalis.'

'Muwattalis is dead. Hattusilis is emperor now.'

'This visit . . . it's a trick, isn't it?'

'A trick? We have come to visit Egypt, and many more will follow us. The war is over. Really over.'

For long minutes, Uri-Teshup stood motionless in the middle of the grand avenue of Pi-Ramses.

'At last, Majesty!' exclaimed Mat-Hor. 'I despaired of ever seeing you again. Why was I not at your side when you received my countrymen? They would have been delighted to have the chance of admiring me.'

Looking magnificent in a red gown decorated with silver rosettes, Mat-Hor pirouetted in the middle of a ballet of serving-women. Every day, they hunted down the slightest speck of dust, brought fresh jewels and sumptuous garments and changed the hundreds of flowers which scented the queen's apartments.

'Dismiss your servants,' Ramses ordered.

The queen froze. 'But . . . I've no complaints about them.'

It was not a man in love who stood before Mat-Hor, but the pharaoh of Egypt. He must have had that same look in his eyes when he counter-attacked at Kadesh, when he hurled himself alone against thousands of Hittites.

'Leave, all of you,' cried the queen. 'Be off!'

Unaccustomed to being treated like that, the servants withdrew unhurriedly, dropping on the floor the things they were carrying.

Mat-Hor tried to smile. 'What has happened, Majesty?'

'Do you think your behaviour is that of a Queen of Egypt?'

'I maintain my rank, as you demanded.'

'On the contrary, Mat-Hor, you behave like a tyrant and your whims are unacceptable.'

'What have I done wrong?'

'You pestered the head of the Treasury and forced him to withdraw from its stocks riches which belong to the temples. And yesterday you dared to issue a decree claiming possession of precious metals offered to the state by your countrymen.'

The young queen said mutinously, 'I am the queen. Everything belongs to me!'

'You are seriously mistaken. Egypt is governed not by greed and selfishness but by the Rule of Ma'at. This land is the property of the gods; they bequeath it to the pharaoh, whose duty it is to maintain it in good condition, prosperous and happy. What you should have shown in all circumstances, Mat-Hor, is righteousness. When a leader is no longer a model, the whole country rapidly declines to decadence and ruin. By acting as you do, you strike at the authority of Pharaoh and the welfare of his people.'

Ramses had not raised his voice, but his words were more cutting than the edge of a sword.

'I . . . I didn't think—'

'A Queen of Egypt needs not only to think but to act. And you act badly, Mat-Hor. I have annulled your unjust decree and taken precautions to prevent your doing further harm. Henceforth, you will reside in the harem of Mer-Ur, and will come to court only at my command. You will lack for nothing, but all excess will be banished from now on.'

'Ramses, you cannot refuse my love!'

'I am wedded to Egypt, Mat-Hor, and you are unable to understand what that means.'

43

The Viceroy of Nubia could no longer bear Setau's presence or his activities. With Lotus's expert help, Setau had involved himself so far in the economic development of the province of the Far South that he had succeeded in putting all the tribes to work without provoking fighting among them – a feat the viceroy had thought impossible.

What is more, the stone-cutters liked Setau and he was covering the region with temples and shrines to the glory of the pharaoh and the gods who protected him. And this same Setau saw that agricultural work was well organized, had set up a land register and collected taxes!

The viceroy had to face the facts: this snake-charmer, whom he had thought an eccentric with no future, was making a name for himself as an efficient administrator. If Setau continued to obtain such remarkable results, the viceroy's position would become very awkward; he might be accused of incompetence and laziness and lose his post.

It was impossible to negotiate with Setau. Stubbornly refusing to take life easily and reduce his programme of work, he would accept no compromise. The viceroy hadn't even attempted to bribe him; in spite of his rank, Setau and Lotus lived simply, in touch with the natives, and showed no taste for luxury.

There was only one solution: a fatal accident, organized carefully enough for there to be no doubt about the cause of

Setau's death. The viceroy had therefore summoned to Abu Simbel a Nubian mercenary recently released from prison, a man with a past, who had no scruples. A large reward would induce him to act – and quickly.

The night was dark. The four massive statues which embodied Ramses' *ka* and which formed the façade of the great temple gazed into the distance, penetrating times and expanses which human eyes could not perceive.

The Nubian was waiting there. He had a low forehead, protruding cheekbones and thick lips. He was armed with a throwing-spear.

The viceroy identified himself.

'I know who you are,' said the Nubian. 'I saw you in the fortress where I was imprisoned.'

'I need your services.'

'I hunt for my village . . . I lead a quiet life now.'

'You're lying. You've been accused of theft, and there's evidence against you.'

The Nubian planted his spear angrily in the ground. 'Who accused me?'

'If you don't cooperate with me you'll go back to prison, and this time you'll never get out. If you do as I say, you'll be a rich man.'

'What do you want of me?'

'Someone is getting in my way. You must get rid of him for me.'

'A Nubian?'

'No, an Egyptian.'

'Then it'll cost you a lot.'

'You're in no position to bargain,' the viceroy said curtly.

'Who am I to "get rid of"?'

'Setau.'

The Nubian picked up his spear again and brandished it. 'That's worth a fortune!'

'You'll be paid handsomely, providing his death looks like an accident.'

'Understood.'

The viceroy staggered as if drunk and fell on to his backside. Before the Nubian could laugh, as the same thing happened to him. The two men tried to get up, but they lost their balance and fell over again.

'The ground is shaking,' the Nubian exclaimed. 'The Earth God is angry!'

The hill rumbled, the *ka* statues moved. Frozen with shock, the viceroy and his accomplice saw the gigantic head of one of the statues come loose. Ramses' face rolled towards the criminals and crushed them beneath its weight.

Lady Tanit was desperate. Uri-Teshup had not made love to her for more than a week. He left early in the morning, spent the whole day galloping about the countryside, returned home exhausted, ate enough for four, then dropped asleep without saying a word.

Tanit had only dared question him once, and then he had beaten her nearly senseless. Her only comfort was her little tabby cat, and she no longer even had the heart to manage the property she had inherited.

A new day was ending, empty and dull. The cat purred on Tanit's lap. There was the sound of a horse's hooves: Uri-Teshup was returning.

The Hittite appeared, his eyes full of ardour. 'Come here, my beauty!'

Tanit rushed into the arms of her husband, who tore off her gown and threw her down on to the cushions.

'My darling,' she said joyfully. 'You've come back to me!' She was overjoyed by the violence of Uri-Teshup's passion as he devoured her.

Much later, 'What was it that was worrying you so much?' she asked.

'I thought I'd been deserted. But Malfi is alive and he's continuing to unite the Libyan tribes! One of his messengers has contacted me and told me to remain confident. The struggle continues, Tanit, and Ramses is not invulnerable.'

'Forgive me for repeating it, but this Malfi frightens me.'

'The Hittites are held back by their cowardice. Only the Libyans will rouse them from their torpor, and Malfi is the man for the job. We have no choice but violence and all-out war. And you can count on me to win!'

Tanit was sleeping, sated with pleasure. Uri-Teshup was seated on a straw-bottomed chair in the garden, his head full of dreams of bloodshed, looking up at the waxing moon and asking for its help.

'I shall be more use to you than that star,' a woman's voice whispered behind him.

He turned round. 'Mat-Hor! You are taking a huge risk!'

'The queen still has the right to go where she pleases.'

'You seem disillusioned. Has Ramses repudiated you?'

'No, of course not!'

'Then why have you come here in secret like this?'

She looked up at the starry sky. 'You were right, Uri-Teshup. I am a Hittite and I shall always be one. Ramses will never recognize me as his Great Royal Wife. I shall never be Nefertari's equal.' She could not hold back a few tears.

Uri-Teshup tried to take her in his arms, but she shrank from him. 'I am stupid,' she said. 'Why weep over a failure? That is the attitude of a weak woman. A Hittite princess has no right to feel sorry for herself.'

'You and I were born to conquer.'

'Ramses has humiliated me,' said Mat-Hor. 'He has treated me like a servant. I loved him, I was prepared to become a great queen, I submitted to his will – and he has trampled contemptuously on me.'

'Are you determined to take your revenge?'

'I don't know. I no longer know what to do.'

'Keep a clear head,' urged Uri-Teshup. 'To accept humiliation without reacting would be cowardice unworthy of you. And if you are here, it's because you have come to a decision.'

'Be silent!'

'No, I will not be silent! Hatti is not defeated. She can still hold her head high. I have powerful allies, Mat-Hor, and we have a common enemy: Ramses.'

'Ramses is my husband.'

'No, he is a tyrant who despises you and has already forgotten your existence! Act, Mat-Hor. Do as I suggested. You can lay hands on the poison.'

To kill her dream . . . Could she destroy the future she had wanted so much, murder the man with whom she had been madly in love, the pharaoh of Egypt?

'Make up your mind,' ordered Uri-Teshup.

The queen fled into the night.

With a smile on his lips, he climbed up to the terrace of the villa, to be nearer the moon and to thank her.

'Who is that following me?' he demanded.

'It's me, Tanit.'

He seized her by the throat. 'Were you spying on us?'

'No, I—'

'You heard everything, didn't you?'

'Yes, but I won't say anything, I swear!'

'Of course you won't, my dear. You wouldn't make such a fatal mistake. Look, my beauty, look!'

From his tunic Uri-Teshup pulled out an iron dagger, which he pointed at the moon.

'Look hard at this weapon,' he said. 'It killed Ahsha, and it will kill the pharaoh. And it will slit your throat if you betray me.'

44

To celebrate his birthday Ramses had invited Kha and Meneptah to dine, together with Ahmeni, the most loyal of his loyal followers. Ahmeni had had the idea of asking the palace cook to prepare a Ramses' Delight for the occasion, served with a vintage wine from the third year of Seti's reign.

Fortunately for the future of Egypt, there was no dissension between the brothers. Kha pursued his quest for knowledge by studying the ancient texts and the monuments of the past, while Meneptah, in his capacity as commander-in-chief, was responsible for the safety of the kingdom. No other Royal Sons possessed their maturity, their rigour and their feeling for the state. When he judged the moment had come, Ramses would appoint his successor with equanimity.

But who could think of succeeding Ramses the Great who, though now in his sixties, still attracted the eyes of the palace beauties? For a long time now, his reputation had reached far beyond the borders of Egypt, and all the story-tellers, from the south of Nubia to the island of Crete, recounted his legendary exploits. He was the most powerful sovereign in the world, the Son of the Light, and a tireless builder of temples. Never had the gods granted such gifts to a human being.

'Let us drink to Ramses' fame,' proposed Ahmeni.

'No,' the king objected. 'Let us rather celebrate Egypt, our mother, this land which is the reflection of heaven.'

The four men were united in their love of a civilization and a country which offered them so many wonders and to which they dedicated their lives.

'Why isn't Meritamon here?' asked Kha.

'At this moment, she is playing music for the gods,' said Ramses. 'Such is her wish and I respect it.'

'You didn't invite Mat-Hor,' observed Meneptah.

'She is now living in the Mer-Ur harem.'

'But I passed her in the palace kitchens,' said Ahmeni in surprise.

'She should have left the palace already,' said Ramses. 'Tomorrow, Ahmeni, see that my decision has been carried out. Any information about Libya, Meneptah?'

'Nothing new, Majesty. It seems that Malfi is a madman and his dreams of conquest are limited to his sick mind.'

'The Giza ghost has disappeared,' Kha informed them. 'The stone-cutters are working in peace.'

The palace steward presented a missive to the king. It bore Setau's seal and was marked 'Urgent'.

Ramses broke the seal, unrolled the papyrus, read the short message and immediately rose to his feet.

'I'm leaving immediately for Abu Simbel. Finish the meal without me.'

But none of them felt like savouring the marinade, and it was sent back to the kitchens, untouched.

For a moment, the cook was tempted to eat it with his assistants. But this was a royal dish: to touch it would be both an abuse and a violation. With much regret, the cook threw away the festive dish – and, with it, the poison Mat-Hor had poured into it.

Once again, Nubia cast its spell on Ramses. The clarity of the air, the perfect blue of the sky, the enchanting green of the palm groves and the cultivated strip fed by the Nile, combating the inroads of the desert; the flights of pelicans, crested cranes, pink flamingos and ibis; the scent of mimosa; the magical ochre colour of the hills. All this allowed the soul to commune with the hidden forces of nature.

Ramses remained in the bows of the ship bearing him swiftly towards Abu Simbel. He had reduced his escort to the minimum and had himself selected a tireless crew of elite sailors, accustomed to the risks of navigation on the Nile.

Not far from their destination, while the king was taking some refreshment in his cabin, seated on a folding chair with ivory-encrusted feet shaped like ducks' heads, the boat reduced speed.

Ramses called out to the captain, 'What is happening?'

'There's an army of crocodiles on the bank, Majesty, each of them at least fifteen cubits long! And hippopotami in the water. For the moment we can't continue. I even advise Your Majesty to disembark. The animals seem restive, and they might attack us.'

'Sail on, Captain. You have nothing to fear.'

'Majesty, I assure you—'

'Nubia is a land of miracles.'

With their hearts in their mouths the sailors resumed their course. The hippos moved restlessly. On the bank, an enormous crocodile shook its tail, darted forward, then came to a standstill again.

Ramses came out on deck. He had sensed the presence of his ally, even before seeing him. A huge bull elephant parted the lower branches of an acacia with his trunk and trumpeted so loudly that it made hundreds of birds fly off and petrified the sailors.

Some of the crocodiles took refuge on a grassy strip, half submerged; others hurled themselves on the hippopotami, which defended themselves vigorously. The battle was short, then the Nile was calm again.

The elephant trumpeted again for Ramses, who waved his hand in greeting. Many years before, the young Ramses had saved a wounded elephant calf. Now an adult, the animal, with its huge ears and heavy tusks, appeared whenever the king had need of him.

'Shouldn't we capture this monster and take him back to Egypt?' suggested the captain.

'Respect freedom,' said Ramses sternly, 'and be careful to put no obstacle in its way.'

Two mounds projecting far out, a creek, golden sand, a valley separating the two overhanging rocks, acacias scenting the light air, the magical beauty of the Nubian sandstone . . . The sight of Abu Simbel moved Ramses' deeply. He had created there two temples embodying the union of the royal couple which he and Nefertari formed for ever.

As the king had feared, Setau had not exaggerated: the site had been well and truly the victim of an earthquake. The head and torso of one of the four seated *ka* statues had collapsed.

Setau and Lotus greeted the monarch.

'Was anyone injured?' Ramses asked.

'Two dead,' said Setau, 'the Viceroy of Nubia and an ex-prisoner.'

'What were they doing together?'

'I don't know.'

'Any damage inside the temples?'

'See for yourself.'

Ramses went in. The stone-cutters were already at work. They had shored up the damaged pillars of the great hall and straightened those which threatened to collapse.

'Has the building dedicated to Nefertari also suffered?' asked Ramses.

'No, Majesty,' said Setau.

'May the gods be thanked.'

'The work will be dealt with rapidly and every trace of this disaster will be wiped out. The statue will be more difficult, but I've several ideas to put to you.'

'Don't try to repair it.'

'You . . . you're not going to leave the façade in this state?'

'The earthquake was a message from the god of the earth. Since he has remodelled this façade, we must not go against his will.'

The decision shocked Setau, but Ramses was inflexible. Only three statues would perpetuate the presence of the royal *ka*; the fourth, mutilated one would bear witness to the inherent imperfection of all human work, which must eventually show signs of wear. The broken stone giant, far from detracting from the majesty of the ensemble, emphasized the power of the other three.

Ramses, Setau and Lotus dined under a palm tree. The snake-charmer had not asked the king to anoint himself with asafoetida, the resinous gum from the roots of some kinds of giant fennel, whose nauseating stench kept snakes away, but had offered him the red fruit of a shrub* containing an antidote to snake venom.

'You have increased the number of offerings to the gods,' Ramses said to Setau, 'built up stocks of food in the royal granaries, established peace in this turbulent province, built temples throughout Nubia, and have always preferred truth to lies. What would you think about becoming the representative of the justice of Ma'at here?'

'But that's the viceroy's prerogative!'

'I hadn't forgotten that, my friend. You are the new Viceroy of Nubia, appointed by a decree dating from the thirty-eighth year of my reign?'

Setau searched for words to protest, but Ramses didn't give him time.

---

* *Capparis decidua*. (This would be the thorny, trailing bush that gives capers used in pickling. Trans.)

'You can't refuse. For you, too, this earthquake is a sign. Your life takes on a new dimension from today. You know how much I love this region. Take great care of it, Setau.'

The snake-charmer wandered off into the fragrant night. He needed to be alone to take in the decision which made him one of the foremost personalities of the state.

'Will you allow me, Majesty, to ask an impertinent question?' asked Lotus.

'This is a special evening. Of course I will.'

'Why have you waited so long to appoint Setau viceroy?'

'He had to learn to administer Nubia without any thought of such an appointment. Now he lives his vocation and answers a call which has gradually filled his life and his whole being. No one has succeeded in corrupting or degrading him, because the will to serve this province inspires every one of his actions. And he needed time to become aware of this.'

45

Ramses entered the great temple of Abu Simbel to celebrate the dawn rite alone. He followed the path of light which led to the innermost sanctuary and which shone first on the seated statues of Amon and the royal *ka*, then on those of the royal *ka* and Ra. The pharaoh, rather than the man entrusted with this role on earth, was associated with the hidden god and the divine light and with the two great creative gods who, united under the name of Amon-Ra, formed a complete being.

The fourth statue, that of Ptah, remained in the shadows. In his capacity as son of Ptah, Ramses was the builder of his realm and his people. He was also the one who transmitted the Word, by virtue of which all things became real. The king thought about Kha, the High Priest of Ptah, who had chosen the path of this mystery.

When the king emerged from the great temple, a soft light bathed the wooded esplanade and began to bring out the warm colour of the Nubian sandstone, whose mineral gold was a reminder of the flesh of the gods. Ramses made his way towards the temple dedicated to Nefertari, for whom the sun rose. This sun, the nourishing father of Egypt, would rise until the end of time for the Great Royal Wife who had illuminated the Two Lands with her beauty and wisdom.

The queen, immortalized by sculptors and painters, inspired Ramses with a longing to pass into the Hereafter and rejoin her at last. He begged her to take him by the hand, to emerge from these walls where she dwelt, eternally young and beautiful, in the company of her brothers the gods and her sisters the goddesses, she who clothed the world with green and caused the Nile to sparkle. But Nefertari sailed on in the ship of the sun, and simply smiled at Ramses. The king's task was not completed; a pharaoh, whatever his suffering as a man, belonged to the celestial powers and his people. Nefertari, an imperishable star, with her sweet face and wise words, would continue to guide Ramses, helping him to keep the country on the path of Ma'at, until the time when the latter would grant him rest.

The day was drawing to a close when Nefertari's magic prompted the king to return to the outside world in which he had no right to weaken.

On the esplanade were hundreds of Nubians in festive garb. The tribal chiefs and their high officials, wearing wigs dyed red, golden earrings, white gowns down to their ankles, and kilts decorated with floral designs, were laden with gifts: panther-skins, gold rings, ivory, ebony, ostrich feathers and eggs, bags filled with precious stones, fans.

Accompanied by Setau, the most senior chief advanced towards Ramses. 'Homage to the Son of the Light,' he said.

'Homage to the Sons of Nubia, who have chosen peace,' said Ramses. 'May these two temples of Abu Simbel, so dear to my heart, symbolize their union with Egypt.'

'Majesty, the whole of Nubia already knows that you have appointed Setau your viceroy.'

A deep silence reigned over the assembly. If the chiefs disapproved of this decision, unrest would start again. But Ramses would never repudiate Setau. He knew that his friend was born to administer this region and that he would make it happy.

The chief turned to Setau, who was, as usual, dressed in his antelope-skin tunic. 'We thank Ramses the Great for having chosen the man who knows how to save lives, who speaks from his heart and wins ours.'

Moved almost to tears, Setau bowed down before Ramses.

And what he saw terrified him: a horned viper was gliding over the sand towards the king's foot. He tried to cry out to warn the king but he was hailed and carried in triumph by the Nubians, in a great chorus of cheers, and his warning cries were drowned in the din of jubilation.

Just as the viper reared up to strike, a white ibis swooped down from the sky, plunged its beak into the reptile's head and flew off with its prey. Those who had witnessed the scene had no doubts: it was Thoth, in the form of an ibis, who had saved the monarch's life. And since Thoth had shown himself in this way, as viceroy Setau would govern justly and wisely.

Freeing himself from the crowd of his followers, the latter finally managed to approach the king.

'To think that that viper—'

'What were you afraid of, Setau? You immunized me yourself. You must have confidence in yourself, my friend.'

Twice as bad, if not three, ten times worse! Yes, it was worse than Setau had imagined. Since his appointment he had been overwhelmed with work and had to grant audiences to a thousand and one people coming with requests, each more urgent than the last. In a few days he realized that human beings were quite shameless when it came to defending their own interests, even to the detriment of that of others.

In spite of his wish to obey the king and carry out the mission which had been entrusted to him, Setau was tempted to give up. It was easier to capture dangerous snakes than to resolve the conflicts between rival factions.

But the new Viceroy of Nubia had the benefit of two unexpected helpers. The first was Lotus, whose metamorphosis astonished him. He already knew the lover with delightful initiatives, the Nubian liana who knew how to draw enchanting pleasures from her husband's body, the sorceress who could speak the language of snakes. Now she assisted him with the assurance of a woman born to power. Her beauty, unimpaired in spite of the passage of years, was an incalculable advantage when he had discussions with tribal chiefs: they forgot their quarrels, and some of their demands, as they gazed on the ravishing form of the viceroy's wife. In short, she charmed more than just reptiles.

The second ally was still more surprising: Ramses himself. His presence during Setau's first discussions with the senior officers of the Egyptian fortresses was decisive. In spite of their somewhat narrow minds, the officers realized that Setau was not a puppet and that he had the support of the king. Ramses did not utter a single word, leaving his friend to express himself and prove his worth.

At the end of the ceremony to mark the viceroy's installation in the Buhen fortress, Setau and Ramses walked along the ramparts.

'I have never known how to thank you,' said Setau, 'but—'

'No one could have prevented you from asserting yourself; I simply let you have a little time, that's all.'

'You have given me your magic, Ramses, and that force is irreplaceable.'

'The love of this country has taken over your life, and you have accepted the fact because you are a true warrior, passionate and sincere, like this earth.'

'A warrior whom you ask to consolidate the peace!'

'Yes, but peace is the sweetest of foods.'

'You'll be leaving again soon, won't you?' asked Setau.

'You are the viceroy, and your wife is remarkable. It's up to you to make Nubia prosperous.'

'Will you return here, Majesty?'

'I don't know.'

'And yet you, too, love this country.'

'If I lived here, I'd sit under a palm tree on the banks of the

Nile, facing the desert, and I would watch the sun run its course while thinking of Nefertari, and not worry about the affairs of state.'

'Today, for the first time,' said Setau, 'I'm beginning to feel a little of the weight of the burden you bear on your shoulders.'

'That's because you no longer belong to yourself.'

'I haven't your strength, Majesty. I'm afraid this burden may be too heavy for me.'

'Thanks to the snakes, you have vanquished fear. Thanks to Nubia, you will exercise power without becoming its slave.'

Serramanna practised not only boxing, using a dummy made of rags, but also archery, running and swimming. However this orgy of physical exercise did nothing to relieve his loathing of Uri-Teshup. Contrary to his hopes, the Hittite had neither lost his head nor made any mistake which would have allowed the Sardinian to arrest him. And his grotesque union with Tanit was beginning to look like a respectable marriage to which the great families of Pi-Ramses were growing accustomed.

Just as Serramanna was dismissing a ravishing Nubian dancer, whose cheerful sensuality had calmed him a little, one of his underlings rushed in.

'Have you had breakfast, my boy?' asked the Sardinian.

'Well, sir . . . '

'Nile perch, kidneys in sauce, stuffed pigeon, fresh vegetables. That suit you?'

'Oh *yes*, sir.'

'When I'm hungry, my ears are blocked. Let's eat. You can talk afterwards.'

When the meal was over, Serramanna lay back on the cushions. 'What brings you here, my boy?'

'As you told me to, sir, I've been keeping a discreet watch

on Lady Tanit's house while she was away. A man with curly hair and wearing a multicoloured gown went to the door three times.'

'Did you follow him?'

'You didn't tell me to, sir.'

'So I've no reason to be angry with you, eh?'

'Well, sir . . . The third time I did follow him and I wondered if I hadn't made a bad mistake.'

Serramanna rose, and his enormous hand fell on the young man's shoulder. 'Well done, lad! Sometimes it's necessary to know when to disobey. Did you find out anything interesting?'

'I know where he lives.'

46

Serramanna had hesitated for a long time. Should he take direct action and make this suspect talk, or should he first consult Ahmeni? Previously he'd not have thought twice about it; but the former pirate had become an Egyptian and he now believed that respect for justice was a value which allowed human beings to live together peaceably and without affronting the gods. So he went to Ahmeni's office at a time when the latter was working alone by the light of oil-lamps.

Ahmeni was eating some bean broth, freshly baked bread and honey cakes, as he read from wooden tablets. And the miracle continued: no matter how much he ate, he never put on weight.

'It's not a good sign,' he said to Serramanna, 'when you visit me so late.'

'You're wrong. I'm on the track of something interesting, but I haven't yet taken any action.'

Ahmeni was amazed. 'Has Thoth taken you under his ibis wing to protect you and inspire you with a little wisdom? You've done the right thing, Serramanna. For the vizier, respect due to others is no laughing matter.'

'It's in connection with a rich Phoenician, Narish, who lives in a grand house. He has visited Lady Tanit on several occasions.'

'Courtesy visits from a compatriot, perhaps.'

'Narish didn't know that Tanit and Uri-Teshup were on an official journey with the queen. Since they got back, he's been only once – in the middle of the night.'

'Are you by any chance,' asked Ahmeni, 'having Tanit's house watched without permission?'

'Not at all. I owe this information to a watchman responsible for security in the district.'

'You not only take me for a fool, but you also act the diplomat! This is a new Serramanna.' He stopped eating. 'You've made me lose my appetite!'

'Have I made a serious blunder?' the Sardinian asked anxiously.

'No, you've presented the facts shrewdly and correctly. It's the name Narish which worries me.'

'He's a wealthy man and probably influential, but why should he escape justice?'

'He's more influential than you know. Narish is a merchant from Tyre, responsible, with our minister for foreign affairs, for preparing the king's visit to Phoenicia.'

The Sardinian flared up. 'It's a trap! Narish is in contact with Uri-Teshup.'

'He does business with his countrywoman Lady Tanit, a rich businesswoman herself. There's no proof that he's plotting with the Hittite.'

'Don't let's fool ourselves, Ahmeni.'

'I'm in a difficult position. After spending several months in Nubia, to establish Setau's authority, Ramses has taken over the dossiers of our northern protectorates and our commercial partners. The links with Phoenicia had become somewhat slack and he decided to tighten them up by an official visit. You know the king, the risk of an attack won't make him withdraw.'

'We must pursue the inquiry and prove that this Narish is an accomplice of Uri-Teshup!'

'Did you think we were going to sit and do nothing?'

271

The waters of the Nile reflected the gold of the setting sun; in the homes of rich and poor alike, the evening meal was being prepared. The souls of the dead, who had wandered abroad in the company of the day-star and fed on its energy, were returning to their Houses of Eternity, to be regenerated by another form of energy, silence.

However, that evening, the dogs guarding the huge necropolis of Saqqara remained on the alert, for the site had two distinguished visitors: Ramses the Great and his son Kha, who was more elated than usual.

'I'm delighted to welcome you to Saqqara, Majesty!'

'Have you completed your work and discovered the *Book of Thoth*?'

'Most of the ancient structures have been restored, and we are putting the finishing touches to them. As for the *Book of Thoth*, it's just possible that I'm now piecing it together, page by page, and it is in fact one of these pages that I'd like to show you. During your long stay in Nubia, Ptah's masterbuilders and craftsmen have worked without respite.'

His son's joy delighted Ramses. He had rarely seen him so happy.

The vast site of Saqqara was dominated by the main pyramid of Djoser and Imhotep, the first structure to use freestone, whose steps formed a stairway to the sky. But it was not to this extraordinary monument that Kha led his father. He took a newly discovered path, winding towards the north-west of the pyramid.

A shrine with raised pillars, whose bases were adorned with stelae dedicated to the deities by high officials of the state, marked the entrance to a subterranean temple. It was guarded by priests holding torches.

'A bull's tail is attached to Pharaoh's ceremonial kilt,' Kha reminded him, 'for the bull is power above all else. And this power is that of the bull Apis, which allows the Lord of the

272

Two Lands to overcome all obstacles. It was Apis who carried the mummy of Osiris on his back in order to resurrect him by his journey across the sky. I swore to build a sanctuary for the Apis bulls, befitting the greatness of their dynasty. This work is now complete.'

The king and his son followed the torch-bearers into the temple. From generation to generation, the soul of Apis had passed from animal to animal without any break in the transmission of his supernatural strength. Each Apis bull rested in an enormous sarcophagus placed in a shrine. Mummified like humans, the animals had been buried with the treasures of their reign: jewels, precious vases and even tiny figurines with the head of a bull which would come magically alive in the Hereafter, to prevent them suffering any fatigue. The builders had hollowed out and built impressive galleries linking the shrines where the mummified bulls slept peacefully.

'Every day,' Kha explained, 'special priests make offerings in every shrine to let the great soul of Apis grant the pharaoh the strength he needs. I have also had a hospital built, where patients will be lodged in chambers with white plastered walls. There they will undergo sleep cures. Won't Neferet be delighted?'

'Your work is magnificent, my son. It will last for centuries.'*

'Apis is approaching you, Majesty.'

Emerging from the shadows, a colossal black bull advanced slowly towards the pharaoh. The reigning Apis had the bearing of a peaceful monarch. Ramses thought of the terrifying moment when his father had made him confront a wild bull in Abydos. So many years had passed since that episode, which had decided the destiny of the Son of the Light.

The bull came closer.

* In 1850 the French Egyptologist Auguste Mariette discovered the site of the funerary shrines of the bull Apis, known as the Serapeum.

Ramses stood his ground. 'Come to me in peace, my brother,' he said. He touched the bull's horn and the animal licked his hand with its rough tongue.

The senior officials at the secretariat for Foreign Affairs expressed effusive praise and approval for Ramses' plan, congratulating the pharaoh on his remarkable initiative, which was appreciated by all the principalities under the protection of Egypt and Hatti. No one had uttered the slightest criticism or even made any suggestions; were not Ramses the Great's thoughts inspired by the gods?

When Ahmeni entered the king's office, he immediately sensed that all was not well. 'Shall I send for Neferet?' he offered.

'She'll not be able to cure the sickness I'm suffering from.'

'Let me guess: you can't bear flattery.'

'I shall soon have reigned for thirty-nine years, thirty-nine years of spineless, hypocritical courtiers, notables who shower praises on me instead of thinking for themselves, so-called responsible officials who can't live without my decisions – am I supposed to be happy?'

'Did you have to live to be more than sixty to discover what courtiers are like? This moment of weakness is not like you, Majesty. And who do you think *I* am? The gods did not grant me your greatness and breadth of vision, but all the same I say what I think.'

Ramses smiled. 'And you don't approve of my official visit to Phoenicia, do you?'

'According to Serramanna, you could be vulnerable to attack.'

'It's a risk inherent in any travels in that region. But if my magic is effective, what do I have to fear?'

Ahmeni sighed. 'As it is certain that Your Majesty will not abandon this plan, I shall reinforce the security arrangements as far as possible. But is it really essential for you to go to

Tyre? Our commercial agents are capable of resolving many of the problems.'

    'You underestimate the importance of my intervention.'

    'So you have a secret plan.'

    'Your intelligence is a great consolation, Ahmeni.'

47

Uri-Teshup rose late and breakfasted in the garden, in the sun.

'Where's my wife?' he asked the steward.

'The Lady Tanit had business to settle in town.'

The Hittite was not pleased. Why hadn't she told him she had to go out? As soon as she returned he shouted at her, 'Where've you been?'

'I have to see to my property from time to time.'

'Who did you meet?'

'A rich compatriot.'

'What's his name?'

'Are you jealous, my dear?'

Uri-Teshup boxed her ears. 'Don't play games with me; answer me when I question you.'

'You . . . you hurt me!'

'His name!'

'Narish. He'd like to increase the exchanges with Egypt and even act as intermediary for Ramses' forthcoming visit to Phoenicia.'

Uri-Teshup kissed her on the lips. 'Fascinating, my poppet. That's what you should have said straight away, instead of provoking me stupidly. When are you to see this Narish again?'

'We finished our business and I—'

'Think of a new excuse for working with him and get as

much information as possible out of him about this journey. With your powers of seduction, you won't have much trouble.'

Tanit tried to protest, but Uri-Teshup began to make love to her. She fell under his spell and abandoned herself to him. She found it impossible to resist her husband's desire.

'All banquets are cancelled,' Tanit announced to Uri-Teshup, who was having a manicure.

'Why?'

'The bull Apis has just died. During the period of mourning no festivities are allowed.'

'What a ridiculous custom!'

'Not for Egyptians.' Tanit dismissed the manicurist. 'It's Pharaoh's strength itself which is at stake,' she explained. 'He has to discover a bull which can be the new reincarnation of Apis. Otherwise his prestige will decline.'

'Ramses won't have any difficulty.'

'It isn't all that simple, because the animal must have very definite characteristics.'

'What are they?'

'A priest has to be questioned who is a specialist in the worship of Apis.'

'See that we are invited to the funeral ceremony.'

The mortal remains of the old bull Apis, who had died in his enclosure at the temple in Memphis, had been laid on a funerary bed, in the Hall of Purity where, like an Osiris, he had been honoured with a ceremony attended by Ramses and Kha. Resurrection rites had been recited for the deceased; Apis, the magical power of Ptah, the god of builders, had to be treated with the honour due to his role.

When the mummification was completed, the bull had been placed on a strong wooden sledge and taken to the royal ship, which bore him across the Nile. Neither Uri-Teshup nor

Tanit had been admitted to watch the mysterious rites, but they managed to find a talkative priest who was pleased to show off his knowledge.

'To become an Apis, a bull must have a black coat with white markings, a white triangle on its forehead, a crescent on its chest and another on its side, and the hairs of its tail must be alternately black and white.'

'Do many animals meet these criteria?' asked the Hittite.

'No, there's only one bull so fashioned by the gods.'

'What if Pharaoh couldn't find it?'

'He would lose all his strength and many misfortunes would befall the country. But Ramses will not fail in his task.'

'We are all sure of that.'

Uri-Teshup and Tanit withdrew.

'If this creature exists,' said the Hittite, 'we must find it before Ramses does, and kill it.'

Ahmeni looked anxious and tired. It wasn't surprising. Ramses himself had never been able to make his friend slow down the pace of his work, in spite of his many aches and pains.

'There's a lot of good news, Majesty! For example—'

'Begin with the bad news, Ahmeni.'

'Who told you?'

'You've never been able to hide your feelings.'

'As you wish. Emperor Hattusilis has just written to you.'

'Our diplomats correspond regularly. What is unusual about this?'

'He writes to you, his brother, because Mat-Hor has complained of the way you have treated her. Hattusilis is astonished and asks for an explanation.'

Ramses looked angry.

Ahmeni went on, 'She has probably slandered you to provoke her father's anger and stir up discord again between our two peoples.'

'We must reply suitably to my brother Hattusilis.'

'I've taken my inspiration from letters written by Ahsha and I have an letter to submit to you which should appease the emperor.' He showed the king a draft, written on a wooden tablet worn down by being scraped clean many times.

'An elegant diplomatic style,' judged Ramses. 'You continue to make progress.'

'May I entrust the final composition to a scribe with a perfect hand?'

'No, Ahmeni.'

'Why not?'

'Because I shall draw up the reply myself.'

'Forgive me, Majesty, but I fear . . .'

'Are you afraid of the truth?' asked Ramses. 'I shall simply explain to Hattusilis that his daughter is incapable of performing the duties of a Great Royal Wife and that she will live peacefully from now on, in a luxurious retreat, while Meritamon will be at my side for official ceremonies.'

Ahmeni was alarmed. 'Hattusilis may be your brother but he's also a very touchy monarch. Such a blunt reply might provoke an equally violent reaction.'

'No one should take offence at the truth.'

'Majesty . . .'

'Go back to your urgent business, Ahmeni. My letter will leave for Hatti tomorrow.'

Uri-Teshup had chosen his wife well: beautiful, sensual, loving, received in high society, and rich, very rich. Thanks to Lady Tanit's fortune, he had been able to hire a con-siderable number of informers who were to let him know where there were adult bulls with black coats with white markings. As Ramses had not yet begun his search, Uri-Teshup hoped to steal a march on him.

Officially Lady Tanit hoped to buy some herds and in-tended to acquire some good breeding-stock before launching into cattle-rearing. The search had begun around Pi-Ramses, then extended to all the provinces between the capital and Memphis.

'What is Ramses doing?' Uri-Teshup asked Tanit when she returned from the palace, where she had met the officials from the White Double House who were responsible for enforcing the sovereign's economic policy.

'He spends most of his time with Kha. Father and son are reformulating the ancient ritual for the enthronement of the new Apis.'

'Has that damned bull been found yet?'

'It's up to the pharaoh, and the pharaoh alone, to identify it.'

'So why is he doing nothing?'

'The mourning period isn't over yet.'

'If we could dump the dead body of the new bull in front of Apis's temple, Ramses' fame would be destroyed!'

'My steward has a message for you.'

'Show me quickly!'

Uri-Teshup snatched a fragment of limestone out of Tanit's hands. According to a game-beater, a bull meeting the required criteria had been spotted in a little village to the north of Memphis. Its owner was asking an exorbitant price for it.

'I'm leaving immediately,' Uri-Teshup announced.

48

In the middle of the sunny afternoon, the villagers were dozing. Two little girls were playing with their dolls near a well, under a group of palm trees. Close by, their mother was mending wicker baskets.

When Uri-Teshup rode into this peaceful world, the little girls were scared and ran to their mother, who was herself frightened by the violence which emanated from the long-haired horseman.

'You, woman, tell me where I can find the owner of a strong black bull.'

The woman shrank back, clutching her children to her.

'Tell me, or I'll beat you.'

'Just outside the southern end of the village, a farm with an enclosure . . . '

Uri-Teshup galloped off in the direction she indicated. In a few minutes, he saw the enclosure. In it, a magnificent bull, with a black coat with white markings, stood chewing the cud. The Hittite leapt to the ground and examined the bull closely: it did indeed bear all the distinctive marking of an Apis! He ran to the main building of the farm, where labourers were bringing in forage.

'Where's the owner?' he demanded.

'Over there, in the shade.'

Uri-Teshup had reached his goal; he would pay what was

asked, without arguing.

The owner, who was lying on a mat, opened his eyes. 'Did you have a good journey?'

The Hittite froze. 'You!'

Serramanna rose slowly to his feet, unfolding his enormous frame. 'So you're interested in breeding cattle, Uri-Teshup. Excellent idea! It's one of Egypt's strong points.'

'But you aren't—'

'The owner of this farm? Indeed I am! A fine property, which I could afford to buy thanks to Ramses' generosity. I shall spend a peaceful old age here. Don't you want to buy my best bull?'

'No, I don't. I—'

'When Ahmeni and I noticed that you were getting restless, he had an amusing idea: to paint the Apis bull's characteristic markings on this creature's coat. This little joke will remain between you and me, won't it?'

The mourning period would soon be over and the ritualists were beginning to be anxious: why hadn't the king started out in search of the new Apis?

Ramses had made several visits to the underground temple of the mummified bulls, and had worked for whole days on the ritual from the First Dynasty which allowed the Apis to be resurrected. Now he was listening to his son, the High Priest of Ptah, telling him of the continuous action of the god of builders, at work in the heavens, as in beehives or in the depths of the mountains. Ptah's creative words were revealed in men's hearts and then formulated in language, since all living thought must be embodied in a correct and beautiful form.

A week before the crucial day, even Kha could not hide his anxiety. 'Father, the mourning period . . . '

'I know, my son. The successor to the dead Apis exists. Don't worry.'

'If it's far from here, the journey will take time.'

'Tonight I shall sleep in the Temple of Apis, and I shall ask the gods and Nefertari to guide me.'

At nightfall, the king remained alone with the dynasty of the Apis bulls. He knew each one by name and appealed to the one soul that linked them all. Lying on a crude bed in a priest's cell, Ramses abandoned his mind to sleep, not to the simple rest of the body and senses, but to dreams that could rove like tireless birds. As if his being had suddenly been provided with wings, the king rose above the earth, high in the sky, and he could see.

He could see Upper and Lower Egypt, the provinces, towns and villages, great temples and small shrines, the Nile and the irrigation channels, the desert and the cultivated fields.

A strong north wind blew the boat with its two white sails towards Abydos. Ramses stood in the bows and enjoyed admiring his country as he drifted with the water, a pleasure of which he could never tire.

Kha had announced to the ritualists and the court, with an air of great authority, that he was leaving with his father to identify the Apis bull and bring it back to Saqqara. The High Priest knew the dramatic consequences of failure, but refused to contemplate it.

'We have arrived,' he told the king.

'This journey has seemed short. When so much beauty surrounds us, time stands still.'

The entire priesthood of Abydos welcomed the king at the landing-stage.

The High Priest greeted Kha, then asked, 'Has His Majesty come to prepare the mysteries of Osiris?'

'No,' Kha replied. 'Ramses is convinced that the new incarnation of the Apis bull is here.'

'If it were, we would have informed His Majesty! What

does he base his information on?'

'Only he knows.'

The High Priest was filled with dismay. 'Have you tried to reason with your father?'

'He is Ramses.'

Everyone expected the king to explore the surrounding countryside, but he walked unhesitatingly towards the desert, towards the tombs of the pharaohs of the First Dynasty. Their mummies rested in Saqqara, their luminous beings lived on in Abydos. The tombs were shaded by tamarisk trees.

Under the trees, Ramses saw it: a magnificent black bull, which raised its head to look at the man who came towards it. It was exactly the scene that the pharaoh had gazed on in the dream vouchsafed him by the community of Apis bulls. The creature showed no sign of fierceness. One would have sworn it was meeting an old friend again after a long separation.

The bull had a white triangle on its forehead, white crescents on its chest and side, and black and white hairs alternating on its tail.

'Come, Apis. I am taking you to your home.'

When the royal ship drew alongside the main quay in the port of Memphis, the whole town was already rejoicing. The dignitaries of Pi-Ramses had left the capital and come to admire the new Apis, whose strength would allow the pharaoh to reign for many more long years. Even Ahmeni had undertaken the journey, not to take part in the festivities but because he was the bearer of bad news.

The bull and the king disembarked side by side amid cheers, and made their way towards the Temple of Ptah where, in a vast enclosure near the sanctuary, the incarnation of Apis would now live, surrounded by cows each more magnificent than the last.

In front of the gate of the enclosure an ancient rite took place. A lady of high birth, known and respected, and of an excellent reputation, faced the bull. She lifted her gown and revealed her private parts. In this way, while the crowd laughed, the priestess of Hathor greeted the seed-sower who would impregnate the cows, animals sacred to the goddess, and ensure the continued lineage of the Apis bulls.

From the front row of the spectators, Uri-Teshup didn't know where to look. This strange scene, this shameless woman who was also laughing heartily, this impassive bull and all these people lost in worship of Ramses. This Ramses who seemed indestructible!

Anyone else would have given up; but Uri-Teshup was a Hittite warlord, and Ramses had stolen his throne. He would never forgive him for having reduced the Hittite nation, once victorious conquerors, to a timorous bunch bowing down before the former enemy.

The great double gates of the temple closed. While the people danced and sang, ate and drank, at Pharaoh's expense, Ramses and Kha and a college of ritualists celebrated the enthronement ritual for the new Apis, of which the culminating point was the bull racing with the mummy of Osiris on its back, the reconstituted and reanimated body of the god who could vanquish death.

'How can anyone like travelling so much?' grumbled Ahmeni. 'And all this time, there are worrying and urgent matters accumulating on my desk!'

'If you have taken the trouble to come here,' Ramses remarked, 'you must have an important reason.'

'You're going to accuse me again of disturbing a period of festivities.'

'Have I done so?'

Ahmeni muttered something inaudible, then said, 'Emperor Hattusilis has replied surprisingly quickly. You only have to read between the lines to sense his anger. He disapproves of your attitude, and he is making scarcely veiled threats.'

Ramses was silent for several minutes. 'Since my arguments haven't convinced him, we shall try different tactics. Take a new papyrus, Ahmeni, and your best writing-brush. My suggestions will surprise my brother Hattusilis.'

49

'The negotiations are completed,' Tanit told Uri-Teshup, 'and Narish has left again for Tyre, to be there to welcome Ramses with the mayor of the city and local notables.'

The Hittite grasped the hilt of the iron dagger, which never left him.

'Haven't you obtained any more confidential information?'

'The itinerary isn't a secret and the king will be accompanied by Meneptah, who will lead two elite regiments. Any attack against them would be doomed to failure.'

Uri-Teshup was furious. Malfi didn't yet have enough men at his disposal to fight a battle on this scale.

'It's strange all the same,' Tanit added. 'The senior officials of the White Double House haven't made any particular demands, as if the pharaoh wasn't really interested in economic problems. And yet there are some contentious points which Egypt usually has plenty to say about.'

'What do you conclude from this?'

'That Ramses is hiding the real aim of his journey.'

Uri-Teshup was puzzled. 'You're probably right. Well, find out what it is.'

'How?'

'Go to the palace, get the courtiers to talk, steal documents, anything – use your wits, Tanit!'

'But, my dear—'

'Don't argue. I have to know.'

Ramses marched at the head of his army, immediately behind Meneptah and the scouts. Throughout the journey his son had continuously checked the security arrangements The king himself had shown no signs of anxiety.

'If you reign,' he said to Meneptah, 'don't forget to visit our protectorates at regular intervals; if Kha does, remind him to do the same. When Pharaoh is away for too long, rebellion tends to disturb the harmony; when he is nearby, hearts are appeased.'

The path round the foot of Mount Carmel, sloping gently down to the sea, was wide and safe. The sea. It was a strange sight for many of the Egyptian soldiers, an incredible, endless expanse of water. The experienced soldiers told the younger ones that they mustn't swim too far out, or they might be dragged under the water by an evil spirit. It was safe, though, to splash about in the foam at the water's edge.

In spite of the old hands' comforting words, the young recruits were not reassured. The succession of huge waves, breaking against rocky spurs which jutted out into the sea, made them miss the banks of the Nile.

They found the countryside less forbidding: cultivated fields, orchards and olive groves were evidence of the agricultural wealth of the region. But the ancient city of Tyre faced the open sea; an inlet formed a sort of impassible ditch, a protection against any attack by an enemy fleet. The new city had been built on three small islands separated by shallow channels with dry docks along them.

The Tyrians were watching Pharaoh and the soldiers from the top of the watchtowers. A delegation, led by Narish, came to meet the Lord of Egypt. They exchanged warm greetings and Narish guided Ramses enthusiastically through the narrow alleyways of the city. Meneptah kept his eyes glued to the rooftops, from where danger could erupt at any moment.

Tyre was dedicated to trade: the sale of glassware, gold and silver vases, cloth dyed purple, and many other goods which passed through the port. Houses four or five storeys high crowded close to each other.

The Mayor of Tyre, an intimate friend of Narish, had put his luxurious home at Ramses' disposal. It was built at the very end of the city, overlooking the sea. Its flower-filled terrace was a wonder to behold, and the owner of this huge dwelling had carried sophistication so far as to furnish it in the Egyptian style, in order to make the pharaoh feel at home.

'I hope everything will be to your satisfaction, Majesty,' said Narish. 'Your visit is a great honour. This evening you will preside over a banquet which will go down in our history. Can we hope that our trade connections with Egypt will expand?'

'I have no objections, but there is one condition,'

'That we reduce our profits. I suspected as much. We are not against this, providing that we can make up for it by increasing the number of transactions.'

'I was thinking of another condition.'

In spite of the mild air, Narish felt the blood run cold in his veins. After the peace treaty, Egypt had agreed to the region being under Hittite control, even if, in fact, it enjoyed real independence. Was a disastrous wish for power urging Ramses lay hands on Phoenicia, at the risk of breaking the treaty and provoking war?

'What are your demands, Majesty?'

'Let us go to the port. Meneptah will accompany us.'

On the king's orders, the latter had to be satisfied with a reduced escort.

At the extreme western end of the port were some hundred men of varying ages and origins, naked and in chains. Some tried to retain at least an appearance of dignity, others stared blankly into space.

Curly-haired Tyrians were discussing prices, either for

individuals or for batches. They counted on making considerable profits on the sale of these slaves, who were all in good health. There promised to be hard bargaining.

'I require these men to be freed,' demanded Ramses.

Narish was amused. 'They are worth a great deal. Allow the city of Tyre to make you a gift of them, Majesty.'

'This is the real reason for my journey. No Tyrian who wishes to trade with Egypt must traffic in slaves.'

The Phoenician was shocked, and it was all he could do to keep calm and not protest vigorously. 'Majesty,' he said, 'slavery is a law of nature. Trading societies have always practised it.'

'There's no slavery in Egypt,' said Ramses. 'Human beings are the gods' flock and no individual has the right to treat another as an object without a soul, or as merchandise.'

Narish had never heard such wild talk. If the speaker had not been the Pharaoh of Egypt, he would have thought him a madman.

'Weren't your prisoners of war reduced to slavery, Majesty?'

'They were sentenced to hard labour for periods that varied according to the seriousness of the accusations made against them. When they were freed they could do as they pleased. Most of them remained in Egypt, and many of them founded families.'

'Slaves are essential for a great many works!' protested Narish.

'The law of Ma'at insists on a contract between the one who orders a piece of work and the one who carries it out. Otherwise there can be no joy in any work, from the most sublime to the most humble. And this contract is based on each side giving his word. Do you think the pyramids and the temples could have been built by gangs of slaves?'

'Majesty, such ancient customs cannot be changed.'

'I am not naive, and I am aware that most countries

continue to practise slavery. But now you know my demands.'

'Egypt may lose some important markets.'

'The main thing is for her to preserve her soul. Pharaoh is not the patron of merchants, but the representative of Ma'at on earth and the servant of her people.'

Meneptah felt as though Ramses' words had been engraved on his heart. For him the journey to Tyre would remain a major step.

Uri-Teshup was so on edge that to calm his nerves he had chopped down a hundred-year-old sycamore tree that shaded a lake where ducks loved to swim. Lady Tanit's gardener was so horrified that he had gone to hide in the hut where he kept his tools.

'There you are, at last!' the Hittite exclaimed when his wife arrived back home.

Tanit gazed at the sorry sight. 'Was it you who—'

'This is my own home and I do what I like here! What did you find out at the palace?'

'Let me sit down. I'm tired.'

The little tabby cat jumped on to its mistress's lap; she stroked its head automatically and it purred.

'Speak, Tanit!'

'You'll be disappointed. The true aim of Ramses' journey was to combat slavery, which continues to expand in Tyre and the region.'

The Hittite slapped her hard. 'Don't try to make a fool of me!'

In an attempt to defend its mistress the little cat scratched Uri-Teshup, who seized it by the scruff of its neck and slit its throat with his iron dagger.

Tanit was spattered with blood and ran in horror to take refuge in her chamber.

50

Ahmeni was relieved. Serramanna was depressed.

'Ramses has returned safe and sound from Phoenicia, and I can breathe again,' the former said. 'Why are you in such a bad mood?'

'Because the Narish trail has led to a dead end.'

'What were you hoping for?'

'Proof that he was doing shady business with Lady Tanit. I could have threatened to arrest her if she didn't tell me the truth about Uri-Teshup.'

'You're obsessed with that man! Take care it doesn't end up clouding your judgment.'

'Are you forgetting that he murdered Ahsha?' demanded Serramanna.

'You've still got no proof.'

'Unfortunately, you're right about that.'

The Sardinian felt he was growing old. Him, respecting the law! He had to admit his failure and accept it. Uri-Teshup had proved cunning enough to escape Egyptian justice.

'I'm going to bed,' he said morosely.

'A new mistress?'

'Not even that. I'm tired and I'm going to sleep.'

'A lady to see you, my lord,' Serramanna's steward announced.

'I haven't sent for a girl.'

'She isn't a "girl", my lord, she's a lady of quality. I asked her to sit and wait in the guest room.'

Serramanna was intrigued and strode across the reception hall. 'Tanit!'

The lovely Phoenician rose, burst into tears and flung herself into his arms. Her hair was unkempt, and there were ugly bruises on her face. 'Protect me, please!' she implored him.

'I'd like to, but from what or whom?'

'From the monster who's made me his slave!'

Serramanna was careful not to show his satisfaction. 'If you want me to act officially, Lady Tanit, you must make a complaint.'

'Uri-Teshup cut my cat's throat, he chopped down a sycamore in my garden and he never stops beating me.'

'Those are offences for which he can be fined, or even sentenced to hard labour. But that won't be enough to prevent him harming you.'

'Will your men keep watch over me?'

'My men form the king's personal bodyguard and they can't intervene in a private matter. Unless, of course, it becomes a state matter . . . '

Drying her tears, Tanit freed herself from Serramanna's arms and looked him straight in the face. 'Uri-Teshup wants to assassinate Ramses. His ally is the Libyan Malfi – they concluded an alliance in my own home. Uri-Teshup killed Ahsha with an iron dagger that he never lets out of his sight. And he wants to kill the king with that same dagger. Is it a state matter now?'

A hundred men were deployed around Lady Tanit's house. Archers climbed the trees overlooking the garden, others clambered on to the roofs of neighbouring houses.

Was Uri-Teshup alone or with the Libyans? Would he take the servants hostage if he realized he was surrounded?

Serramanna had insisted they approach in complete silence, knowing that the slightest mistake would warn the Hittite.

That was exactly what happened. One of the men missed his footing while climbing the surrounding wall and fell into some bushes. An owl hooted. Serramanna's men froze. They stayed still for a few minutes, then the Sardinian gave the order to advance.

Uri-Teshup had no chance of escaping, but he would not surrender without a fight. Serramanna hoped to capture him alive and bring him to trial before the vizier.

Serramanna and a dozen of his men crawled along the ground, which was damp with dew, until they reached the paving round the house. There was a light in Tanit's bedchamber. They stormed inside.

Tanit's maid screamed with fright and dropped her terracotta oil-lamp, which broke, plunging the room into darkness. For a few minutes confusion reigned; the mercenaries fought invisible opponents and attacked furniture with their swords.

'Calm down!' shouted Serramanna. 'Let's have some light, quickly!'

Other lamps were lit. The trembling maid was held prisoner by two soldiers, who threatened her with their swords.

'Where is Uri-Teshup?' Serramanna asked.

'When he realized that my lady had disappeared, he mounted his best horse and galloped off as fast as he could.'

In his frustration, the Sardinian smashed a piece of Cretan pottery. The Hittite's soldier's instinct had saved him: sensing that he was in danger, he had fled.

For Serramanna, being admitted into Ramses' austere office was like entering the innermost recesses of the country's most secret sanctuary.

Not only Ramses but Ahmeni and Meneptah were there.

'Lady Tanit has gone back to Phoenicia after giving

evidence before the vizier,' Serramanna told them. 'Uri-Teshup was seen by several people, riding in the direction of Libya. So he has joined his ally Malfi.'

'Pure hypothesis,' said Ahmeni.

'No, it's a certainty! Uri-Teshup has nowhere else to hide and he won't ever give up the fight against Egypt.'

'Unfortunately,' Meneptah said regretfully, 'we can't locate Malfi's camp. He's continually on the move. But, when you think about it, our failure is reassuring. It proves that he hasn't succeeded in gathering a real army.'

'We must not relax our vigilance,' ordered Ramses. 'The alliance of these two evil, violent creatures is a considerable danger.'

Serramanna adopted his most dignified manner. 'Majesty, I have a request to make to you.'

'Yes, Serramanna?'

'I'm convinced we'll find this monster Uri-Teshup again somewhere. I ask for the privilege of fighting him, in the hope of killing him with my own hands.'

'Granted.'

'Thank you, Majesty. Whatever the future holds, thanks to you I have had a good life.' The Sardinian withdrew.

'You seem annoyed,' Ramses said to Meneptah.

'After endlessly travelling across more or less hostile regions, Moses and the Hebrews are approaching Canaan, which they consider their Promised Land.'

'Moses must be delighted.'

'Perhaps, but the tribes in that region certainly aren't. They're afraid of that bellicose people. That's why I once again request permission for military intervention, to nip this danger in the bud.'

'Moses will continue his quest to the end and he will find a land where his followers can live as they wish. That is as it must be, my son, and we shall not intervene. One day we may have discussions with this new state and perhaps become allies.'

'And what if it becomes an enemy?' asked Meneptah.

'Moses will not become the enemy of his birthplace. Concern yourself with the Libyans, not with the Hebrews.'

Meneptah did not insist. Although he was not convinced by his father's arguments, he accepted that it was his duty to obey.

'We have received news from your brother Hattusilis,' Ahmeni said.

'Good or bad?'

'The emperor hasn't made up his mind.'

Even when the sun beat down, Hattusilis felt cold. He could never manage to get warm inside his citadel with its thick stone walls. Standing with his back to the wood fire that crackled in a vast fireplace, he again read to Putuhepa the Pharaoh of Egypt's proposals.

'Ramses' audacity is incredible! I send him a letter of reprimand and he dares to reply that I should send him another Hittite princess to set the seal on another diplomatic marriage and consolidate the peace. Better still, that I myself go to Egypt!'

'That's a wonderful idea,' Putuhepa said. 'An official visit by you will be striking proof that the peace concluded between our two peoples is irreversible.'

'You're not serious! Me, the Emperor of Hatti, present myself like a subject of Pharaoh!'

'No one's asking you to humble yourself. You can be certain we shall be received with all the honours due to our rank. The letter of agreement is drawn up; you have only to put your seal on it.'

'We must think about it a little longer and start discussions.'

'The time for parleying is past. We must prepare to set out for Egypt.'

'Have you by any chance appointed yourself head of the

Hittite diplomatic service?'

'My sister Nefertari and I built the peace. The Emperor of Hatti must consolidate it.'

Putuhepa's innermost ardent thoughts were of the most attractive man she had ever known, Ahsha, who now dwelt in the paradise for the righteous. For him this day was a day for rejoicing.

51

When Mat-Hor heard the news which was exciting the whole of Egypt, namely the announcement of her parents' official visit, she thought she was back in favour. True, her existence in the Mer-Ur harem was luxurious and her position offered her countless pleasures of which she never tired, but in reality she was living in a gilded cage. She did not reign; she was a wife in name only, deprived of all power.

She wrote a long, vitriolic letter to Ahmeni, demanding that she be allowed to carry out the duties of the Great Royal Wife and welcome the Emperor and Empress of Hatti, and ordering an escort to take her back to the palace in Pi-Ramses.

The reply, signed by Ramses, was scathing: Mat-Hor would not be present at the ceremonies and would remain in the Mer-Ur harem. She flew into a rage, then paused to reflect: what better way to harm the pharaoh than by preventing Hattusilis's arrival? Intrigued by this idea, she contrived a meeting with the priest of the crocodile god, whose reputation as a ritualist was well established.

'In Hatti,' she told him, 'we often consult soothsayers to find out about the future. They read the entrails of animals.'

'Isn't that a little . . . crude?' asked the priest.

'Do you use other methods?'

'It's up to the pharaoh to ascertain the future.'

'But you, the priests, do you hold the secret of certain

methods?'

'There is a body of state magicians, Majesty, but their training is long and demanding.'

'Don't you ever question the gods yourselves?'

'Under certain circumstances, and with the king's permission, the High Priest of Amon questions the creative power, and the god replies through his oracle.'

'And everyone submits to the god's decision, I suppose.'

'Who would dare resist the will of Amon?'

Sensing the priest's reluctance, Mat-Hor did not importune him any further. That day, after ordering her staff not to mention her absence, she set out for Thebes.

Sweet-smiling death remembered at last that Nebu, the High Priest of Amon, had reached a venerable age. Nebu died in his little house near the sacred lake of Karnak, in the certainty of having given good service to the hidden god, the principle of all life, and to the pharaoh Ramses, his representative on earth.

Bakhen, the Second Prophet of Amon, immediately informed the king, who came to pay tribute to Nebu, one of those upright men thanks to whom the Egyptian tradition was perpetuated, whatever the attacks made by the forces of evil.

The silence of mourning weighed on the vast temple of Karnak. Ramses celebrated the dawn ritual, then met Bakhen near the gigantic scarab at the north-west corner of the sacred lake; it symbolized the rebirth of the sun after its victory over darkness.

'The time has come, Bakhen,' said Ramses. 'You have come a long way since our first meeting in the distant past, and you have never given a thought to yourself. The splendour of the Theban temples is partly owing to you; your administration is irreproachable and everyone is pleased with your authority. Yes, the time has come to appoint you High Priest of Karnak and First Prophet of Amon.'

Bakhen's deep, hoarse voice shook with emotion. 'Majesty, I don't think . . . Nebu, he . . . '

'Nebu proposed you as his successor, and he was a good judge of men. I hand you the staff and the gold ring, insignia of your new dignity. You will govern this sacred city and will see that it does not deviate from its role.'

Bakhen was already taking a grip on himself. Ramses felt that he was buckling down there and then to his countless tasks, without thinking of the prestige which such an enviable title conferred on him.

'I have to speak my mind, Majesty. Here in the South, certain notables are shocked by your decision.'

'Are you referring to the official visit of the Emperor and Empress of Hatti?'

'Exactly.'

'Several notables in the North share their opinion, but this visit will take place, for it will consolidate the peace.'

'A number of priests wish to consult the oracle. If Amon grants his consent, there will be an end to all protests.'

'Prepare the ceremony for the oracle, Bakhen.'

On the advice of one of the administrators of the Mer-Ur harem, Mat-Hor had knocked at the right door, that of a rich Syrian merchant; no event in the life of Thebes escaped his notice. He lived in a sumptuous house on the east bank, not far from the temple of Karnak, and received the queen in a hall with two pillars, decorated with paintings of cornflowers and irises.

'What an honour, Majesty, for a humble merchant!'

'This conversation will not have taken place and we shall never have met. Is that clear?'

She presented the Syrian with a gold necklace and he smiled as he bowed to her.

'If you give me the help I need, I shall be very generous.'

'What is it that you wish?'

'I'm interested in the oracle of Amon.'

'The rumour is confirmed: Ramses is in fact going to consult it.'

'Why?'

'He will ask the god to approve your parents' visit to Egypt.'

Luck was on Mat-Hor's side. With fate having done the best part of the work, it only remained for her to finish it.

'And if Amon refuses?' she asked.

'Ramses will be obliged to submit. And I daren't imagine the Emperor of Hatti's reaction if that happened! But Pharaoh is the brother of the gods. The oracle's reply cannot be negative.'

'I insist that it must be.'

'How . . . ?'

'I repeat, help me and you will become very rich. How does the god reply?'

'Priests carry the boat of Amon and the First Prophet questions the god. If the boat moves forward, the reply is "yes"; if it moves back, it means "no".'

'Bribe the men who carry the boat, and see that Amon rejects Ramses' proposal.'

'That's impossible.'

'You must manage to replace the most obstinate men with ones you can rely on. Give potions to those who prove incorruptible, to make them ill. If you succeed I'll shower you with gold.'

'The risks . . . '

'You no longer have any choice, merchant. You are my accomplice now. Don't back out and don't betray me, or I shall show no mercy.'

When the Syrian was alone, looking at the bags of gold nuggets and precious stones which the Hittite had given him as an advance on his future fortune, he reflected for a long time. Some people asserted that Mat-Hor would never regain the trust of the king, but others were convinced that she would; and some priests in Karnak, jealous of Bakhen's rise to power, were ready to play a nasty trick on him.

It was impracticable to bribe all the men carrying the boat, but it would be enough just to buy off the strongest; the god would hesitate, unsure whether to go forward or back, and then would clearly demonstrate his refusal.

The game was playable – and the wealth so tempting!

Thebes was in a state of excitement. Everywhere in the city and all over the countryside, it was known that 'the great celebration of the divine audience' was to take place, during which Amon and Ramses would once more demonstrate that they were in communion.

Every personality of the great city of the South was present in the courtyard of the temple where the ritual was to take place. The mayor, administrators, property-owners: no one would miss this exceptional event at any price.

When the boat of Amon left the cover of the temple and emerged into the sunlight, all held their breath. In the middle of the boat of gilded wood was the inner shrine containing the divine statue. The statue was hidden from human eyes, yet it was this living effigy which would make the decision.

The bearers advanced slowly over the silver paving. Bakhen, the new High Priest of Amon, noticed several new faces among them, but he had been told that several of those entitled to carry out this duty had been prevented by a stomach upset from taking part in the ceremony.

The boat halted in front of the pharaoh.

Bakhen spoke. 'I, the servant of Amon, I question you in the name of Ramses, the Son of the Light. Is the Pharaoh of Egypt right to invite the Emperor and Empress of Hatti to this country?'

Even the swallows ceased swooping around in the blue sky. As soon as the god replied positively, Ramses would be greeted by universal acclamation.

Bribed by the Syrian merchant, the strongest bearers exchanged glances and tried to step back. In vain. They thought that their colleagues who were determined to go forward were resisting them, but that would not last long, so they made a decisive effort.

But a strange force obliged them to advance. Dazzled by a light which shone out from the shrine, they gave up the struggle.

Amon approved the decision of his son Ramses. The rejoicing could begin.

52

Stooping slightly, his hair greying, but his eye still inquisitive, he looked at first glance like a rather ordinary man whom no one need fear. But there could be no doubt about it: it was the Emperor of Hatti himself, wrapped in a thick woollen cloak to protect him from the feeling of cold which, winter or summer, never left him. It was he, the head of a warlike, victorious nation, the supreme commander of the Hittite troops at Kadesh; Hattusilis, undisputed lord of a rugged land where he had wiped out all opposition.

And Hattusilis had just set foot on Egyptian soil, followed by two women, Empress Putuhepa and a timid young Hittite princess.

'It's impossible,' murmured the Emperor of Hatti, 'absolutely impossible. No, this is not Egypt.'

Yet he was not dreaming: it was indeed Ramses the Great who came towards his former enemy to embrace him.

'How fares my brother Hattusilis?'

'I grow old, brother Ramses.'

The flight of Uri-Teshup, who from now on was as much the enemy of Egypt as of Hatti, and who was wanted for murder, had removed any obstacle to Hattusilis's official visit.

'Nefertari would have appreciated this extraordinary moment,' Ramses said to Putuhepa, who looked magnificent in her long scarlet gown, adorned with Egyptian gold jewels which the pharaoh had presented to her.

'All through our journey, I never stopped thinking of her,' the empress said. 'However long you reign, she will always be your only Great Royal Wife.' Her words smoothed away any diplomatic problems.

Pi-Ramses was in festive mood in the light of the scorching summer sun. The City of Turquoise was illuminated to welcome the thousands of dignitaries who had come from all the cities of Egypt to be present at the arrival of the sovereigns of Hatti and the many ceremonies planned in their honour. Knowing that Amon had given Ramses his consent, the population welcomed the illustrious visitors enthusiastically.

The imperial couple were dazzled by the beauty and wealth of the capital. Standing beside the pharaoh in his chariot drawn by two caparisoned horses, Hattusilis went from surprise to surprise.

'Does my brother enjoy no protection?'

'My personal bodyguard keeps watch,' Ramses replied.

'But all these people, so close to us . . . We cannot be safe!'

'Look at the expression in my people's eyes, brother. You will see neither hatred nor aggression. Today, they thank us for having established peace and we share in their rejoicing.'

'A population that is not governed by terror . . . how strange! And has Ramses succeeded in raising an army capable of resisting Hatti's might?'

'The Egyptians all love their country just as the gods love it.'

'You were the one, Ramses, who prevented me from being victorious, you and no one else. In the last few minutes, I've stopped regretting it.' He removed his woollen cloak; he no longer felt cold. 'This climate suits me,' he said. 'A pity . . . I'd have liked to live here.'

The first reception given at the Pi-Ramses palace was on a grand scale. There were so many delicious dishes that

Hattusilis and Putuhepa could only take bites here and there, while sipping from goblets filled with a remarkable wine. Delightful bare-breasted musicians charmed their ears and eyes, while the empress admired the elegant gowns worn by the noble ladies.

'I would like these festivities to be dedicated to Ahsha,' suggested Putuhepa. 'He gave his life for peace, for this happiness which both our peoples now enjoy.'

The emperor approved but looked vexed. 'I regret that our daughter is not present,' he remarked.

'I shall not go back on my decision,' stated Ramses. 'Although Mat-Hor has made grave mistakes, she will remain the symbol of peace and, in this capacity, will have the honour she deserves. Must I be more precise?'

'Better not, brother Ramses. It is sometimes good not to know some details.'

So Ramses avoided mentioning the arrest of the Syrian merchant, who had denounced Mat-Hor, thinking to clear himself by slandering the queen.

'Does Pharaoh wish to converse with his future wife?' asked Hattusilis.

'That will not be necessary. We shall celebrate this second marriage of convenience with pomp and ceremony and our two peoples will be grateful. But the time for sentiment and desire has passed.'

'Nefertari is indeed unforgettable,' said Hattusilis, 'and rightly so. I don't think that the princess I have chosen, who is pretty but unintelligent, is capable of conversing with Ramses the Great. She will discover the pleasure of living in Egypt and will never cease to enjoy it. As for Mat-Hor, who did not love Hatti, every day she will appreciate more and more her adopted country, where she was so anxious to live. With age, she will become more reasonable.'

The emperor had just sealed the fate of two Hittite princesses. In this fortieth year of Ramses' reign, there no longer existed any motive for a quarrel between Egypt and Hatti. Intense joy lit up Empress Putuhepa's brown eyes.

The gateways, obelisks, statues, great open courtyards, colonnades, scenes of offerings, silver pavings, all fascinated Hattusilis. He was also interested in the House of Life, with its books, storehouses, stables, kitchens and offices where scribes were at work. He was most impressed by his discussions with the vizier and his ministers; the structure of Egyptian society was as grand as the architecture of its temples.

Ramses invited Hattusilis to burn incense to delight the nostrils of the gods and attract them to the homes men had built for them. The empress took part in the ritual for appeasing dangerous forces, performed by Kha with his accustomed rigour. And then came the visit to the temples of Pi-Ramses, in particular the sanctuaries devoted to foreign gods; and the emperor was able to rest and relax for a moment in the palace gardens.

'It would have been regrettable if the Hittite army had destroyed so beautiful a city,' he said to Ramses. 'The empress is delighted with her stay. Since we are at peace, will my brother allow me to ask a favour?'

Hattusilis's relative passivity was beginning to arouse Ramses' curiosity. The emperor was fighting against the spell Egypt cast on him, and the strategist was now getting the upper hand.

'The empress and I are dazzled by so many wonders, but it is sometimes necessary to think about less cheerful things,' Hattusilis went on. 'We have signed a mutual assistance pact, in the event of any attacks against our respective countries, and I would like to see the state of the Egyptian army. Would the pharaoh allow me to visit the main barracks of Pi-Ramses?'

If Ramses replied 'military secret' or led the emperor to

smaller barracks, Hattusilis would know that he was up to something. It was the moment of truth, for which he had agreed to make this journey.

'Meneptah, my younger son, the commander-in-chief of the Egyptian army, will take the Emperor of Hatti to visit the main barracks of Pi-Ramses.'

At the end of the banquet organized in honour of Empress Putuhepa, Hattusilis and Ramses took a little stroll round a pool covered with blue and white water-lilies.

'I feel something which up to now has been foreign to me,' Hattusilis said. 'Trust. Only Egypt is able to create beings as great as you, brother Ramses. To have succeeded in creating genuine friendship between two sovereigns formerly prepared to destroy each other is nothing short of a miracle. But you and I are growing old and should be thinking of our succession. Whom have you chosen among your many Royal Sons?'

'Kha is a man of learning, profound, thoughtful, capable of appeasing minds under all circumstances, and of convincing people without giving offence. He would be able to preserve the unity of the kingdom and would deliberate long before making any decision. Meneptah is brave, he can command and administer, and he is loved by the military and feared by the senior officials. Both of them are capable of reigning.'

'In other words, you have still not made up your mind. Well, fate will send you a sign. With such men I have no worries about the future of Egypt. They will know how to continue your work.'

'And have you chosen your own successor?'

'It will be a nonentity, chosen from among nonentities. Hatti is declining, as if the peace has cut off her virility and removed all ambition. But I have no regrets, for there was no other choice. We shall at least have experienced a few tranquil years and I shall have given my people a happiness they had never known before. Unfortunately, my country will not be able to develop and it will disappear. Ah . . . I have another request to make to you. In my capital, I am not accustomed to walking so much and my feet hurt. I've been given to understand that the head physican of the kingdom is very competent and, what is more, is a very beautiful woman.'

Neferet left the great reception hall of the palace, where she was conversing with Putuhepa, and came to take a look at the imperial toes.

'It's a complaint which I'm familiar with and which I can treat,' she said after her examination. 'In the first instance I shall apply an ointment made from red ochre, honey and hemp. Tomorrow morning I shall use another remedy, made of acacia and jujube leaves, ground malachite and the inside of a mussel, all pounded together into a powder. This second ointment will give you a pleasant cooling sensation, but you must also keep your ankles bandaged when you walk.'

'If I offered you a fortune, Neferet, would you come back to Hatti with me and become my personal physician?'

'You know that I would not, Majesty.'

'Then I shall never conquer Egypt,' Hattusilis said with a slight smile.

53

Fine-Shanks was whistling a song in praise of Ramses, as he made his way towards the north-west border of the Delta, with his donkey laden with pottery. Not far from the coast, washed by the waves of the Mediterranean, the pedlar took winding paths to reach a little fishing village, where he was certain of selling his goods.

Fine-Shanks was proud of the name given him by the girls who watched the men running races on the damp sand at the edge of the sea. For more than two years, no competitor had beaten him. And the girls admired the efforts of the naked athletes displaying their strength to captivate them. Thanks to his strong legs, he was the fastest runner to the west of the Delta and had lost count of his conquests.

This success had more than one good side, for these young ladies loved jewellery and Fine-Shanks had to do a great deal of business to keep up his reputation as a great and generous champion. So he enthusiastically travelled back and forth along every path to make the greatest possible profit from his trading.

Some cranes flew overhead; low clouds were blown across the sky by the wind. Observing the position of the sun, Fine-Shanks realized that he would not reach his destination by nightfall. It would be better to stop at one of the reed huts which were found at intervals along the road. It was wiser, too, because when darkness fell on the coastal region, dangerous creatures emerged from their lairs and attacked foolhardy travellers.

Fine-Shanks unloaded his donkey, fed it, and then lit a fire with a flint and tinder. He ate two grilled fish and drank some water kept cool in a jar. Then he lay down on his mat and fell asleep.

As he was dreaming of his next race and his new triumph, a noise woke him. The donkey was scraping the ground with its front hoof. Between him and his master, that was a clear signal: danger.

Fine-Shanks rose, put out the fire and hid behind some thorn-bushes. It was as well he did, for some thirty armed men, wearing helmets and breastplates, appeared out of the shadows. The moon was full that night, which enabled him to see their leader clearly. He was bare-headed, with long hair, and his chest was covered with a mat of red hair.

'There must have been a spy here and he's fled!' exclaimed Uri-Teshup, planting his spear in the ground.

'I don't think so,' objected Malfi, 'Look at all those pots and this donkey. It was a travelling merchant who decided to stop and rest here.'

'All the villages to the west of this zone are under our control. We must find this spy and kill him. We must spread out.'

Four years had passed since the visit of Emperor Hattusilis and Empress Putuhepa. Relations between Egypt and Hatti remained stable and the spectre of war had vanished. Regular waves of Hittite visitors came to admire the countryside and the cities of the Delta.

Ramses' two Hittite wives got on wonderfully. Her pampered existence had caused Mat-Hor's ambitions to fade, while her compatriot greedily enjoyed the daily fare. They both acknowledged without regret that Ramses the Great, at sixty-six, had become a legend in his lifetime, beyond their reach. And the pharaoh, perceiving that no destructive passions burned in the hearts of the two queens, allowed them to be present at certain official ceremonies.

In the forty-third year of his reign, at Kha's insistence, Ramses had celebrated his fifth regeneration feast, in the presence of the community of gods and goddesses, who came to the capital in the form of statues animated by the *ka*. From now on, the pharaoh would have to have more frequent recourse to this ritual in order to be able to bear the burden of age, which weighed more and more heavily on him.

Ramses regularly had to consult Neferet. Ignoring her illustrious patient's bad temper on the occasions when he had difficulty accepting that he was getting old, she cured his toothache and curbed the pain and swelling in his joints. Thanks to her treatment, his vitality remained intact, and he did not slacken the pace of his work.

After awakening the divine power in its sanctuary and celebrating the dawn ritual, Ramses usually had discussions with the vizier, Ahmeni and Meneptah. He then left it to this trio to put his instructions into practice. In the afternoon he studied the great state rituals with Kha and suggested changes in the wording.

The king was gradually detaching himself from the administration of the country, which was in excellent hands. And he often went to Thebes to see Meritamon and to meditate in his Temple of a Million Years.

One day, when Ramses was returning from Karnak, where Bakhen was carrying out his tasks to general satisfaction, he was greeted at the port of Pi-Ramses by Meneptah, who looked anxious.

'I've had a worrying report, Majesty.'

Meneptah himself drove the royal chariot swiftly back to the palace. He said, 'If the facts are proved, Majesty, I am guilty of irresponsibility.'

'What do you mean?'

'The oasis of Siwa, near the Libyan border, is said to have been attacked by an armed gang commanded by Malfi.'

'When did this happen?'

'About ten days ago, but I've only just been told.'

'Why are you unsure about it?'

'Because the name of the officer responsible for the security of the oasis is given wrongly. But that may be because of the urgency in the heat of the moment. If the oasis has indeed been attacked, we must react. If it is indeed Malfi, we must nip the rebellion in the bud.'

'Why do you think that you are responsible?' asked Ramses.

'Because I wasn't vigilant enough, Majesty. The peace with Hatti has made me forget that war could break out in the west. And that damned Uri-Teshup is still at liberty . . . Allow me to leave for Siwa with a regiment and crush these insurgents.'

'In spite of your thirty-eight years, Meneptaph, you still have the fire of youth! An experienced officer can carry out this mission. As for you, put our troops on a state of alert.'

'I can swear that they were Libyan bandits,' Fine-Shanks repeated to the sleepy border-guard.

'You're talking nonsense, young man. There are no Libyans round here.'

'They wanted to kill me! I've run till I'm out of breath, and if I hadn't been a champion, they'd have caught me. They had helmets, breastplates, swords, spears – a real army!'

The border-guard yawned again, then gave the young man a nasty look. 'Strong beer goes to your head. Give up drinking! Drunkards come to a bad end.'

'It was a full moon,' Fine-Shanks insisted. 'I even saw their leader before I ran off. A big man with long hair and a red hairy chest.'

These details roused the border-guard. Like all officers in the army, the police and the customs, he had received a drawing of the criminal Uri-Teshup, with the promise of a good reward for anyone who helped get him arrested.

The guard flourished the portrait under Fine-Shanks's nose. 'Is that their leader?'

'Yes, that's him.'

All along the desert strip to the west of the Delta, between the Egyptian territory and the sea, the military administration had built forts, round which hamlets had grown up. They were separated from each other by one or two days' fast chariot ride, and the garrisons were ordered to warn the generals in Pi-Ramses and Memphis of any suspicious movements by the Libyans. If there was one region which the high command thought was under rigorous surveillance, this was it.

When the military governor of the border zone received an alarmist report based on statements by a travelling merchant, he took care not to transmit it to his superiors. Nevertheless, the possibility of capturing Uri-Teshup led him to send a patrol to the place where the Hittite was said to have been spotted.

Nakti and his men, snatched from their peace and quiet, had undertaken forced marches into an inhospitable region, infested with mosquitoes, with only one idea in their heads, to finish this unpleasant mission as quickly as possible.

Nakti cursed at every step he took. When would he finally be transferred to Pi-Ramses, to comfortable barracks, instead of pursuing non-existent enemies?

'A fort's in sight, sir.'

The border-guards will probably take us for fools, thought Nakti, but at least they'll give us something to eat and drink, and we can leave tomorrow morning.

'Look out, sir!' A soldier pulled Nakti back. On the path, a huge black scorpion was ready to attack. If the officer, lost in thought, had taken one more step, he would have been stung.

'Kill it,' the officer ordered his saviour.

The soldier did not have time to bend his bow. Arrows flew from the battlements of the fort and killed the Egyptians. With the precision of trained archers, the Libyans commanded by Uri-Teshup slew all the members of Nakti's patrol.

The Hittite himself slit the throats of all the wounded with his iron dagger.

54

As he did every morning, the military governor of the border zone with Libya made his way to his office to consult the reports sent from the forts. This didn't usually take long, because there was usually only one comment on the wooden tablets: 'Nothing to report.'

That morning, no reports had come in. There was no need to look far for the culprit: the soldier responsible for distributing the messages must have overslept. The governor was furious, and swore to demote him to junior laundryman.

In the courtyard of the fort, a soldier was sweeping half-heartedly, and two young footsoldiers were practising with short swords. The governor hurried to the quarters occupied by the couriers and scouts.

There was no one sleeping on the mats.

The governor was dumbfounded and wondered what on earth was going on. No reports, and no sign of the soldiers responsible for distributing them. What could possibly have caused this mess?

The officer stood open-mouthed as Libyans, with feathers in their hair, suddenly broke through the gate of the fort with a beam-ram and rushed inside.

They killed the sweeper and the two footsoldiers with their battle-axes and then smashed the skull of the petrified governor, who had not even tried to run. Uri-Teshup spat on the corpse.

'The oasis of Siwa has not been attacked,' a senior officer told Meneptah. 'It was false information.'

'Any casualties?'

'Neither casualties nor rebellion. I went there for nothing.'

Left alone Meneptah was racked by anxiety. If his attention had been diverted like this, it must have been done to conceal an attack somewhere else. Only Ramses would be able to appreciate the extent of the danger.

Just as Meneptah was climbing into his chariot, his armour-bearer came running to him. 'General, a message from a garrison near the Libyan border. There's been a massive attack against our forts! Most of them have already fallen and the governor of the region is said to have been killed.'

Never had Meneptah's horses galloped so fast. Leaping from his chariot before it had even come to a halt, he raced up the stairs of the palace. With the support of Serramanna, he interrupted the audience the pharaoh was giving to some provincial governors.

Meneptah's expression was enough for Ramses to realize that something serious had happened. He dismissed his guests, promising them a future discussion.

'Majesty,' declared Meneptah, 'the Libyans have probably invaded the north-west of the Delta. I don't know the full extent of the disaster.'

'Uri-Teshup and Malfi!' exclaimed Serramanna.

'There is in fact mention of the Hittite in the disjointed report I've received. And Malfi has managed to unite the Libyan clans that were at each other's throats. We must act swiftly and forcefully. Unless, of course, it's a question of a new trap, like the one at Siwa.'

If the main body of the troops was engaged to the north-west of the Delta, and it was in fact a trap, Malfi would attack near Thebes without encountering any resistance. He would put the sacred city of Amon to fire and the sword.

The future of Egypt depended on Ramses' decision.

'Majesty,' Serramanna said timidly, 'you promised me . . .'

'I haven't forgotten: you will come with me.'

With his cruel black eyes set in a square face, Malfi was thought by his men to be the embodiment of a desert demon, who had eyes in the back of his head, and could tear any enemy to pieces with fingers as sharp as blades. Nearly all the Libyan tribes had placed themselves under his command because he had been able, after long parleyings, to stir up their old hatred for Egypt. Faced with the ferocity of the Libyan warriors, the Egyptians, weakened by being long accustomed to peace, would flee. And the presence of the Hittite Uri-Teshup, whose reputation for bravery was now established, would galvanize the conquerors.

'Over there, less than two hours' march away,' said Uri-Teshup, pointing with his right hand, 'are the first villages of the Delta. We'll soon occupy them. Then we shall destroy Pi-Ramses, whose defences will have been reduced to a minimum. You will be proclaimed pharaoh, Malfi, and the remains of the Egyptian army will place themselves under your sovereignty.'

'Is your plan certain to work?' asked Malfi.

'It is, because I know Ramses well. The diversion at Siwa will have worried him and he'll be convinced that we've decided to open several fronts. His priority will be to protect Thebes and his temples, so he'll send two regiments to the South, probably under the command of Meneptah. The third will ensure the safety of Memphis. Since Ramses is vain enough to believe that he's invincible, he himself will lead the fourth regiment against us. We shall face only a few thousand men, Malfi, and we shall easily defeat them. I ask you for only one favour: let me kill Ramses with my dagger.'

The Libyan nodded. He would have preferred to have had more time to give his troops further training, but the alarm given by a pedlar had forced him to bring the attack forward.

Malfi was not frightened of one single regiment. The Libyans were eager to fight; their keenness, reinforced by drugs, would give them the advantage over the timid Egyptians. The men received only one order: no quarter was to be given.

'Here they come,' announced Uri-Teshup.

Malfi's eyes shone with the desire for vengeance. He was at last going to avenge the honour of Libya, flouted by the pharaohs for so many centuries, raze prosperous villages to the ground and burn the crops. He would make the survivors slaves.

'Ramses is leading his troops,' announced the Hittite excitedly.

'Who is that on his right?'

Uri-Teshup's face darkened. 'Meneptah.'

'Wasn't he supposed to command the troops massed at Thebes?'

'We'll kill both father and son.'

'And who's the man on the king's left?'

'Serramanna, the head of his personal bodyguard. Fate is favouring us, Malfi! I shall flay that man alive.'

Footsoldiers, archers and chariots were deployed on the horizon, in perfect order.

'That's not just one regiment,' said Malfi.

In his dismay, Uri-Teshup did not know what to say. The vast plain was gradually filling with Egyptian soldiers.

The Libyan and the Hittite had to face the facts: Ramses had taken the risk of coming to meet them with the four regiments of Amon, Ra, Ptah and Set. The entire Egyptian striking force was preparing to swoop down on their enemies.

Malfi clenched his fists. 'You said you knew Ramses well, Uri-Teshup!'

'His strategy is insane! How dare he take so many risks?'

Malfi realized that retreat was impossible. The Nubian archers, commanded by their viceroy, Setau, barred the way.

'One Libyan is worth at least four Egyptians,' Malfi shouted to his men. 'Attack!'

While Ramses stood impassively in his chariot, the Libyans hurled themselves at the first line of Egyptians. The footsoldiers knelt down in order to facilitate the aim of the archers, who decimated the enemy. The Libyan archers retaliated, but less effectively. Their second wave of attack, too uncoordinated, broke against the footsoldiers of the Set regiment. Then the Egyptian chariots counter-attacked. On Meneptah's orders they broke through the ranks of the rebels who, in spite of Malfi's curses, began to scatter.

The fugitives clashed with Setau's Nubians, whose arrows and spears wreaked destruction. From now on, the outcome of the battle was in no doubt. Most of the Libyans, realizing they were outnumbered, threw down their arms.

Wild with fury, Malfi gathered his last remaining followers round him; Uri-Teshup had disappeared. Forgetting the coward who had deserted him, the Libyan had only one idea in his head: to massacre as many Egyptians as possible. His first victim would be none other than Meneptah, who was within spearshot.

In the thick of the fray, the two men's eyes met. In spite of the distance between them, Ramses' son could sense the Libyan's hatred.

Their two spears rent the air simultaneously.

Malfi's grazed Meneptah's shoulder; Meneptah's sank into Malfi's forehead. The Libyan stood motionless for a few seconds, then staggered and fell.

Serramanna was enjoying himself. He had lost count of the number of Libyans he had cut to pieces with his heavy, double-bladed sword, which he handled with great skill. With

Malfi's death, his last followers had surrendered, and the Sardinian could take a rest.

He turned toward Ramses, and what he saw terrified him.

Wearing a helmet and protected by a breastplate which hid the mat of red hair on his chest, Uri-Teshup had managed to infiltrate the Egyptian lines and was approaching the royal chariot from the rear. He was about to assassinate Ramses.

Running like mad, forcing a way through the Royal Sons, Serramanna succeeded in getting between the chariot and Uri-Teshup, but could not avoid the Hittite's violent blow: the iron dagger bit deep into his chest.

Although mortally wounded, Serramanna still had enough strength to seize his sworn enemy by the throat, and strangle him with his two enormous hands.

'You've failed, Uri-Teshup, you're beaten!'

The Sardinian did not loosen his grip until the Hittite stopped breathing. Then, like a huge cat feeling the approach of death, he turned to lie on his side.

Ramses cradled the head of the man who had just saved his life.

'You have won a great victory, Majesty . . . And thanks to you I have had a good life.'

Proud of his last exploit, the big Sardinian departed for the Hereafter, giving up the ghost in Ramses' arms.

55

Vases and ewers of solid silver with gold rims, each weighing over one hundred and sixty deben, gold and silver offering-tables weighing more than three quintals, a barque of gilded pinewood from Canaan, more than a hundred and forty cubits long, gold plaques to adorn the pillars, four quintals of lapis-lazuli, eight of turquoises: such were some of the treasures Ramses gave to the temples of Thebes and Pi-Ramses to thank the gods for saving Egypt from invasion.

And this forty-fifth year of his reign had seen the foundation of a new Temple of Ptah in Nubia, at Gerf Hussein, where an old sacred cave had been transformed into a sanctuary by Setau. The king had inaugurated this miniature Abu Simbel, which was also hollowed out of a sandstone cliff. There, as on many other sites, colossal statues of the monarch in his form as Osiris had been erected.

When the festivities were over, Ramses and Setau watched the sun set over the Nile.

'You are becoming an indefatigable builder, Setau.'

'The example comes from above, Majesty. The fire of Nubia burns so fiercely that it must be channelled into the stones of temples. They will be your voice speaking to posterity, won't they? And then we shall have plenty of time to rest for ever. Our brief life is the place for effort, and it is that alone which grants us long life.'

'Are you having any difficulties with your new duties?'

'Nothing serious. During your reign, Ramses, you have killed off war. The peace with Hatti, the peace in Nubia, the peace imposed on Libya . . . that work is as beautiful as the most magnificent building and will count among your greatest creations. Wherever he may be, Ahsha must be happy!'

'I often think of Serramanna's sacrifice. He gave his life to save me.'

'All those close to you would have done the same, Majesty. How could it be otherwise, since you will speak for us when confronted with the Hereafter?'

The sycamore planted in the first year of Ramses' reign, in the garden of the palace in Thebes, had grown into a magnificent tree spreading its beneficial shade. Ramses was accustomed to sit under its foliage, listening to his daughter play the lute, accompanied by the song of the bluetits.

As every day, in all the temples of Egypt the priests had purified themselves with water from the sacred lakes and performed the rites in the name of Pharaoh. As every day, food had been brought to all the sanctuaries, great and small, to be offered to the gods before being redistributed to humans. As every day, the divine power had been awakened and Ma'at had been able to say to the king, 'You live through me, my fragrant dew revives you, your eyes are Ma'at.'

Meritamon put down her lute at the foot of the sycamore.

'You are the Queen of Egypt, Meritamon,' said Ramses.

'When you speak to me like that, Majesty, it means you are preparing to disturb my peace and quiet.'

'Old age is claiming me, Meritamon. Bakhen watches over the prosperity of Karnak and his days are filled with more tasks than there are hours in which to do them. You, my daughter, must be the guardian of my Temple of a Million

Years. Thanks to its magic, your mother and I were able to overcome adversity. You must ensure that rites are celebrated at the right time, so that the energy of the House of Ramses continues to exert its influence.'

Meritamon kissed his hand. 'Father, you know that we shall never be parted.'

'Fortunately, no man can escape death,'

'But the pharaohs have triumphed over her. Although she has struck you some hard blows, you have resisted her and I even think you have tamed her.'

'She will have the last word, daughter.'

'No, Majesty. Death has missed the chance of destroying you. Today your name is present on all the monuments in Egypt and your fame has spread beyond our borders. Ramses can no longer die.'

The Libyans' rebellion had been crushed, peace reigned, Ramses' prestige never ceased to grow, but the difficult dossiers continued to pile up on Ahmeni's desk; he grew more and more grumpy. Neither Meneptah nor Kha could solve the insoluble problem which had left the king's private secretary at a loss. Even the vizier declared himself unqualified to deal with it. Who could he turn to, except Ramses?

'I'm not reproaching Your Majesty for travelling,' declared Ahmeni, 'but when you are far from the capital, troubles have a tendency to accumulate.'

'Is our prosperity in danger?'

'I persist in thinking that, in the construction of a monument, the most minute detail can be the cause of its ruin. I don't work on the grand scale. I deal with the problems of daily life.'

'Spare me a long speech!'

'I've received a complaint from the mayor of Sumenu, in Upper Egypt. The sacred well on which the region depends has dried up, and the local priests admit they can't do anything about it.'

'Have you sent any experts there?'

'Are you accusing me of not doing my job properly? An entire army of experts has failed. And I find myself with this unmanageable well and a population in distress!'

Several housewives had gathered beside one of the channels which irrigated the fields outside Sumenu. They came in mid-afternoon to wash dishes, at some distance from the washerwomen, for whom a different stretch of the channel was reserved. They chatted, exchanged confidences and tittle-tattle and didn't hesitate to criticize all and sundry. The one with the readiest tongue was Brunette, the pretty wife of a carpenter.

'If the well has dried up,' she said, 'we should leave the city.'

'We can't!' protested a servant-girl. 'My family has lived in Sumenu for generations, and I don't want my children to be brought up anywhere else.'

'Without the water from the well, how will you manage?'

'The priests must do something!'

'They've failed. Even the most knowledgeable among them can't save the well.'

An old man, lame and blind, approached the women. 'I'm thirsty. Please give me something to drink.'

Brunette replied forcefully, 'Stop hanging around and bothering us! Work for your living and you'll get something to drink.'

'Fortune has been unkind to me, I've been ill and—'

'We've heard that tale too often. Be off, or we'll stone you!'

The blind man retreated, and the conversation resumed.

'And what about me? Will you give me some water?'

The women turned round, subdued by the authority in the

325

voice of the elderly man who addressed them. From his impressive bearing, it was clear that he was a powerful person.

'My lord,' said Brunette, 'we'll give you whatever you ask for.'

'Why did you rebuff that unfortunate man?'

'Because he's a good-for-nothing and he's always bothering us.'

'Remember the law of Ma'at: "Do not mock the blind, do not deride a dwarf, do not harm the lame, for we are all, healthy or infirm, in the hands of the gods. Let no one be abandoned and left without care".'

The housewives lowered their eyes in shame, but Brunette retorted, 'Who are you, to talk like that?'

'The pharaoh of Egypt.'

Petrified, Brunette ran and hid behind her companions.

'There is a curse on Sumenu's main well because of your contemptuous and contemptible behaviour to this unfortunate man. That is the conclusion I have reached after spending several days here.'

Brunette prostrated herself before Ramses. 'If we change our ways, will it be enough to save our well?'

'You have angered the god whose dwelling it is, and I must appease him.'

When the monumental statue of Sobek, in the form of a man with a crocodile's head, seated on a throne, was brought out of the sculptors' workshop in the Sumenu House of Life, all the inhabitants of the city crowded around as it passed. Hauled on round logs by a team of stone-cutters, it slid slowly over the damp soil to the main well, where Ramses was waiting.

The king recited prayers beseeching Sobek to cause the water to flow from Nun, the primeval ocean surrounding the earth, water essential to the survival of human beings. Then he ordered the artisans to lower the god to the bottom of the well, where he would perform his life-giving work.

326

The very next day the Sumenu well once more supplied the inhabitants of the city with precious water, and they organized a banquet at which the blind man and Brunette sat next to each other.

56

Hefat, the son of an Egyptian father and a Phoenician mother, had had a brilliant career. A diligent scholar, an outstanding student at the Academy of Memphis, where his mathematical gifts had astounded his exacting teachers, he had hesitated for a long time between several posts before entering the central Water Service, which managed the waters of the Nile, from forecasting the floods to the methods used in irrigation.

With the passing years, Hefat had inevitably gained the ear of the vizier, of ministers and provincial heads. His skill in flattering his superiors had allowed him to rise steadily in the service, and people forgot that he had modelled himself on Shanaar, the pharaoh's elder brother. Shanaar had been a traitor to his country, but nevertheless a courtier and politician whose ambition fascinated Hefat. He had wisely avoided openly taking sides with Shanaar, who had come to a bad end.

Now a dynamic fifty-year-old, married with two children, Hefat seemed an official in a settled position, at the top of a government department whose every mechanism he controlled with an iron hand. No one would have dreamt that he was the last surviving member of a network of influential people set up by Shanaar in his plan to usurp the throne.

These distant memories would have remained buried in the past, if he had not encountered the merchant Narish, whose fortune had dazzled him. He had realized that he, too, given his position and his abilities, could become very wealthy.

When dining with the Phoenician, Hefat's eyes had been opened. Ramses would soon be seventy, and he would hand over the government of the country to men trained in the traditional ways; they were incapable of taking the initiative. Kha was a mystic, distanced from the demands of government; Meneptah blindly obeyed his father and would be helpess when the latter was no longer there; and Ahmeni, the ageing scribe, would be dismissed.

The more one thought about it, the more clearly one saw that the existing power structure was much weaker than it seemed. Obliged, as Ramses was, to have recourse to the magic of the regeneration feasts, and to Neferet's treatment, his strength was declining.

The time had come to strike a decisive blow and realize Shanaar's dream.

Meneptah showed the ambassador from Hatti into the audience chamber of the Pi-Ramses palace. The diplomat was alone, without the usual host of bearers of gifts.

He bowed to Ramses. 'Majesty, I bring you sad news: your brother the Emperor of Hatti has died.'

Many scenes, from the battle of Kadesh to the emperor's visit to Egypt, flooded into the pharaoh's memory. Hattusilis had been a formidable adversary before becoming a loyal ally. Together, Ramses and he had built a better world.

'Has his successor been named?' asked Ramses.

'Yes, Majesty.'

'Is he resolved to respect the peace treaty?'

Meneptah gritted his teeth.

'The decisions of our late emperor are binding on his successors,' the ambassador replied. 'Not a single clause of the treaty will be challenged.'

'You will send my condolences and my expressions of

affection to Empress Putuhepa.'

'Alas, Majesty, the empress was already unwell, and the emperor's death precipitated her end.'

'Assure the new Lord of Hatti of my friendship and goodwill. He is to know that he can always count on Egypt's help.'

As soon as the ambassador had left, Ramses addressed his son. 'Get in touch immediately with our informers. They must send me a detailed report on the situation in Hatti immediately.'

Hefat was entertaining Narish in his fine house in Pi-Ramses. He introduced his wife and two children to him, proud of their excellent upbringing and the fine future assured them. After a pleasant meal, during which they talked of this and that, the head of the Water Service and the foreign merchant retired to a summerhouse built of sycamore wood with small, delicately worked pillars.

'Your invitation to me is an honour,' said Narish, 'but forgive me for speaking plainly: why am I here? I am a merchant and you a senior official. We have nothing in common.'

'I heard that you were not pleased with Ramses' trade policy.'

'His ridiculous challenge to the validity of slavery does harm us, it's true. But Egypt will eventually understand that she is isolated and that her position is untenable.'

'That could take many years. And you and I would like to get rich without delay.'

The Phoenician was intrigued. 'I can't quite follow your gist, Hefat.'

'Today, Ramses enjoys undivided power. But it was not always so. And this absolute power hides a serious weakness: his advanced age. Not to mention the unfitness of the two favourites for the succession, Kha and Meneptah.'

'I don't meddle in politics, especially not in those of Egypt.'

'But you believe that profit is all-powerful, don't you?'

'Isn't that the future of mankind?'

'Let us bring that future nearer! Both of us, if for different reasons, have a grudge against Ramses, an elderly king, now incapable acting vigorously. But that is not the main thing. We could take advantage of the decline in the strength of the central power to carry out a fantastic commercial operation.'

'What sort of operation?'

'Put at the lowest estimate, tripling the wealth of Phoenicia. And that is certainly well below the truth. Needless to say, the instigator of this happy event, you, Narish, would be praised to the skies.'

'And what about you?'

'To begin with, I prefer to remain in the background.'

'What is your plan?'

'Before I reveal it, I must be sure of your silence.'

Narish smiled. 'My dear Hefat, a verbal promise is valid only in Egypt. If you launch into business you must immediately abandon this archaic morality.'

Hefat hesitated: if the Phoenician betrayed him, he'd end his days in prison. Then he said, 'Very well, Narish, I'll explain everything to you.'

As Hefat spoke, Narish asked himself how such a crazy plan could have taken root in the mind of one of Pharaoh's subjects. But he himself would not run any risk, and Hefat was right: if the operation succeeded, a phenomenal fortune was promised them, and Ramses' reign would end in disaster.

Meneptah could not get the Libyan episode out of his mind. He, the supreme commander responsible for the safety of the territory, had not been able to foil Malfi's manoeuvre. Without Ramses' perceptiveness and daring, the rebels would have invaded the Delta, sacked the capital and killed

331

thousands of Egyptians.

Profiting from this experience, Meneptah had himself inspected the forts responsible for watching the movements of the Libyan tribes and giving the alarm in case of danger. He had made essential transfers, tightened discipline and stressed the crucial nature of the work done by the soldiers assigned to this thankless task.

Meneptah did not believe that the Libyans had been finally defeated. True, Malfi had disappeared, but others, equally eager for revenge, equally full of hatred, would replace him and preach all-out war with Egypt. So he had undertaken to reinforce the protection of the north-west region of the Delta, with the full agreement of Ramses.

But how would the situation develop in Hatti? Did the death of Hattusilis, an intelligent and realistic sovereign, mark the beginning of an internal crisis, which the ambassador had tried to mask by his reassuring words? Among the Hittites, it was common to seize the throne by using poison or the dagger. And the old emperor might have been mistaken in believing that he had crushed all forms of opposition.

While waiting impatiently for reliable news from Hatti, Meneptah kept his regiments on a war footing.

Although he did not scorn fish, Wideawake had a marked preference for red meat. As bright-eyed as his forebears, Ramses' dog valued his conversations with his master; a meal without a good discussion did not taste the same.

The king and Wideawake were finishing their midday meal and their conversation when Meneptah arrived.

'Majesty, I've read all our informers' reports, and I've had a long talk with our principal agent in Hattusa.'

Ramses poured some wine into a silver goblet and handed it to his son. 'Don't conceal anything from me, Meneptah. I want to know the exact truth.'

332

'The ambassador from Hatti did not lie to us. Hattusilis's successor is firmly resolved to respect the peace treaty and to maintain excellent relations with Egypt.'

57

The Nile floods. A miracle renewed every year, a gift from the gods which kindled the fervent gratitude of the population to the pharaoh, the only one who could cause the waters of the river to rise and enrich the soil. Since the beginning of Ramses' reign, the life-giving water which flowed from the depths of the celestial ocean had never failed. And the rise in the water level this year was remarkable: twenty cubits!

The peace with Hatti was confirmed and the summer promised great possibilities of excursions from one settlement to another, in the many boats repaired during the winter. Like all his compatriots, Hefat marvelled at the sight of the Nile transformed into a lake out of which rose hillocks on which villages were built. His family had left for Thebes to spend a few weeks with his parents, and he was free to do whatever he liked.

While the peasants were resting, those responsible for irrigation worked without respite. But Hefat watched the floodwaters with a different eye. While the reservoirs were filled up, separated by earthworks, which were breached as and when required, Hefat congratulated himself on his brilliant idea. It was going to make him richer and more powerful than Ramses the Great.

The senior officials of the Egyptian government had

requested an audience with Ramses to put to him a suggestion which they thought reasonable. Although they had not conferred together, they had all arrived at the same conclusion.

The king listened to them attentively. He advised them against taking the step with which they wished to succeed, but without giving a categorical refusal. Interpreting this as encouragement, the head of the Treasury, whose courage his colleagues appreciated, made his way to Ahmeni's office that evening, after the latter had sent his staff home.

Though now nearing his seventieth year, Ahmeni hadn't changed from the student who had sworn loyalty to Ramses, before it was clear that the latter's fate was to become Pharaoh. He was still pale, slightly built, as thin and hungry as ever, in spite of all the food he put away, perpetually suffering from backache, yet able to endure stresses and strains which would have felled a giant, a determined worker, exact and meticulous, sleeping only a few hours a night and reading every dossier himself.

'Is there a problem?' he asked the head of the Treasury.

'Not exactly.'

'What is it, then? I'm busy.'

'We had a meeting with the vizier and—'

'Who's we?'

'Well, the head of the White Double House, the minister for agriculture, the—'

'I see. And what was the purpose of this meeting?'

'To tell you the truth, there were two.'

'Let's hear the first one first.'

'For your services to Egypt, your colleagues in the higher echelons of government would like to make you the gift of a house in the locality of your choice.'

Ahmeni put down his writing-brush. 'Interesting. And the second purpose?'

'You have worked hard, Ahmeni, much harder than the

administration demands. Probably, because of your dedica-
tion, you haven't thought about it, but isn't it time for you to
retire? A peaceful retirement in a comfortable house, not to
mention enjoying everyone's respect. What do you think?'

Ahmeni's silence seemed a good omen.

'I knew that you would listen to the voice of reason,' said
the delighted head of the Treasury. 'My colleagues will be
pleased to learn your decision.'

'I'm not so sure of that.'

'I beg your pardon?'

'I shall never retire,' declared Ahmeni passionately, 'and
no one except Pharaoh will make me leave this office. Until
he asks for my resignation, I shall continue to work at my own
pace and according to my own methods. Is that quite clear?'

'We thought that in your own interests—'

'Don't think it any more.'

Hefat and Narish met again at the Egyptian's house, on a hot
summer's day. The merchant much appreciated the cool, light
beer served to him, which helped the digestion.

'I wouldn't like to seem vain,' said Narish, 'but I think I've
done an excellent job; the Phoenician merchants are ready to
purchase Egypt. But you, Hefat, are you ready to sell?'

'I haven't changed my mind.'

'I need to know the exact date.'

'I can't infringe the laws of nature, but we haven't long to
wait.'

'No serious obstacles?'

'Thanks to my position, none.'

'Won't you need the seal of the High Priest of Memphis?'

'Yes, but that's Kha, who's given over to his spiritual
quest and his love of ancient stones. He won't pay any
attention to the document he signs.'

'One detail worries me,' said the Phoenician. 'Why do you
hate your country?'

'Thanks to our arrangement, Egypt will scarcely suffer and will finally be opened up to the external world, which will sweep away its old superstitions and its outdated customs, as Shanaar wished. He wanted to do away with Ramses and I shall be the one to destroy this tyrant. The Hittites, the Libyans and the magicians all failed and Ramses is no longer on his guard. But I, Hefat, shall be victorious.'

'The answer is no,' Ahmeni told the head of Two Falcons province, a sturdy fellow with a determined chin.
'Why?'
'Because no province shall benefit from special privileges, to the detriment of the others.'
'But I've received encouragement from the central administration!'
'Possibly, but no department is authorized to lay down the law. If I followed our senior officials in all circumstances, Egypt would be ruined.'
'Is your refusal final?'
'The irrigation system will not be modified, and the water from the holding-reservoirs will be released at the usual time and not before.'
'In that case, I demand to see the king!'
'He will receive you, but don't waste his time.'
Handicapped by Ahmeni's unfavourable opinion, the head of the province had no chance of winning Ramses' approval. He had no choice but to return home.
Ahmeni was curious. Whether by courier or in the course of conversation, six heads of important provinces had asked him to confirm the decision taken by the Water Services at Memphis: to release the water from the holding-reservoirs early, in order to increase the area available for cultivation.
To do so would be a double mistake, Ahmeni believed, since, on the one hand, such development was unnecessary and, on the other hand, irrigation had to be progressive, not

sudden. Fortunately, the Water Service officials were not aware that the majority of the provincial heads, with exemplary discretion, always consulted the king's private secretary before venturing on to slippery ground.

If he had not had so many problems to solve, Ahmeni would have liked to lead an inquiry to identify the person responsible for these aberrations. He began to study a report about the plantations of willow trees in Middle Egypt, but couldn't concentrate and stopped reading. This matter was too serious to ignore.

Ramses and Kha passed through the gateway which gave access to the Temple of Thoth in Khmun, crossed a courtyard flooded with sunshine, and were welcomed by the High Priest of the god on the threshold of the covered temple. The king and his son marvelled at the halls, to which only the servants of Thoth, the patron of scribes and scholars, were admitted, and stood in meditation in the sanctuary.

'My quest ends here,' declared Kha.

'Have you found the *Book of Thoth*?'

'I thought for a long time that it consisted of one ancient piece of writing, hidden in a temple library. But I eventually realized that each one of the stones of our sanctuaries is one of the letters of this book, written by the god of knowledge to give meaning to our life. Thoth has transmitted his message in every sculpture and every hieroglyph, and it is up to us to assemble what is scattered, in the same way as Isis put together the scattered pieces of the body of Osiris. Our whole country, father, is a temple in the likeness of the sky; and it is the pharaoh's duty to keep this book open so that the eyes of the heart can decipher it.'

No poet, not even Homer, could have found words to describe the joy and pride that Ramses felt on hearing what his wise son had said.

58

Although simple, Hefat's idea would be amazingly effective: to release too soon the water accumulated in the irrigation reservoirs and attribute the mistake to the administration, and in the first instance to Kha, who was responsible for affixing his seal on the document, giving it his theoretical authority as supervisor of the channels.

Reassured by the falsified studies Hefat had sent them, the heads of provinces had fallen into the trap and would think they had extra reserves at their disposal to develop the farmlands and enrich their regions. When the accumulation of mistakes became known, it would be too late. There would not be sufficient water for irrigation and there would be no hope for the crops.

The accusations would be levelled at an authority higher than Kha: Ramses himself.

Then Narish would act, in conjunction with the Phoenician merchants, who would offer the produce which Egypt needed – at an exorbitant price. The Treasury would be forced to accept their conditions, and the elderly pharaoh would be swept away in the storm, while Hefat would reap enormous profits from the transaction. If luck was with him, he would drive out the vizier and take his place; if not, once he had made his fortune he would settle in Phoenicia.

There was one final formality to be gone through: asking

Kha to affix his seal. Hefat would not even have to meet the High Priest, who would order his secretary to perform this task.

The secretary received Hefat warmly. 'You are in luck. The High Priest is here and will be glad to receive you.'

'There's no need,' Hefat protested. 'I don't want to bother him.'

'Follow me, please.'

Hefat felt nervous as he was shown into the library where Kha, dressed in a tunic which looked as if it had been cut out of a panther-skin, was studying some papyri.

'I am glad to meet you, Hefat.'

'For me it is a great honour, my lord, but I didn't mean to interrupt your work.'

'In what way can I help you?'

'A simple administrative matter.'

'Show me the document.' Kha's voice was grave, his tone authoritative; he did not at all resemble the dreamer Hefat had imagined.

'This is an unusual suggestion which requires close study,' said Kha.

Hefat's blood froze in his veins. 'No, my lord, it's quite a common way of facilitating the irrigation, nothing more.'

'You are too modest! As I'm unable to express an opinion, I shall hand this document to a competent person.'

Another specialist, thought Hefat, reassured. He would have no difficulty in convincing him, given his high position in the Water Service.

'Here is the person who will judge you,' announced Kha.

Ramses was dressed in a wide-sleeved gown of fine linen, and wore on his wrists his two famous gold bracelets with the central lapis-lazuli design depicting a wild duck.

The pharaoh's eyes pierced Hefat's heart and forced him to step back till he bumped into the shelves loaded with papyri.

'You have made a serious mistake,' declared Ramses, 'in

340

thinking that your knowledge was sufficient to let you ruin your country. Do you not know that greed is an incurable disease which makes one blind and deaf? For an official, you've been very stupid to think that Egypt is governed by incompetents.'

'Majesty, I beg you to—'

'Don't waste your words, Hefat; you are not worthy to use them. In your behaviour I see the mark of Shanaar, the weakness which leads a man to destroy himself by betraying Ma'at. Your future is now in the hands of the judges.'

It was Ahmeni who, thanks to a rigorous inquiry, had saved the country from a very real danger. The king would have liked to reward him, but how, without angering him? Between the two men, a simple glance of understanding was enough, and Ahmeni returned to work.

And the seasons and the days had passed, simple and happy, until the spring of the fifty-fourth year of Ramses the Great's reign. Against Neferet's advice, the king had made a decision. Reinvigorated by his ninth regeneration feast, he wished to travel through the Egyptian countryside.

The month of May saw the return of extreme heat, beneficial to the king's stiff joints. It was harvest time. The peasants, using wooden-handled sickles, cut the stalks of the ripe corn high up; then the ears were gathered into sheaves and taken to the threshing floors by tireless donkeys. Building the stacks of straw needed expert hands, able to erect low pyramids which would remain intact for a good part of the year. Two long sticks were planted in the stacks to reinforce them.

As soon as the pharaoh entered a village, the elders presented him with a table of offerings loaded with ears of corn and flowers; then he sat down under a shelter and listened to their grievances. The scribes took notes and sent them to Ahmeni who had insisted on reading all the reports made during the journey.

The king noted that, on the whole, agriculture was in good shape and, though things could never be perfect, there were no problems which could not be dealt with. The complainants were not aggressive, with the exception of a peasant from Beni Hassan, whose vehemence shocked the pharaoh's entourage.

'I spend my days digging,' he complained, 'and my nights repairing my tools, I chase after my animals, which are always running away, and then there comes the inspector of taxes who goes for me and fleeces me! With his army of vultures he treats me like a thief, beats me because I can't pay and imprisons my wife and children! How can I ever be happy?'

Everyone feared a fierce reaction from Ramses, but he was unmoved.

'Have you any other criticisms?' he asked.

The peasant was astonished. 'No, Majesty, no.'

'One of your family is a scribe, isn't he?'

The man could not hide his embarrassment. 'Yes, but—'

'He has taught you a classical text learnt in all the schools for scribes: how to praise one's own profession, the better to run down the others. You recited it fairly well. But do you really suffer from all the troubles you've just described to me?'

'Well, some of the animals do run away and go from one field to another, and that makes trouble.'

'If you can't get on with your neighbours, appeal to the village judge. And never accept an injustice, however small it may be. In that way you will help Pharaoh to govern.'

Ramses inspected many enclosures of cereals and ordered the grain measurers to be exact in handling the bushel. Then he inaugurated the harvest festival in Karnak, by beginning to fill one of the large granaries in the domain of Amon. Priests and dignitaries noted that, in spite of his age, the Lord of the Two Lands still had a strong hand and his actions were steady.

Bakhen accompanied his illustrious guest along a path through lush fields near the temple, to reach a landing-stage. Ramses had finally admitted to being tired and had agreed to be carried in a litter.

Bakhen was the first to notice a lazy fellow who, instead of working with his comrades, was sleeping under a willow tree. He hoped that the king would not see him, but Ramses' eye was still sharp.

'That fault will be punished,' the High Priest promised.

'For once, be lenient. I was the one who had willow trees planted throughout Egypt, wasn't I?'

'That man will never know what he owes you, Majesty.'

'I've sometimes been tempted like him to fall asleep under a tree, and forget the burden of my duties.'

Not far from the landing-stage, Ramses ordered the bearers to put him down.

'Majesty,' said Bakhen anxiously, 'why walk?'

'Look at that little shrine over there. It's in ruins.'

A modest sanctuary to the goddess of the harvest, a female cobra, had suffered from the weather and neglect; weeds grew between the loose stones.

'That is a *real* fault, Bakhen,' stated Ramses. 'Have that shrine restored and enlarged. Equip it with a stone gate and see that a statue of the goddess, made by the sculptors of Karnak, is placed inside it. It was the gods who fashioned Egypt. We must not neglect them, even in their most modest aspects.'

The Lord of the Two Lands and the High Priest of Amon placed wild flowers at the foot of the shrine, in homage to the *ka* of the goddess. High in the sky a falcon hovered and circled.

59

On the way back to the capital, Ramses stopped at Memphis to talk to Kha, who had just completed the restoration of the monuments of the Old Empire, and had added more adornment to the subterranean temple of the Apis bulls.

At the landing-stage he was met by Neferet, who looked as beautiful and elegant as ever.

'How are you feeling, Majesty?' she asked.

'I'm a bit tired, and my back aches a little, but my body is holding up. You seem distressed, Neferet.'

'Kha is very ill.'

'You don't mean . . . ?'

'I know what ails him but I cannot cure this sickness. Your son's heart is worn out. No remedies can help any more.'

'Where is he?'

'In the library of the Temple of Ptah, surrounded by the texts he has spent so much time studying.'

The king went immediately to his son. As he neared his sixtieth year, the High Priest's stern bony face had grown more serene. In his deep blue eyes there shone the inner peace of a person who, his whole life through, had been prepared to meet the Hereafter. No fear distorted his features.

'Majesty! I did so much hope to see you again before I departed.'

Pharaoh took his son's hand.

'Would Pharaoh permit his humble servant to rest in the Mountain of Life, as a friend who has been useful to his master, for there is no greater happiness. Permit me to travel to the fair lands of the West and arrive there as one of those who have been close to you. I have tried to respect Ma'at, I have carried out your commands and performed the missions which you have entrusted me with . . . '

Kha's grave voice gradually faded. Ramses gathered the memory of it to himself to keep as an unfailing treasure.

Kha was buried in the temple of the Apis bulls, near those beloved creatures whose animal form concealed the expression of the divine power. Ramses had placed a gold mask on the face of the mummy, and had chosen the funerary furnishings: furniture, vases and jewels, masterpieces created by the craftsmen of the Temple of Ptah and destined to accompany Kha's soul along the fair and pleasant paths of eternity.

The old king directed the funeral ceremony with surprising vigour, mastering his emotion as he opened his son's eyes and mouth so that he could depart alive into the Otherworld.

At every moment Meneptah stood ready to offer his father his assistance, but Ramses showed no weakness. Nevertheless, Ahmeni sensed that his lifelong friend was having to draw from his innermost depths the strength he needed, to set an example of dignity in the face of the new tragedy which had befallen him.

The lid was placed on Kha's sarcophagus, and the tomb was sealed.

When he was out of sight of the courtiers, Ramses wept.

It was one of those hot, sunny days that Ramses loved. He had left it to a priest to celebrate the dawn rite in his stead, and he was not to have his usual discussion with the vizier until late in the morning. In an attempt to forget his pain, the king intended to work as usual, although he lacked his accustomed energy.

But his legs were paralysed and he could not rise. He called his steward in a peremptory voice.

A few minutes later, Neferet was at the king's bedside.

'This time, Majesty, you are going to have to listen to me and do as I say.'

'You ask too much of me, Neferet.'

'In case you were still in doubt, your youth has definitely flown, and you must change the way you live.'

'You are the most formidable opponent I've ever had to contend with.'

'Not me, Majesty: old age.'

'Tell me what to expect. And see that you don't hide anything from me!'

'You will be able to walk again tomorrow, but you'll have to use a stick; and the stiffness in your right hip will make you limp a bit. I shall try to ease the pain, but rest is essential, and from now on, you must spare yourself all effort. Don't be surprised if you occasionally feel some weakness, with an impression of paralysis; it won't last if you receive daily massage. Some nights you will have difficulty in stretching out full length; soothing ointments will help you. And frequent mud baths in Faiyum will complete your treatment.'

'Treatment every day? You seem to think I'm a helpless old man!'

'I've already told you, Majesty, you're no longer young, You'll no longer be able to drive your own chariot, but if you are a good patient, you will prevent your health deteriorating too fast. Daily exercise, like walking or swimming, provided you don't overdo it, will maintain your mobility. Your general state of health is fairly satisfactory for a man who, all his life, has refused to take any rest.'

Neferet's smile consoled Ramses. No enemy had ever

defeated him except this accursed old age, which Neferet's favourite author, the sage Ptah-hotep, had complained of. But he had been a hundred and ten when he composed his *Maxims*. Accursed old age, whose sole advantage was to bring him nearer to those dear ones whom he so longed to join in the fertile fields of the Otherworld, where weariness did not exist.

'Your weakest point,' added the physician, 'is your teeth; but I'll watch them to prevent any risk of infection.'

Ramses complied with Neferet's demands. In a few days he recovered some of his strength, but he had come to realize that his body, worn out by too many battles and ordeals, was now nothing but an old instrument on the point of breaking.

Accepting this was his last victory.

In the silence and darkness of the Temple of Set, the formidable power of the skies, Ramses the Great made his last decision.

Before making it official, in the form of a decree which would have the force of law, the Lord of the Two Lands summoned his vizier, ministers, senior officials and all the dignitaries occupying posts of responsibility. The only absentee was Meneptah, whom he had sent to the Delta to make a detailed report on the area's economy.

The king had long discussions with the men and women who, day by day, continued to build Egypt. During all these interviews Ramses was seconded by Ahmeni, whose many notes proved invaluable.

'You haven't made *too* many mistakes,' he told his private secretary.

'Have you spotted a single one, Majesty? If you have, please let me know!'

'That was merely a form of words, to express my satisfaction.'

'All right,' grumbled Ahmeni. 'But why did you send your

supreme commander off on such an eccentric mission?'

'Don't tell me you haven't guessed.'

Leaning on his stick, Ramses walked slowly along a shady path, accompanied by Meneptah.

'What are the results of your investigations, my son?'

'The taxes in the Delta region that you asked me to inspect were based on 8760 taxpayers; every cattle-owner is responsible for 500 beasts, and I have compiled a register of 13,080 goatherds, 22,430 poultry-keepers and 3920 donkey-drivers who between them are in charge of several thousand donkeys. The crops have been excellent with very few tax-evaders. As too often, the administration has proved over-critical, but I told the petty chiefs firmly that they were not to importune honest folk but should worry more about the cheats.'

'You have good knowledge of the Delta, my son.'

'This mission has taught me a lot. By talking to the peasants I felt the heartbeat of the country.'

'Aren't you forgetting the priests, the scribes and the military?'

'I have mixed with them a great deal, but I'd had little direct contact with the men and women of the land.'

'What do you think of this decree?' Ramses handed Meneptah a papyrus written in his own hand.

His son read it aloud. 'I, Ramses, Pharaoh of Egypt, elevate Prince Meneptah, royal scribe, guardian of the seal, supreme commander of the army, to the rank of Sovereign of the Two Lands.'

Meneptah gazed at his father, who was leaning on his stick.

'Majesty . . . '

'I do not know how many years of life fate will grant me, Meneptah, but the time has come to make you a partner on the throne. As my father acted, so do I act; I am an old man. You

348

are a mature man who has just overcome the last obstacle that I set before him. You know how to govern, to administer and to fight. Take the future of Egypt into your hands, my son.'

60

Twelve years had passed and Ramses, now aged eighty-nine, had been reigning over Egypt for sixty-seven years. In accordance with his decree, he now left the cares of government to Meneptah, but the latter frequently consulted his father who, as far as the inhabitants of the Two Lands were concerned, was still the reigning pharaoh.

The king lived part of the year in Pi-Ramses and the rest in Thebes, always accompanied by his faithful Ahmeni. In spite of his great age and his many aches and pains, the latter continued to work in his own way.

Ramses started the day by listening to music composed by Meritamon, then he decided to take his daily walk in the countryside near his Temple of a Million Years. His stick was now his best ally, as every step was becoming difficult.

On the occasion of the fourteenth regeneration feast, celebrated the year before, Ramses had spent the whole night talking to Setau and Lotus, who had made Nubia into a rich and prosperous province. The sturdy snake-charmer was now also an old man and even the lovely Lotus had yielded to the onslaught of age. How many memories they had shared! All the many exhilarating times they had lived through! And not one of them had spoken of a future which none of them could shape.

At the side of the road an old woman was baking bread in

an oven. The smell delighted the king. 'Will you give me a piece of your bread?' he asked.

With her failing eyesight, the woman did not recognize the king. 'This is a thankless job that I do.'

'And it deserves its reward, naturally. Will this gold ring satisfy you?'

The old woman peered at the jewel, which she polished on the hem of her skirt. 'With this I could buy myself a fine house. Keep your ring and eat my bread. Who are you, anyway, to own such treasures?'

The golden crust was baked to a turn. It brought back memories of tastes enjoyed in childhood, for a moment letting the king forget the afflictions of old age.

'Keep the ring,' he said. 'You bake the best bread I've ever tasted.'

Ramses liked spending an hour or two in the company of a potter. He liked to watch his hands kneading the clay to shape a jar which would serve to keep water cool or to preserve food. Did not the god with the ram's head ceaselessly create the world and mankind on his potter's wheel?

The king and the craftsman did not exchange a single word. Together they listened to the music of the wheel and silently participated in the mysterious transformation of shapeless matter into a useful and well-proportioned object.

Summer was awakening, and Ramses was thinking of leaving for the capital, where the heat would be less overpowering. Ahmeni no longer left his office, which was always airy by virtue of its high windows, and the king was surprised not to find him working at his desk.

For the first time in his long career, not only had his private secretary granted himself a few moments' rest in the middle of the day, but he was exposing himself to the sun, at the risk of burning his pale skin.

'Moses is dead,' Ahmeni declared in distress.

351

'Did he realize his dream?'

'Yes, Majesty, he found his Promised Land, where his people will now live in freedom. Our friend has reached the end of his long quest. The fire which burned in him has been transformed into a land where water flows freely and honey abounds.'

Moses . . . one of the architects of Pi-Ramses, the man whose faith had triumphed over many years of wandering, a prophet whose zeal was inexhaustible. Moses, the son of Egypt and the spiritual brother of Ramses. Moses, whose dream had become reality.

The king's luggage and that of his private secretary stood ready. They would embark for the North before the end of the morning.

'Come with me,' the pharaoh ordered Ahmeni.

'Where do you want to go?'

'Isn't this a beautiful day? I would like to rest beneath the acacia of my Temple of a Million Years, under the tree planted in the second year of my reign.'

The expression in the monarch's voice made Ahmeni anxious. 'We are just about to leave, Majesty.'

'Come, Ahmeni.'

The great acacia of the Temple of a Million Years shone in the sun, and its leaves rustled in the light breeze. Ramses had planted many acacias, tamarisks, fig trees, perseas, pomegranates, willows and other representatives of the tree family that he so loved.

Wideawake, the old heir to a dynasty of faithful companions to the king, forgot his aching joints to follow Ramses. Neither he nor his master was worried by the noisy dance of the bees which tirelessly gathered the nectar from the blossoms of the magnificent acacia, whose fragrance delighted animals as well as humans.

Ramses sat down, leaning against the trunk of the tree.

352

Wideawake curled up at his feet.

'Do you remember, Ahmeni, the words spoken by the goddess of the Western Acacia, when she welcomes souls into the Hereafter?'

'"Receive this cool water. May your heart be soothed by this divine water, which comes from the ritual lake of the necropolis. Receive this offering, so that your soul may dwell in my shade."'

'Our celestial mother offers us life,' Ramses said, 'and she it is who places the spirits of the pharaohs among the tireless, indestructable stars.'

'Perhaps you are thirsty, Majesty. I'll go and fetch—'

'Don't go, Ahmeni. I am weary, my friend, a fatal fatigue overcomes me. Do you remember when we used to discuss true power? According to you, only Pharaoh was capable of exercising it, and you were right, providing he respects the Rule of Ma'at, by struggling ceaselessly against the dark. If that power weakens, the solidarity between heaven and earth disappears, and mankind is given over to violence and injustice. The history of a reign must be that of a celebration, my father said; the humble as much as the great must receive their sustenance from Pharaoh, and the one must not be neglected to the detriment of the other. Today women come and go as they please, children laugh, old men rest in the shade of trees. Thanks to Seti, thanks to Nefertari, thanks to those near and loyal to me, who have laboured for the greatness and influence of our civilization, I have tried to make this land happy and to act righteously. Now, the gods must judge me.'

'No, Majesty, do not leave us!'

Wideawake sighed. An intense sigh, deep as the primeval ocean, peaceful as a sunset over the Nile. And the last representative of the dynasty of Wideawakes passed away at his master's feet.

Summer was awakening, and Ramses the Great had just

entered eternity, beneath the Western Acacia.

Ahmeni did something that he had never dared to do during eighty years of an unfailing friendship: he took the pharaoh's hands in his and kissed them passionately.

Then Pharaoh's sandal-bearer and private secretary assumed the scribe's posture and, with a new brush, traced hieroglyphs on a tablet of acacia wood.

'I shall devote the rest of my life to writing your history,' he promised. 'In this world and in the next, no one will forget the Son of the Light.'